Realism Today
Aspects of the Contemporary West German Novel

Realism Today

ASPECTS OF THE CONTEMPORARY WEST GERMAN NOVEL

KEITH BULLIVANT

OSWALD WOLFF BOOKS
BERG PUBLISHERS
Leamington Spa / Hamburg / New York
Distributed exclusively in the US and Canada by
St. Martin's Press, New York

Published in 1987 by
Berg Publishers Limited
24 Binswood Avenue, Leamington Spa, CV32 5SQ, UK
Schenefelder Landstr. 14K, 2000 Hamburg 55, FRG
175 Fifth Avenue/Room 400, New York, NY 10010, USA

British Library Cataloguing in Publication Data

Bullivant, Keith
  Realism today: aspects of the contemporary
West German novel.
  1. German fiction — 20th century —
History and criticism
  I. Title
  833′.914′09   PT1334
ISBN 0–85496–521–1

Library of Congress Cataloguing-in-Publication Data

Bullivant, Keith.
  Realism today.
  "Oswald Wolff books."
  Bibliography: p.
  Includes index.
  1. German fiction—Germany (West)—History and
criticism.   2. German fiction—20th century—History and
criticism.   3. Realism in literature.   I. Title.
PT772.B84   1987   833′.912′0912   86–31018
ISBN 0–85496–521–1

Printed in Great Britain by Billings of Worcester

Contents

For Henner

Foreword

It has not been my intention in this study of the contemporary West German novel to consider in detail the body of existing literature on the German branch of literary realism. Rather, I offer a reading of the development of ideas on realism and the German novel since the beginning of the nineteenth century, which may help to explain the particular nature of the German novel up to the Second World War and, at the same time, cast some light on the nature of literary debate since 1945. The approach I have adopted means, inevitably, that the picture drawn is far from complete, but, as an ideal-type analysis, it enables features peculiar to the German novel tradition to be highlighted. In the first half of this book, consideration of this tradition and the role it has played in literary criticism in the Federal Republic affords a framework of reference to the more detailed examination of the recent novel in the second half. While the categories used in Part II overlap somewhat at times, they are designed to give a sense of overview and to aid orientation within a vigorous and complex literary scene. The choice of texts for close analysis was dictated, to some extent, by my desire not to duplicate existing studies of individual works, and in certain cases there is a degree of special pleading for works that have not received the recognition they deserve. The selection is, however, essentially a reflection of my own sense of what constitute the key realist novels over the last fifteen years; others will, of course, have their own ideas on this.

Work on this volume has been supported generously by the British Academy, the German Academic Exchange Service and the University of Warwick and I am grateful to these bodies for that assistance. I should also acknowledge the services of the Deutsches Literaturarchiv in Marbach and of Mr Richard Parker of the University of Warwick Library. At all stages of the work on this volume I have been lucky to have the constant advice, criticism and support of my colleagues, various Writers in Residence at the University of Warwick and of friends in Cologne and Herrsching. I can only hope that the shortcomings of this work, for which I alone am responsible, do not cause them too much disappointment. I should

1

add a final word of thanks to the forbearance during the final phase of this work of my wife Jean, and of John-Paul and Matthew, who went without a proper summer holiday and for much of a year saw little of a father who spent all his time 'playing with the Amstrad'.

Keith Bullivant
Crowdecote, September 1986

PART I

The Anti-Realist Tradition

1

Away from Reality: Aspects of the German Novel of the Nineteenth and Twentieth Centuries

In 1974 a public dispute took place in West Germany between the novelist Uwe Timm and Jörg Drews, a professor of literary criticism at Bielefeld University and former literary editor of the *Süddeutsche Zeitung*. The acrimonious argument was remarkable not only for the vigour of, in particular, Drews' language, but also for the fact that there was in no way bad blood between them: their quarrel was about realism. This particular controversy, to which we shall return later, tellingly illustrates the passions that can be unleashed by the term 'Realismus' in German literary discussions. Within English and American Studies the concept of realism is not without its problems, but there is a complete absence of the vehemence and the frequently dismissive tone of German debates on the subject over the years.[1] To be confronted with such condemnation of realist writing is a shock to the reader of English and American novels, who is very much aware of a realist novel tradition that extends from the eighteenth century right up to the present, with a general acceptance among novelists, critics and scholars as to the continued viability of realist writing. This is not so in Germany; we can observe in recent times a 'differentness' about the German literary situation, stemming essentially from a resistance to realism rooted in a long-established tradition of anti-realism.

In the English-speaking world there is no dogmatic view of what actually constitutes realism. It might be described at this point — although this working understanding of the term will need constant scrutiny — as starting from the epistemological premise that empirical reality can be comprehended, if only partially, by the individual, with the realist work of literature relating the experience of reality by

---

1. It is impossible to list here the body of relevant literature in English and American studies, but we would refer readers to David Lodge, *The Novelist at the Crossroads*, London, 1971; J.P. Stern, *On Realism*, London, 1973; and John Halperin (ed.), *The Theory of the Novel*, New York & London, 1974, esp. pp. 213–70.

an individual or individuals in a given social situation, but at the same time holding up the realist picture of the given world against the utopian vision of a life of true human dignity. While a discussion of the subject cannot exclude matters of style, there is no rigid canon of what constitutes realist writing and no restriction of it to one particular period; we speak, rather, of 'different realisms at different times and in different contexts'.[2] In Germany the most prevalent view of realism, not only with reference to German literature, is of it referring specifically to a particular epoch, as an essentially historical phenomenon. It is understood as the 'Bezeichnung für einen historisch begrenzten Kunstwillen und -stil, der sich vor allem im Roman des neunzehnten Jahrhunderts geltend machte, in der Praxis wie in der Theorie'.[3] This historically delimited realism is characterised in the German novel by ' "Gegenständlichkeit", unvoreingenommene, vorbehaltslose, "objektive" Aufnahme der tatsächlichen Wirklichkeit . . . , dies alles mehr oder weniger verklärt, ästhetisch erhoben, verschönt, vergoldet . . .'.[4]

Alongside this established understanding of realism as an historical phenomenon we find in German literary theory and criticism the widely-held view that in modern society it is just not possible to write realist works — where realism is defined, again, by that of the nineteenth century. The first major proponent of this position was Brecht, who, setting his face firmly against Georg Lukács's advancement of precisely such realism as the appropriate model for would-be Socialist Realists, advocated avant-garde literature as the only suitable means of reflecting reality:

> Schon für die Beschreibung der Prozesse, in denen ein Mensch des Spätkapitalismus steht, sind die Formen des Rousseauschen Erziehungsromans oder die Techniken, mittels derer die Stendhal und Balzac die Karriere eines jungen Bourgeois beschrieben, außerordentlich überholt. . . . Die Arbeiten von Joyce und Döblin weisen, und das in großer Weise, den welthistorischen Widerspruch auf, in den die Produktionskräfte mit den Produktionsverhältnissen geraten sind.[5]

The ideas put forward by Brecht in the context of the so-called

2. John W. Loofbourow, 'Realism in the Anglo-American novel', in Halperin, *The Theory of the Novel*, p. 257.
3. Roy Pascal, 'Fortklang und Nachklang des Realismus im Roman', in Werner Kohlschmidt (ed.), *Spätzeiten und Spätzeitlichkeit*, Berne & Munich, 1962, p. 137.
4. Richard Brinkmann, 'Zum Begriff des Realismus für die erzählende Dichtung des neunzehnten Jahrhunderts' in idem (ed.), *Begriffsbestimmung des literarischen Realismus*, Darmstadt, 1969, p. 222.
5. Brecht, 'Notizen zur realistischen Schreibweise', in idem, *Über Realismus*, Leipzig, 1968, p. 170.

'Expressionismusdebatte' have had a powerful part to play in more recent literary debates in the Federal Republic; whereas, however, Brecht was demanding a new form of realism appropriate to the modern age, his arguments have been used extensively to support anti-realism, making it clear that this position is not restricted to those, like him, on the Left. This broadly based antipathy to realism was equally noticeable earlier in this century: ideas similar to Brecht's are found in Hermann Broch's theoretical pronouncements on the novel. In the Fifties, before Brecht had been rediscovered, Erich Kahler, whose origins are in the George-Kreis, put forward in his 'Übergang und Untergang der epischen Kunstform' ideas strikingly similar to those advanced in the Seventies by critics and scholars steeped in Brecht. Kahler felt that technological progress had shaken fundamentally artistic concepts such as realism, that 'die Realität, mit der wir es heute zu tun haben, . . . in Tiefe und Tragweite unmeßbar über jene vordergründliche Sphäre hinausgerückt [ist], die das Substrat des "Realismus" im Verstande des neunzehnten Jahrhunderts gewesen ist'. The result, he claims, is that 'in unserer kollektiven und übertechnisierten Zivilisation das Individuum und der individuelle Vorgang seine repräsentative Bedeutung verloren hat. Nicht mehr kann daher eine erfundene individuelle Geschichte das allgemeine, das wesentliche Geschehen unserer Epoche ausdrücken'.[6]

One thing is particularly striking about the examples which the participants in this debate give to illustrate the type of novel that is no longer possible: they are predominantly French, less frequently Russian or English, but almost never German. We thus have the absurd situation that a whole body of theory about the constraints upon the modern German novel is built up which takes virtually no account of the German novel tradition as such. This suggests immediately that the novel of so-called German realism is particularly problematical in this context, and indeed it is. Although Fritz Martini has tried energetically to rebuff the charge made by a number of non-German critics and scholars that the German novel of the nineteenth century was relatively short on realism, there is little doubt that the finest products of the period are, compared with those of other European countries, more 'idealistic' and, as is implied by the term frequently used to describe it, more 'poetic'. Moreover, the use of specifically non-German examples to support a particular view of the modern novel suggests that the interrelationship between society and literature, to which Brecht and Kahler allude, was different in Germany from that in other countries and

6. *Neue Rundschau*, 1953, pp. 2, 34.

thus produced a different view of the novel. That this was indeed so emerges, we would argue, from nineteenth-century German theories of the genre.

While Henry Hatfield is undoubtedly right in seeing a significance in Goethe's reworking of the essentially realist *Wilhelm Meisters Theatralische Sendung* into the far more reflective *Lehrjahre*, we would view Hegel's theoretical pronouncements on the novel, which for him was 'die moderne bürgerliche Epopöe', as the essential source of the specifically German view of the form since 1800. Hegel's starting-point is the lack 'des ursprünglich poetischen Weltzustands, aus welchem der eigentliche Epos hervorgeht'. The heroic, the source of the epic, has in modern times had to give way to 'einer fest einge-richteten bürgerlichen Ordnung und einem prosaischen Weltlauf', and, since the world has become unpoetic, the novel's task is to strip off the prosaic from the actions of the characters 'und dadurch eine der Schönheit und Kunst verwandte und befreundete Wirklichkeit an die Stelle der vorgefundenen Prosa setzen'. For Hegel 'die lebendige subjektive Besonderheit der Individuen' is far more worthy of artistic treatment than external reality and one of the most appropriate topics for the novel is 'der Konflikt zwischen der Poesie des Herzens und der entgegenstehenden Prosa der Verhältnisse'.[7] In such a novel — and though Hegel is thinking of *Wilhelm Meisters Lehrjahre*, the only *Bildungsroman* he knew, his formulation is an uncanny anticipation of a number of later ones — 'schrauben sich nun die subjektiven Wünsche und Forderungen in diesem Gegen-satze ins Unermeßliche in die Höhe'.[8]

The emphasis on the superiority of inner, as opposed to external, life and the consequences for the novel of Hegel's view of the modern world are subsequently taken up — and, indeed, intensified — by Fr.Th.Vischer in his *Aesthetik*. As with Hegel, Vischer's point of departure is 'die prosaische Einrichtung der Dinge . . . , die Erkäl-tung der Umgangsformen, de[r] allgemeine Zug zur Mechanisie-rung der technischen Produkte'. Faced with the threat posed by emergent industrialisation, the novel has to take upon itself the task of restoring 'der Poesie auf diesem Boden der Prosa ihr verlorenes Recht'. As with Hegel, 'das eigentliche Thema des Romans' lies in the conflict 'der inneren Lebendigkeit mit der Härte der äußern Welt'; however, Vischer here goes further than Hegel in stressing that this theme is vital as a means of rescuing 'die Idealität' from the threat of prosaic reality 'durch die Rückführung auf ein vertieftes

7. G.W.F. Hegel, *Werke*, 15, Frankfurt, 1970, p. 393.
8. *Werke*, 14, p. 219.

inneres Leben'. The clear implication is — and this is the central concern of, for example, Immermann's *Die Epigonen* — the advocacy of a turning-away from the new, real world into an inner one in which the 'Gewinnung des Poetischen' is still possible, since 'die Geheimnisse des Seelenlebens . . . die Stelle [sind], wohin das Ideale sich geflüchtet hat, nachdem das Reale prosaisch geworden ist'.[9]

This view of the novel as essentially anti-realist — formulated here by one of the so-called German realists! — seems to have achieved wide acceptance by the mid-century, with only the social novels of Willkomm, Prutz and Scherr breaking the mould. By this time, however, in the theoretical pronouncements of, for example, Otto Ludwig, we note the absence of a philosophical justification of the modern novel; the emphasis is rather on the calling of the true artist to portray not 'die gemeine Wirklichkeit', but 'poetische Wahrheit'. For Ludwig, the task of the novelist is 'Ausmalung . . . des Gewöhnlichen im Leben mit dem Lichte der Idee';[10] literature has to create 'realistische Ideale' and, to do this, 'wahre Poesie' has to 'sich ganz von der äußern Gegenwart loslösen, sozusagen von der wirklichen Wirklichkeit'.[11] Even in the *Grenzboten*, the literary magazine edited by Julian Schmidt and Gustav Freytag, which was seen as *the* mouthpiece of literary realism, realist writing was understood as mediating 'eine der Natur abgelauschte Wahrheit, die uns überzeugt, so daß wir an die künstlerischen Ideale. glauben'. Perhaps the clearest formulation of these by now well-established views on the novel had been made some time earlier by Schopenhauer in his 'Zur Metaphysik des Schönen und Aesthetik', where he claimed: the 'Aufgabe des Romanschreibers . . . besteht darin, daß man mit dem möglichst geringen Aufwand von äußerm Leben das innere in die stärkste Bewegung bringe'. Moreover, Schopenhauer makes it obvious that this sort of idea generated two criteria for the evaluation of a work of literature; for him a novel would 'desto höherer und edlerer Art seyn, je mehr *inneres* und je weniger *äußeres* Leben er darstellt'.[12]

The theoretical position contained in this statement had thus evidently become a more or less normative critical canon, the strength of which after the mid-nineteenth century can perhaps best be illustrated by an examination of the literary debates among, of all people, the German Naturalists. Given that the initial impetus to the German Naturalist movement came from French literature, it might

9. Vischer, *Aesthetik*, Stuttgart, 1857, 3.Teil, 2.Abschnitt, pp. 1304–8.
10. Ludwig, *Gesammelte Schriften*, Bd.6, Leipzig, 1891, p. 75.
11. *Gesammelte Schriften*, Bd.5, p. 411.
12. Schopenhauer, *Sämmtliche Werke*, Bd.6, Leipzig, 1908, pp. 473–4.

reasonably have been expected that theoretical discussion would have centred on Zola's *Le roman expérimental* and on analysis of his novels. This was to some extent true of the Munich Naturalists, and especially of Michael Georg Conrad, but a body of major theorists rejected the Zola model as inappropriate and defined the new literature they wished for very much in terms of the established canon identified above. Thus in Wilhelm Bölsche's *Die naturwissenschaftlichen Grundlagen der Poesie* — a title which would seem to suggest an affinity with Zola — the 'gesunder Realismus' he propagates is intended to reconcile 'Ideal und Wirklichkeit' and to expose 'das Ideale in der natürlichen Entwickelung'.[13] The Brothers Hart, two of the leading Berlin Naturalists, cling to a concept of 'Poesie' redolent of Ludwig, and which can never be attained through a realist 'Schriftstellerroman'. Literature has to strive to achieve 'die rechte Mitte . . . zwischen erdfrischem Realismus und hoher Idealität'; indeed, the highest art goes further than this. It transfigures ('verklärt') 'ursprüngliche, individuell gefärbte *Natur* zum Ideal'.[14] The Harts' model for such writing is not Zola, but rather the Goethe of *Werther*. These and other similar pronouncements go some way towards explaining why German Naturalists achieved so little in the novel, but their real interest for us here is what they tell us about the entrenchment of the specifically German novel tradition. Only the normative canon can explain the uniformly idealist nature of major German novels — in the sense of a concern with inner life and with abstract problems of the self — not only in the nineteenth century, but also after 1900. The novels of Robert Musil, Otto Flake, Hermann Hesse and Hermann Broch clearly belong in this context, as do those of Thomas Mann. Mann, in fact, himself makes a specific connection with these ideas; in his Princeton lecture of 1939, 'Die Kunst des Romans', he cites in full Schopenhauer's remarks, quoted earlier, on the nature of the novel and declares his belief in their continued validity.

Given this particular view of the novel, it ought no longer to be altogether surprising that the major German novels of the nineteenth and twentieth centuries are so different from their European counterparts. Still to be explained, however, is *why* the German path was unique. Erich Auerbach attributes the otherworldliness of the German novels to 'the traditional attitudes of the particular corner of the land in which they were rooted'.[15] But this is not really very

13. Bölsche, *Die naturwissenschaftlichen Grundlagen der Poesie*, Munich, 1976 (Leipzig, 1887), p. 51.
14. Heinrich & Julius Hart, *Kritische Waffengänge*, Berlin, 1884, Heft 2, p. 55.
15. Auerbach, 'Germinie Lacerteux', in *Mimesis*, Princeton, 1971 (3rd edn.), p. 516.

satisfactory, and neither is Fritz Martini's rejection of this sort of criticism as inappropriate. For Martini the 'Verinnerlichung' is entirely justified, since it was the only way 'in der Prosa des Romans als Wiedergabe einer verhärteten Wirklichkeit das dichterische Sprechen zu retten . . .',[16] but he tells us nothing at all about the reasons for this response being confined to German prose; in fact, he aligns himself here in his very phraseology with the aesthetic canon of Vischer, Ludwig, etc. A partial answer to the problem is provided by Otto Ludwig, who identifies a specifically social cause for the 'Intensität' of the German novel, as opposed to the 'Extensität' found in the English one: 'Wir haben kein London, in welchem das Wunderbarste natürlich erscheint . . . , keinen Verkehr mit Kolonien in allen Weltteilen, kein so großes politisches Leben'.[17] In his posthumously published papers, Wilhelm Dilthey remarks that it was 'natürlich, daß der eigentliche Kampf mit den realen Faktoren in dieser über die Welt herrschenden Nation [England, KB] ein Übergewicht hatte. Bei uns ward im deutschen Roman der Kampf innerlich'.[18] It therefore seems appropriate to look at German society in the nineteenth century, and particularly at the middle class, to see if any specific features emerge that might lead us further.

In nineteenth-century Europe, in which the enterprise of the middle-class entrepreneur was so dominant, his self-confident class easily attributed to itself the status of a universal class, as Victorian Britain demonstrates. The novelist was an important mouthpiece of this social group, a fact reflected in the prominence enjoyed by discussions of novels of the day, both in the drawing-room and in family magazines. However, the social changes that gathered pace in the second half of the century weakened the claim of the middle class to universality. In the case of Britain the 'Condition of England' novels (Mrs Gaskell's *Mary Barton* and *North and South*, Disraeli's *Sybil*, Dickens' *Hard Times* and Kingsley's *Alton Locke*) clearly proceed from fear of social disintegration brought about by the new urban industrial age, and the solutions put forward, reflecting the shift in the relationship between writer and reading public, are unambiguously personal. It is dangerous, however, to apply such ideas uncritically to the German situation at that time. Although the industrialisation of Germany was delayed by political divisions and the Napoleonic Wars, between ca. 1840 and 1900 it transformed an

16. Martini, 'Zur Theorie des Romans im deutschen "Realismus"', in *Festgabe für Eduard Behrend*, Weimar, 1959, p. 296.
17. Ludwig, *Gesammelte Schriften*, Bd.6, p. 79.
18. Dilthey, *Die große Phantasiedichtung*, Göttingen, 1954, p. 323.

essentially feudal country into a major power with unparalleled speed. Moreover, Germany lacked the sort of middle class that played such a major role in Britain and elsewhere; the emergent country was dominated, in the main, by banks, joint-stock companies and the various German states, while the failure of the 1848 Revolutions effectively excluded the middle classes from political power. The political might of the old guard continued unaltered into the twentieth century, so that Max Weber was driven to complain: 'bei uns [ist] das Bürgertum in seinen breiten Schichten von der Herrschaft ausgeschlossen durch den Feudalismus, der Minister und Fabrikanten beherrscht . . .'.[19]

Thus the optimistic view found in Spielhagen's *Hammer und Amboß* and Gustav Freytag's *Soll und Haben*, that the new age would open up great possibilities for a new middle class, did not become reality, while the old educated one, the 'Bildungsbürgertum', cursed the increasing mechanisation of production as threatening crucial aspects of a cherished existence. Vischer, for example, felt it important that the novel should 'die poetische Lebendigkeit da [suchen], wohin sie sich bei wachsender Vertrocknung des öffentlichen geflüchtet hat: im engeren Kreise, der Familie, dem Privatleben, in der Individualität, im Innern'.[20] Whereas Spielhagen's and Freytag's heroes live for and through their work, Vischer is concerned about the canker of such activity on the authentic existence of his protagonist, who can only save what he holds dear by a process of withdrawal: 'Nur im Privatleben ist der Philister [i.e. the 'Bildungsbürger', KB] noch lebendig. Hier ist die Bildung, wesentlich eine Frucht der humanistischen Studien, so durchgedrungen, daß der Mensch in diesem abgegrenzten Kreise seine Persönlichkeit abgerundet . . . hat'.[21] The change going on is thus seen by Vischer — as it was later by the cultural pessimists and the Conservative Revolutionaries — as endangering the notions of 'Bildung' and personality. But the 'Bildungsbürgertum' was not such a threatened species as Vischer thought: one of the peculiarities of nineteenth-century Germany was that, despite the massive growth of cities, whole regions were virtually untouched by change. In the country and in many a small town (the true home of the 'Bildungsbürger') the traditional pattern of life continued undisturbed, as is reflected in the novels and 'Novellen' of the time. The crude assertion that the German novel of the nineteenth century simply turned its back on social reality is wrong, in that the writers, as members of the

19. Weber, *Gesammelte politische Schriften*, Tübingen, 1958, p. 109.
20. Vischer, *Aesthetik* [1857], p. 1306.
21. Idem, *Aesthetik*, Reutlingen & Leipzig, 1857, 2.Teil, 1.Abteilung, p. 290.

educated middle class, lived by and large far away from the political and commercial centres of the new Germany. This, together with the lack of change in the political power structure, referred to earlier, led to writers dealing, primarily in the 'Bildungsroman', with a concept of individual development that was the only path open to a group excluded from real social power, or else, like any author, drawing the stuff of their novels from their day-to-day experience of rural and small-town life.

Given the peculiar pattern of German social history in the nineteenth century, it is hardly surprising that there emerged a novel tradition different from that of its neighbours. Where efforts were made to transplant foreign models — Dickens and Eugène Suë come most readily to mind in this context — the effect was disastrous in terms of literary quality. The unconvincing nature of even the better social novels further emphasises the difficulties that confronted those who wished to conform to the European novel style. They fail, ultimately, less from the writers' lack of skill, than from their inability to show 'typical characters under typical conditions', which — as Friedrich Engels stressed in his famous letter to Miss Harkness — the great European novels can and do. The central characters of novels like *Soll und Haben* and *Hammer und Amboß* are not so much typical, as the author's pipe-dreams. On the other hand, one undoubted reason for the quality of the German 'Bildungsroman' is that it articulated typical self-awareness and portrayed figures that reflect the sort of group experiences already mentioned.

In the latter part of the nineteenth century, in Germany perhaps more than in other countries, the bewildering speed and all-embracing nature of social change and the growing impenetrability of a complex modern society radically altered the individual's experience of reality, as Georg Simmel showed so early and so perceptively in his essay 'Die Großstädte und das Geistesleben' (1903). In an increasingly atomised society the writer can no longer express so self-evidently the typical or the representative; his view of things becomes an increasingly personal one. This change in the relationship between the writer and society is clearly no real problem for the idealist novel tradition, concerned as it is with the inner world of the self (indeed Broch is able to use it as a *post hoc* justification of the 'Bildungsroman' in 'Das Weltbild des Romans'), but it is of great significance for the realist novel. It is by no means coincidental that, for the comparatist, the German novel joins the main stream of the European tradition with Fontane, who, writing at a time when these changes were being fully felt and when the German experience was no longer different from that of the rest of Western Europe, reflects so sensitively their consequences for narration. Through the clearly ironic voice of the narrator of his work it is made obvious that the social world portrayed is viewed through the eyes of an individual. Another possible way of reflecting in realist prose the increasingly very personal experience of reality was put forward by Arno Holz, who in 'Der erste Schultag' and 'Papa Hamlet' introduces perspectivised narration, whereby events are portrayed more or less simultaneously from the point of view of various protagonists. This technique is later taken over and applied to the epic form of the novel by Alfred Döblin, who always acknowledged his debt to Arno Holz, in *Berlin Alexanderplatz*; after 1945 this technique gains considerably in importance. There is, however, another German writer of the late nineteenth century (and one difficult to integrate adequately into the German tradition) who, we feel, recognised the consequences of social change for realist prose-writing and who in some of his work created a truly realist novel which responded fully to the specific social circumstances, experiences and concerns of the 'Bildungsbürgertum' — Wilhelm Raabe. In our view, his work in many ways prefigures important aspects of the realist novel of today.[22]

Raabe (1831–1910) belongs to the generation which experienced the full force of German social change and watched with sadness the demise of the old world, particularly embodied for him in 'die bürgerstolzen, freien Gemeinwesen des Mittelalters'. Unlike many of his contemporaries, however, Raabe could recognise the opportunities offered by the new age to a younger generation. Given Germany's abrupt transition from feudalism to advanced capitalism, which highlighted the particular problems for established notions of personality — picked up so early by Goethe and Schiller — it is not difficult to understand why the leading proponents of aesthetic theory chose the inward path. There is no doubt that, emotionally, Raabe sided with them, but his work makes it clear that resignation and withdrawal ultimately offered no solution to the difficulties faced by his generation. A number of his works are characterised by a tension born of the sense of living between two worlds and by the presentation of a figure new to the German novel: the problematical hero. This protagonist — as Lucien Goldmann has demonstrated in his *Cultural Creation in Modern Society* — became increasingly central to the European realist novel from the late nineteenth century onwards. He attempts to embody, or in some

22. Cf. in this connection my article, 'Wilhelm Raabe and the European novel', *Orbis litterarum*, 1976, 31, pp. 263–81.

way to keep alive through his involvement with social life, crucial and authentic human values seemingly threatened by a world seen as increasingly reified and degraded. Raabe adds particular force to this clash between personal and external, alien values in *Die Chronik der Sperlingsgasse* (1856), *Pfisters Mühle* (1884), *Stopfkuchen* (1891) and *Die Akten des Vogelsangs* (1896), through the use of the reminiscence-technique, which facilitates vivid contrasting of the (narrative) present with the (narrated) fondly remembered past by means of intercutting. This allows the most forceful literary expression of Raabe's ambivalent attitude to the new age, but has inevitable consequences for the novel form, as then conceived — indeed, Raabe did not call any of these works a novel and the narrator of *Die Chronik der Sperlingsgasse* is at pains to stress that he is not writing one. They all have a seemingly chaotic structure, no omniscient third-person narrator, no linear chronology or sense of individual development in the central character. Today we unhesitatingly class these highly individualistic, not to say idiosyncratic, presentations of experience in prose as novels; in their day, however, they represented a radical break with the established understanding of a novel. They also show that it was indeed possible to break away from the idealist tradition and to generate a form of the realist novel adequate to the particular experiences of the 'Bildungsbürgertum'. Raabe's stylistic and formal innovations also call into question the German equation of realism with the 'traditional' novel (and hence a *passé* form); at the same time the comparison with Fontane, who has just as little to do with the canonised German novel tradition, yet whose (successful) solution to the problems of realist narration in the latter part of the nineteenth century is so different from Raabe's, makes it clear how wrong German authors, critics and scholars are to view realism as being an historically delimited and essentially homogeneous style of writing. Moreover, these two writers represent the beginnings of an alternative realist novel tradition in Germany that is continued by, amongst others, Heinrich Mann, Döblin, Arnold Zweig, Remarque and Kästner in the Twenties and Thirties, and by a substantial body of novels in the Seventies. Fontane and Raabe offer markedly different formal solutions to the problems posed to the writer by a radical shift in the nature of the relationship of the individual subject to reality and these solutions point forward to the range of styles adopted by modern realist writers. At the same time, the break with the quietism of the idealist novel, the utopian dimension in their depiction of the individual social experience, links such authors back to the main thrust of European realism and forward to the realist novel of the Twenties and Thirties and of the

15

Seventies. But there can be no doubt that, even long after 1945, the anti-realist novel tradition, born of the peculiar German experience in the early part of the nineteenth century, remained dominant. The following chapters will seek to demonstrate the amazing endurance of this aesthetic canon.

2

West German Literature and Realism 1945–65

One of the distinctive features of German intellectual and political life, from the failure of the 1848 Revolution on into the twentieth century, is the tendency of the German 'Bildungsbürgertum' to aestheticise political and social phenomena — in the way in which, for example, fascism was seen as a threat to German 'Geist'.[1] There are clear indications that this tradition continued in the immediate post-war situation. Amongst the educated middle classes the political defeat of Germany, the destruction of the cities and the problem of the regeneration of the country were seen primarily as areas where it was necessary for the 'Geist' to reassert itself. Thomas Mann took up the question of Germany's war guilt in very much the same terms as he had used in the *Betrachtungen eines Unpolitischen* and there was a noticeable revival of interest in Oswald Spengler's historical pessimism; perhaps the most dominant trend was the turning to the tradition of German Classicism as the source of a necessary German rebirth. Karl Jaspers pronounced that the Germans faced the task, 'Goethes Welt anzueignen, durch Übersetzung seiner Wahrheit in die eigene Welt', while E.R. Curtius saw Goethe's legacy as 'eine Kraft, an der die deutsche Jugend genesen und erstarken kann'.[2] An important publication in this connection was Friedrich Meinecke's *Die deutsche Katastrophe* (1946). He believed it to be essential to return to the 'ewigen, ehernen, großen Gesetzen unseres Daseins', and this task was the special duty of those few who would come to form 'eine Gemeinschaft gleichgerichteter Kulturfreunde, der ich am liebsten den Namen einer "Goethegemeinde" geben möchte'.[3] Similar ideas, uncannily close to those of the Conservative Revolution of the Twenties, were also put forward by Gottfried Benn.

Given this general intellectual climate, it should not be surprising to find similar ideas in the area of literary theory. In a 1947 edition

1. Cf. Karl Jaspers, *Rechenschaft und Ausblick*, Munich, 1958, p. 56.
2. E.R. Curtius, 'Goethe, Jaspers, Curtius. Ein Schlußwort in eigener Sache', *Die Zeit*, 2.6.1949.
3. *Die deutsche Katastrophe*, 3rd edn., Wiesbaden, 1947, pp. 157, 174.

of *Karussell*, Joachim G. Boeckh expressed the hope 'daß die Erziehung als geistige Aktion ihren Rang in Deutschland wieder bekommt, den sie seit langem zugewiesen erhalten hat durch den "Wilhelm Meister", durch den "Nachsommer" und nun wieder durch das "Glasperlenspiel" '.[4] Hesse — who was praised in literary circles for his 'transparent realism', i.e. one that leads back 'zu Quellen aus hohen humanitären Bildungselementen'[5] — Ernst Jünger and Gottfried Benn, named in 1948 by the (then) influential critic Hans Egon Holthusen as the major German writers of the day, represent the continuation of the escapist 'magischer Realismus' in the immediate post-war years. The anti-realist nature of their writing emerges clearly from Jünger's *Das abenteuerliche Herz*, in which literature itself is proclaimed the highest form of reality, in contrast to the 'platten Realitäten der bürgerlichen Welt',[6] while Benn's 'absolute Prosa' is conceived as being 'außerhalb von Raum und Zeit, ins Imaginäre gebannt, ins Momentane, Flüchtige gelegt'.[7] Further support for such a view came from Leonhard Frank, just returned from exile; he claimed: 'Nur das *innere* Bild kann wahr sein. Es gibt nur die *innere* Wahrheit, alles andere ist Lüge'.[8] Significantly, in this context, the post-war writing most highly praised by critics conformed to such anti-realist ideas; obvious examples are Elisabeth Langgässer's *Das unauslösliche Siegel* (1946), Ilse Aichinger's *Die größere Hoffnung* (1948) and Hermann Kasack's *Die Stadt hinter dem Strom* (1947), which was widely considered to be the archetypal novel of the period. Gerhard Pohl described it as 'das Spiegelbild unserer "verlorenen" Epoche . . . eine großartige dichterische Vision alles Werdens, Daseins und Vergehens',[9] and Kasack himself spoke of his desire to create 'Sinnbilder der Realität', 'die unabhängig von der Erscheinungsform ihre "universelle Gültigkeit" behalten'.[10]

The tendency to deal in literature with dictatorship, defeat and the material problems of the immediate post-war period in allegory or other forms of symbolism is the reverse side of an inability to think in any sort of political category. Hans Egon Holthusen, whose *Der unbehauste Mensch* was the most influential critical work of its day, castigated (as 'sinnstörend') any sort of 'Doktrinarismus und Ideologismus, jede Versteifung und Verengung der eigenen Position, die

4. Quoted in Jürgen Manthey, 'Zurück zur Kultur', *Literaturmagazin 7*, 1977, p. 15.
5. Cf. *Freude an Büchern*, 1952–3.
6. Ernst Jünger, *Gesammelte Werke*, Bd. 9, Stuttgart, 1979, p. 173.
7. Benn, 'Der Roman des Phänotyp', *Werke*, Bd. 4, Wiesbaden, 1961, p. 132.
8. R. Adolph (im Gespräch mit Leonhard Frank), 'Die Kunst des Weglassens', *Das literarische Deutschland*, 3, 1950, p. 5.
9. 'Magischer Realismus', *Aufbau*, 1949, Heft 8, p. 653.
10. *Die Welt*, 1947; quoted in Manthey, 'Zurück zur Kultur'.

uns die Offenheit des Horizonts beeinträchtigt'. He was prepared to tolerate the then fashionable existentialism, if only for having 'vor der Psychoanalyse und dem Marxismus das eine voraus, daß seine Fragestellung eine *metaphysische* [my italics, KB] ist', addressing the choice, 'die mir das Kernproblem der Epoche zu enthalten scheint: Gott oder das Nichts, Christentum oder Nihilismus'. The problems of the day were accordingly stripped of specificity and cloaked in more general apocalyptic motifs. This literature tackles neither fascism and its consequences nor the post-war polarisation of the world; instead the time was ripe, according to Holthusen, 'die aus allen Fugen geratene Welt wieder in Ordnung zu denken . . . , das alte Wahre in neuer Sprache wiederherzustellen'.[11]

This notion — emanating, as already shown, from the tradition of German idealism — of a sphere of reality transcending the common world of normal experience informs the critical view of the leading West German literary scholars and academies until well into the Fifties. Frank Thieß, President of the influential Mainzer Akademie für Dichtung und Wissenschaft, considered literature (he used, significantly, the older term 'Dichtung') to be a supra-reality ('Überrealität'), it represented 'durchschaute Wirklichkeit'. He firmly rejected what 'im gemeinen Verstande' was considered as reality, preferring instead that 'tiefere Wirklichkeitsschicht' which he held to be the domain of literature. He had an 'Animosität gegen den Realismus', since it did not address itself to this other, 'die *eigentliche* Wirklichkeitsschicht' beyond the 'Tatsachenbereich der bürgerlichen Existenz'.[12] The strength of the anti-realism of the day emerges vividly from Karl Korn's 1956 account in *Akzente* of a meeting of French and German writers, at which the French had without a second thought spoken of realism and reality, whereas the Germans had set their faces resolutely against 'literarischen Realismus als Parole'. Korn himself rejected the 'Verfälschung von Realität durch die traditionellen Erzählmittel eines längst historisch gewordenen Realismus', but — unlike the rest of his German colleagues, notably Günter Eich — he could actually countenance a modern form of realism, whose task it was to find appropriate symbols for an abstract situation. Ultimately, he too was seeking a 'Symbolismus der Realität', and so it is not surprising that his examples of contemporary realism are Kafka, Joyce and, above all, Kasack. Particularly interesting in this context is a report on the same conference by Günter Eich, whose lyric poetry and 'Hörspiele'

---

11. *Der unbehauste Mensch*, Munich, 1951, pp. 7–33.
12. Thieß, *Dichtung und Wirklichkeit*, Wiesbaden, 1952, pp. 8–12.

were so central to German literature of the Fifties; he claimed not to know 'was Wirklichkeit ist'. For him, to be a writer was to see the world simply in terms of language, but language in a sense that transcended the 'Zeitwort'.[13]

A similar view that literature is not particularly concerned with empirical experience, but rather aims to transcend it by means of language, metaphor or other forms of symbolism, and to create a world of 'schöner Schein', dominates the reviews and essays of the major literary critics of the Fifties, such as Friedrich Sieburg, Günter Blöcker, Holthusen, Curt Hohoff and Karl Friedrich Horst. The vigorous defence of writing conforming to their anti-realist notion of literature led to high esteem for writers whose work today is of little interest, apart from some curiosity as to why they were once rated so highly. In this connection, an exemplary case-study is provided by Gerd Gaiser, acclaimed in the Fifties as a major writer by all these critics and by scholars: he also received several major literary prizes. Gaiser's work, clearly influenced by the experiences of his formative years in the 'bündische Jugend', reflects the post-war revival of interest in the work of Nietzsche, Moeller van den Bruck and the historical pessimism of Oswald Spengler; to this is added an Existentialist criticism of the age, strongly influenced by Heidegger. The dominant feature of Gaiser's writing, and simultaneously the medium of his cultural criticism, is a symbolism derived primarily from classical literature and the Bible, which serves to relativise, in a fundamental way, the temporal specificity in his portrayal of the post-war world. The returning soldier ('Heimkehrer') Oberstelehn in *Eine Stimme hebt an* (1950) is a modern Odysseus or Don Quixote, trying to keep alive eternal values amidst post-war chaos and concerned, above all, that 'die Honigstimme aus Lesbos' — the classical canon of literature — should still be heard. *Die sterbende Jagd* (1953), celebrated in its day as the 'poetic' treatment of the war in the air, presents the pilots, in a manner reminiscent of passages in Ernst Jünger's *In Stahlgewittern*, as the heirs of mediaeval knights. Where any reference seems to locate events most definitely in the Third Reich, the symbolism very quickly intervenes to shift things on to a much more general plane. Thus one speaker, pointing to a picture that is undoubtedly of Hitler or, possibly, Goering, says: 'Gott hat ihn uns geschickt . . . und er muß uns verderben. Ich verstehe das und verstehe das nicht. Aber ich kann nicht austreten und kann es nicht wenden. *Nemo contra Deum nisi Deus ipse*'.[14]

13. Karl Korn, 'Darstellung der Grunderfahrung (Der Schriftsteller vor Realität)', *Akzente*, 3, 1956, pp. 307–14.
14. *Die sterbende Jagd*, Frankfurt, 1957 (Fischer Bücherei), p. 157.

National Socialism, alluded to only very obscurely, is, like all problems in the physical world, the result of the unfathomable machinations of an inscrutable Will, not of human action. The shortcomings of his earthly life can, however, be escaped, in that Gaiser — in much the same terms as Jünger or Frank Thieß — believes in a higher plane of existence, attainable by a few elect, and this he evokes in all his work. Even in *Schlußball* (1958), which was widely (mis-) understood as one of the representative socio-critical novels of the early 'Wirtschaftswunder', 'das eigentliche Leben' is not shown as consisting in a more dignified and satisfying life for all members of society, but as existing in the world of dreams or in a realm beyond the grave. The existence of this supra-reality dominates all Gaiser's novels and stories, finding its fullest expression in *Am Paß Nascondo* (1960), in which the physical world is abandoned completely in favour of the superior dream-world. From today's perspective such a response to the problems of life in re-emergent Germany seems astonishing, with its firm belief in a state bridging life and death, embodying ancient cultural values. But these ideas, drawing on Schopenhauer and Nietzsche, Heidegger, Moeller van den Bruck and Oswald Spengler, clearly struck a chord with educated Germans at the time; Gaiser's reputation at the end of the Fifties was such that Walter Jens was moved to write a full-page article in *Die Zeit*, arguing that he was overrated, while Marcel Reich-Ranicki launched a violent attack in *Deutsche Literatur in Ost und West*, trying to discredit Gaiser as a former Nazi.[15]

Given the strength of the anti-realist tradition examined in the previous chapter, it is not surprising that it continued its dominance in the post-war period, not only in the novel, but also in the lyric, the 'Hörspiel' and the short story. Alfred Andersch probably sensed something of this when in 1948 he declared that it was 'eine große Aufgabe der deutschen Literaturforschung, aufzuklären, warum der reine Realismus in Deutschland niemals zum Durchbruch gekommen ist'.[16] The renewal of idealist literature and literary theory after the Second World War was strong enough to be able to withstand and overcome a very determined campaign for realist literature. In 1947, Friedrich Knapp, criticising the 'Flucht aus der Substanz', which he saw as characteristic of much German literature, urged the adoption of a realism springing 'aus dem Mut und dem Willen zur Erkenntnis'; its great advantage would be that only such a literature is concerned 'mit den wesentlichen Aufgaben der

15. Cf. further in this connection my *Between chaos and order: the work of Gerd Gaiser*, Stuttgart, 1980.
16. Andersch, *Deutsche Literatur in der Entscheidung*, Karlsruhe, 1948, p. 20.

Zusammenschau, der Überwindung und Vereinigung des Widersprüchlichen, der Ergründung und Durchbrechung der Oberfläche'. Realism was for him the healthy 'Antithese zum Individualismus, zu dem . . . deutschen Hang nach dem Tiefsten, dem Unendlichen', and as such was 'die Forderung der Stunde'.[17] Similar ideas are found in Andersch's essay 'Deutsche Literatur in der Entscheidung' (1948), where the professed 'Anti-Symbolist' was at that time optimistic enough to claim: 'Der Haupstrom [of German writers, KB] scheint . . . instinktiv zum reinen Realismus hinzudrängen, bemüht, diesen mit nenen Formen, mit der Intensität unmittelbarer Erlebniskraft zu füllen'.[18] Andersch named Plievier's *Stalingrad* and Kolbenhoff's *Von unserem Fleisch und Blut* as pointers here, to which might be added Erich Kuby's *Brest-Tagebuch*, Erhart Kästner's *Das Zeltbuch von Tumilat* and Hans Werner Richter's *Die Geschlagenen* as early indications of the attempt at producing realist prose. Above all, this endeavour is associated with the initial phase of Gruppe 47 under Richter and Andersch. Looking back on the early years of the group *Der Spiegel* stressed the important influence of the American realists Saroyan, Steinbeck, Dos Passos and Hemingway, whose work was only now becoming known and which, it was felt, set an example of the new realism 'mit humanistisch-Sozialistischem Einschlag' (Richter) that was needed. (Not for the first time the strength of the German anti-realist tradition is indicated by the sense that it was necessary to turn to foreign models.) The most radical — and most famous — demand for realist writing came from Wolfgang Weyrauch, who urged the stripping down of literature to the precise portrayal of problems of survival in the immediate post-war era; this was the formula for 'Kahlschlag' literature: 'Die Methode der Bestandsaufnahme. Die Intention der Wahrheit. Beides um den Preis der Poesie. Wo der Anfang der Existenz ist, ist auch der Anfang der Literatur'.[19] Weyrauch demonstrated the potential (and the limitations) of this technique in his short story 'Das Begräbnis', which is so reminiscent of Holz's 'Sekundenstil'; the overwhelming impression, though, as with Holz, is the impossibility of sustaining such a method of writing at length in a novel, that it is a stylistic cul-de-sac. In retrospect it could be said of the so-called 'Kahlschlag' phase that, as with German Naturalism, more energy was expended on statements of position than on creative writing; its prose monuments are the early works of Richter and Kolbenhoff and some short stories.

17. 'Realismus in der zeitgenössischen Literatur', *Wort und Welt*, 2, 1947, p. 158.
18. *Deutsche Literatur in der Entscheidung*, p. 25.
19. Cf. Hans Werner Richter, '15 Jahre' in Reinhard Lettau (ed.), *Almanach der Gruppe 47*, Reinbek, 1962, p. 10.

The radical realist renewal of German literature did not, however, take place, and neither did the concomitant desire for the linguistic cleansing of literature in the post-war period. The notion of a literary and linguistic 'Stunde Null', prevalent in the Fifties, was, as Urs Widmer and Heinrich Vormweg have shown, only a myth.[20]

It is not possible to find any one cause for the failure of the realist thrust of the Forties and early Fifties. But it is striking that every demand for realism was accompanied by a suspicion of ideology. Despite the humanistic–socialist position proclaimed in *Der Ruf* by the founders of Gruppe 47, the excesses of fascism and the increasingly sharp ideological divisions of the cold war seemed to make it impossible for them to comprehend and to treat the war and the post-war world other than in non-political categories, which in literature easily slid into symbolism. Although much of his writing is informed by sober analysis, Hans Werner Richter, for example, presents National Socialism in his novels as the manifestation of evil; social and political causes are ignored. Heinrich Böll's 'Trümmerliteratur' is concerned with the destruction of basic decent human values, a destruction rendered through metaphor, again in a way that does not bring social causes into the foreground, but rather the interplay of good and bad with human nature. In the short stories of the Fifties this works well enough, but the metaphorical dimension of novels like *Das Brot der frühen Jahre* and *Billard um halbzehn* is at times bizarre and at odds with the closely observed and economical realism of so much of the narration.

Another reason for the relative lack of prominence of the realist novel is the way in which so many writers conceived of the war and its aftermath in Existentialist terms; notable here is the strong influence of Sartre and Camus on German writers. Hans Erich Nossack's *Nekyia* and *Interview mit dem Tode* are obvious examples in this context. It would seem that Alfred Andersch's own writing strayed from the realist path under the same influence. Whereas the presentation of the motives, coloured by Existentialist thought, leading to the desertion described in the autobiographical *Die Kirschen der Freiheit* (1952) provides a psychologically persuasive impression of his experiences in Italy, we see in the later novel *Sansibar oder der letzte Grund* (1956) how Existentialist ideas generate an essentially symbolic treatment of his theme of individual responsibility in the face of oppression. By an ironical coincidence, in the year of this novel's publication *Texte und Zeichen*, a magazine co-

edited by Andersch, announced a competition to find 'einen realistischen, zeit- und gesellschaftskritischen Roman'; a year later the
editors conceded that none of the forty-two manuscripts submitted
met their criteria. It is not known whether *Sansibar . . .* was among
these.

None of these various factors which dulled the realist thrust can,
however, explain adequately why the loud call for realism in the late
Forties was answered so briefly. There are other not unimportant
aspects of this question: for example, Kolbenhoff rapidly lapsed into
relative literary silence and Richter stagnated somewhat as a writer.
Above all, though, attention has to be paid to the literary climate of
the day, in particular to the clear signs that the anti-realist taste of
the conservative critics was shared by the educated middle-class
reading public. Plievier's *Stalingrad* or Böll's novels and short stories
did have a popular success but they were not regarded as consituting
literature in the true sense of the word (*Der Spiegel*, which until
his death did not have a high regard for Böll as a writer, in 1961
labelled him a 'katholischer Fallada'). Literary journals of the day
and the award of literary prizes indicate that real respect was
accorded to the conservative writers already mentioned, lyric poets
such as Celan, Lehmann, Eich and Bachmann, the Existentialists
and, above all, the so-called 'Klassiker der Moderne', such as Rilke,
George, Hofmannsthal, Proust, Joyce and Eliot, whose work was
republished and widely read. An additional factor here was undoubtedly the sense of a need to 'catch up' on modern writers
from other literatures not available in the Third Reich. These
various influences, added to the strength of the idealist tradition,
produced an antipathy to literary innovation that affected both
experimental literature and realism, so that the impression created
by the contemporary literary scene and surveys of German literature
is at variance with the reading of the major literary currents of the
Fifties given by literary histories today. This is made fairly clear by
the negative reception of important works by writers now regarded
as major and whose work has had a considerable influence on later
generations of writers: Wolfgang Koeppen and Arno Schmidt.
Koeppen's first post-war novel, *Tauben im Gras* (1951) constituted a
broad critical treatment of the early Federal Republic. In its use of
montage technique and quotation, the work links back stylistically
to writers like Döblin, Joyce and Dos Passos, but it also anticipates
elements of the 'Sprachrealismus' of the Sixties and Seventies (cf.
Chapter 4); it is not really surprising that it was Helmut Heißenbüttel, more than any other writer, who campaigned vigorously for
recognition of Koeppen's merits. Koeppen's later novel, *Das Treib-*

haus (1953), through its intensive use of interior monologue and the exclusive focus on the experiences of the protagonist Keetenheuve, points forward to another important tendency in the West German novel of the Seventies, when, significantly, Koeppen belatedly received full recognition. But even more important that Koeppen, certainly as far as influence on later writers is concerned, is the case of the early writings of Arno Schmidt. Although soon hailed by Grass and Walser as exciting and stimulating, these works were widely ignored. It was not, again, until the Seventies that Schmidt's stature as a major writer was recognised; his ideas on realism and prose writing then received great attention and they may be regarded as one of the most important stimuli to the novel of the period.

Arno Schmidt's literary theory [21] rests on two seemingly contradictory tendencies. On the one hand he stresses the importance 'für die Beschreibung und Durchleuchtung der Welt durch das Wort (die erste Voraussetzung zu jeder Art von Beherrschung)' of the change since the turn of the century in the writer's relationship to language (articulated initially by Hofmannsthal), as well as the need to develop new forms of prose-writing that reflect adequately the present-day experiences and self-awareness of the writer as mediating subject (RuP, 284). And yet he still sees the task of the 'Dichter' 'als Beobachters und Topographen aller möglichen Charaktere und Situationen . . . doch wohl unter anderem auch, diese dann darzustellen wie solche wirklich sind'. His aim is ultimately 'die getreue Schilderung einer Zeit mit ihren typischsten und feinsten Zügen'. (SH, 180). Such formulations reveal an uncanny closeness to Auerbach's ideas on the mimetic nature of the realist novel and, indeed, to Naturalist notions of the function of the novelist. Modern writing, which for Schmidt begins with Lewis Carroll (cf. TbZ, 257), consists in the fusion of these two elements and is synonymous with prose; in it alone 'wird rhythmisch der Vielfalt der Weltabläufe annähernd gerecht; zumal wenn mit einer erfreulichen Tendenz zu größerer Genauigkeit und Offenheit gekoppelt' (TbZ, 261). Given the increasing isolation of the modern subject the aim of modern literature should be 'die möglichst exakte Wiedergabe des Gemisches aus subjektivem Gedanken-Stromgeschnelle plus Dauerberieselung durch eine Realität' (TbZ, 272), as exemplified by Joyce's use of the stream of consciousness.

The fullest explanation by Schmidt of his theoretical views on

21. References in the text are to the following works by Schmidt: *Das steinerne Herz*, Karlsruhe, 1956 (SH); *Rosen und Porree*, Karlsruhe, 1959 (RuP); *Trommler beim Zaren*, Karlsruhe, 1966 (TbZ); and *Zettels Traum*, Stuttgart, 1970 (ZT).

literature is to be found in the 'Berechnungen' (RuP). Since modern life is for him a 'Bindfaden der Bedeutungslosigkeit', on which is strung 'die Perlenkette kleiner Erlebniseinheiten, innerer und äußerer' (290), the flow of epic narration is today impossible, instead there is a need for 'ein der menschlichen Erlebnisweise gerechter werdendes, zwar mageres, aber trainierteres Prosagefüge', such as he aims at in the trilogy *Brand's Haide*. In these novels Schmidt attempts to blend thought-'photos', which trigger off each and every act of memory, with 'texts', which are intended to explain and comment upon the image. He asserts that, through the amalgam of these 'Foto-Text-Einheiten', the illusion of memory is re-created linguistically and formally. The structure is constantly broken up by 'cuts' (the filmic term renders the effect most clearly here, KB), but the result is a mosaic true to the experience of reality. Schmidt then proceeds from this structuring principle to his idea of the 'Längeres Gedankenspiel' (LG). All experience of objective reality (E I) is accompanied by subjective reflection on this (E II). As with the process of 'Sich-Erinnern' just described, the writer has to incorporate both elements of reality into his text, with the ultimate aim, 'das Zusammen- und Durcheinanderspiel des Alltags eines Menschen . . . getreulich abzubilden. Genau und rücksichtslos — also, mit anderen Worten: WAHR! — vorzuführen, was an der Realität in die betreffende Seifenblasenwelt übernommen wird'.[22] The formulation could have been made by Arno Holz or Alfred Döblin, but, whereas Holz sought to render Schmidt's E II by free indirect speech (FIS) and Döblin by a complex blend of FIS, montage and collage (often making it difficult for the reader to distinguish between E I and E II), Schmidt attempts to mark the difference at all times by clearly distinct forms. In his early work he uses separate blocks of print; however, he very soon conceives the radical solution (rendering the two elements simultaneously on opposite halves of the page) which he put into practice from *Zettels Traum* onwards.

After the publication of *Kaff auch Mare Crisium* (1960) E II is stressed more and more in Schmidt's work; he even goes so far as to state in *Zettels Traum*: 'Das sogenannte Wirkliche Lebm. (Und das viel-wirklichere in unserem Gehirn)' (ZT, VII, 1020). He withdraws into a solipsistic life, his major concern is the cultivation of his 'Bargfelder Ich', although the element of irony continually calls into question the contented isolation of his protagonists. But the generation of 1968 came to discover and appreciate in Schmidt's early work

---

22. Cf. Schmidt's contribution to *Schwierigkeiten, heute die Wahrheit zu schreiben*, Munich, 1964, p. 151.

his sharp, realistic treatment of everyday life in the Third Reich (*Aus dem Leben eines Fauns*), the misery of the refugees in the aftermath of war (*Brand's Haide* and 'Die Umsiedler'), the early years of the 'Wirtschaftswunder' and of divided Germany (*Das steinerne Herz*) and his prescient examination of the dangers of a nuclear catastrophe (*Die Gelehrtenrepublik*). His precise use of language created a vivid word-picture of the first decade or so after the war which, in its realism, contrasted with the literature of this period that they had met at school. Above all, however, this younger generation of writers responded to Schmidt with enthusiasm because they found in his early work an affinity with what they were now demanding of contemporary literature. Their reading of Brecht and Bloch, Barthes and Adorno had made it clear to a good many of them that realistic writing in the manner of the nineteenth century was no longer possible, but they retained a belief in the epistemological claim of realism — in what Schmidt called ' Beherrschung' or 'Durchleuchtung durch das Wort'; in his early work they found a highly persuasive example of modern realism. This is not the place at which to go fully into the influence of Schmidt on the literature of the late Sixties and after, but it seems to be particularly marked in experimental prose writing (Heißenbüttel, Jürgen Becker, Alexander Kluge and Ror Wolf, for example), in the documentary montage-novel and in the use of the 'block' technique in the novels of Härtling and Kempowski. In all these types of writing *objets trouvés* or documentary material (= E I) are combined with subjective commentary (= E II) and the attention is throughout drawn by formal means to the distinction between the two elements and, as in Schmidt's work, the clear message is that the realist novel should reflect the impossibility for the modern, increasingly isolated individual of attaining an unambiguous, 'objective' interpretation of reality.

In the Fifties, though, Schmidt was widely ignored. The dominant literature of the day was, as has been shown, anti-realist; it was 'eine Literatur der Bilder, Gefühle, Aussagen, Reminiszenzen mehr als eine Literatur der Wahrnehmung, der Artikulation des Realen'.[23] Despite the initial claims of the founders, this was increasingly true of the literature emanating from Gruppe 47; instead realism was seen as a solution to problems of writing only for the immediate post-war years. In 1957, looking back at the development of the group, Arnold Bauer observed: 'Die Einengung und Festlegung des Kreises auf einen neuen Realismus in den ersten Nachkriegsjahren ist nicht mehr akut. Nur wenige von den Alten (und noch weniger

23. Vormweg, 'Deutsche Literatur 1945–60'.

die Jungen, inzwischen Dazugestoßenen) verteidigen die realistische Ausgangsposition von 1947'.[24] In retrospect this is not altogether surprising, since there was from the very beginning an
ambivalence in the demands made upon realism, in that it had to be
social realism, and yet it was also stressed — understandably enough
in the context of the day — that it had to be free of dogma, ideology
and the like, which pulled it, rather, in the direction of being an
expression of the *individual's* humanitarian concern for others. But
Stalinism and the tensions of the cold war rapidly led to even this
view of realism widely being called into question, particularly because of its proximity to Socialist Realism, the then official aesthetic
code of the young GDR. In Adenauer's Germany, East German
literature, and by extension much realist writing as such, tended to
be dismissed as propaganda. Moreover, critics observed with scarcely
concealed glee that well-known writers who had returned to the
eastern part of Germany had either written nothing (Becher) or at a
level below that of earlier work (Anna Seghers and Arnold Zweig).
Increasingly, therefore, realism came to be understood as poor
literature. In the *Streit-Zeit-Schrift*, Horst Bingel dismissed it as
identical with 'einen forcierten sozialen Anliegen', while Günter
Busch equated it with Lukács' reflection theory, which to him was
untenable. Karl August Horst, in his review of Lukács' *Wider den
mißverstandenen Realismus* criticised Socialist Realism as concerned
'nicht mit der Wirklichkeit', but rather with a 'geschichtlich-ökono-
mischem Vorurteil'; moreover, the decisive thing in literature was
not 'der soziale Ort, sondern der einzelne Mensch, der die Über-
macht des über ihn verhängten Schicksals wissend durchschaut und
im Kampf mit den Mächten entweder überwindet oder unterliegt'.[25]
That such negative criticism was motivated as much by the political
climate as by literary disagreement, emerged clearly after the building of the Berlin Wall in August 1961, as was particularly evident in
an attack of 1962 by the critic Peter Jokostra published in the
conservative *Die Welt*. Commenting on the planned edition of the
works of Anna Seghers by the Luchterhand Verlag, Jokostra declared that she, as Präsidentin of the East German Schriftstellerver-
band, was actively involved 'an der Knebelung des freien Wortes, an
dem ganz perfiden Mechanismus des Funktionär- und Parteiappa-
rates'.[26] Further proof of the political aspect of criticism comes from
Dieter Wellershoff, who complained in 1969 of the term 'realism'
suffering badly from the proximity to Socialist Realism and all that it

24. *Der Kurier*, Berlin 5–6.10.1957.
25. *Das Spektrum des modernen Romans*, Munich, 1964, pp. 55–8.
26. *Die Welt*, 1.8. 1962.

stood for, and from Jörg Drews, who as late as 1974 used these associations to dismiss all realism (cf. Chapter 3).

This ideological dimension of the weakness of realism in the Fifties is, of course, only part of a complex picture. As far as the shift of ideas within Gruppe 47 in particular is concerned, the literary theories of Walter Jens, then one of its leading figures, are revealing. He rejected the model of American realists like Hemingway and all other such 'epigonales Fabulieren', calling instead for an 'abstrakte Literatur' based on Hofmannsthal's observation in the Chandos-Brief, 'daß die traditionellen Sprachformen nicht mehr genügen, um eine Wirklichkeit zu beschreiben, die sich der Deutung durch das betroffene Individuum mehr und mehr entzieht'.[27] From this correct assertion, which informs any modern notion of realism, Jens — like Adorno — concluded that narrative prose is no longer possible. Newspapers, films, television and radio had superseded the novel as far as narration was concerned, while the reportage conveyed information more accurately than the novel, which 'weder zu verwandeln noch zu informieren versteht, sondern nur Fassaden ableuchtet'. In the same way as 'die Photographie die bildende Kunst zu sich selbst führte', the novel was freed by the reportage to be 'Kunst und nichts als Kunst'; the realist novel was now *passé*. Just what could be achieved in modern 'abstract' literature — the model for which was French avant-garde writing — was for Jens demonstrated by Geman lyric poetry of the Fifties; in it reality appeared only 'als Basis, der terminus technicus fungiert als Fixpunkt, von dem aus man die Tiefe der Zeit und die Weite des Raums, das Dinglich-Konkrete so wie das Poetisch-Abstrakte zu überschauen vermag'. In prose writing, as in this poetry, the times demanded not 'Erzählen, sondern fragendes Stilisieren, nicht "Darauflos-Dichten", sondern problematisches Interpretieren', and as a result the 'begabtesten deutschen Autoren' were trying to escape from 'der stofflich-realistischen Eindeutigkeit, der faktisch-kruden Präokkupation des Romans'. It is exceedingly difficult to tease out of Jens' rather obscure formulations exactly what he was after, but he was most certainly correct in his observation that, at that time, the younger generation was turning mainly to lyric poetry, the 'Hörspiel' and shorter prose forms, rather than the novel. The short story, which in many ways is more important than the novel within the context of much of the Fifties, was particularly attractive, as Jens noted: 'Kein Wunder abermals, daß der auf

---

27. Jens, 'Plädoyer für die abstrakte Literatur', *Texte und Zeichen*, 1, 1955, p. 510. All other quotations from Jens in the text are from *Deutsche Literatur der Gegenwart*, Munich, 1966 (1961), pp. 117–27.

dramatische Stilisierungen, ironische Pointen, lyrische Chiffrierungen und essayistisch-zugespitzte Sentenzen bedachte Nachkriegsautor sich gerade der Kurzform zuwandte: hier allein konnte er, inmitten einer im Ungreifbaren verschwimmenden Umwelt, ein Dauerhaft-Festes, Klassisch-Begrenztes erfinden'. The writer, reacting against ideologies and party politics as compromising his freedom and adopting a free-floating position, compared by Jens to that of a partisan in the French Resistance, essentially viewed the world in aesthetic or existentialist, rather than social, terms. The short story of the Fifties, reflecting this, is characterised by a lack of realism, by its metaphorical, satirical, parabolic, emblematical or grotesque treatment of experience. With the publication of Günter Grass's *Die Blechtrommel* (1959), which despite its many realist descriptive sections, essentially seems to meet Jens' criteria, the already considerable obstacles to the realist novel in West Germany were increased significantly by the achievement of this, the most important postwar German novel.

Given a situation in which a good realist novel like Martin Walser's *Ehen in Philippsburg* (1957) stands out by its very isolation, there is a tendency from a later perspective to view the founding of the Dortmunder Gruppe 61 as a more or less conscious expression of dissatisfaction at the absence of such works (as is the case, for example, in the introduction to the Autoren-Edition's *Kontext 1* of 1976). Indeed, Fritz Hüser, co-founder of the group, attempted to show (in his introduction to the *Almanach* of the group, *Aus der Welt der Arbeit*, 1966) that the new 'Soziale Realismus', as he called it, was a direct response to the prevailing lack of realist writing. He cited essays by Rothe, Andersch and Jens, 'die bewußt machen, wie wenig die beherrschende Realität der industriellen Arbeitswelt einen Niederschlag in der Literatur der Gegenwart gefunden hat. Die Beiträge gaben direkt und indirekt den Anstoß zur Bildung der Dortmunder Gruppe 61'.[28] A closer examination of these essays reveals that the claims made by Hüser and perpetuated by others are less than accurate. Wolfgang Rothe made a general appeal for literature of the industrial world not stemming from, or addressing, a specific social group or class; this does not square with the earliest phase of Gruppe 61. Alfred Andersch, in his essay 'Die moderne Literatur und die Arbeitswelt' (*FAZ*, 24.7.1959), was more concerned with the lack of experience of the real world among the young university trained generation of writers than with a thematic con-

---

28. *Aus der Welt der Arbeit. Almanach der Gruppe 61 und ihrer Gäste*, Neuwied & Berlin, 1966, p. 22.

cern with the world of labour. Hüser's last name, the one to which he attaches greatest importance, is particularly surprising in this context: Walter Jens. Not only do the works produced by Gruppe 61 represent the antithesis of Jens' 'abstract literature', but in the essay mentioned, as elsewhere, he was anxious to show how the 'Raum der Dichtung' had become restricted by the cinema and scientific discoveries; his point was, rather, that the 'Arbeitswelt' could not be portrayed by conventional literary means in modern literature. The reasons for the formation of the group are to be found more locally; with hindsight Hüser's claims appear merely an attempt to give his organisation respectability. The then still strong concentration of the mining industry in the *Ruhrgebiet* kept alive amongst the miners a sense of solidarity that had been lost in other regions and other branches of work in 'Wirtschaftswunderdeutschland' and which was further strengthened by the first recession in the industry at the end of the Fifties. This collective spirit also produced, as well, an interest in the long tradition of mining literature in the area, and the founding fathers of the group, apart from the librarian Hüser, were all associated with mining. Their early novels (such as von der Grün's *Manner in zweifacher Nacht* and Bruno Gluchowski's *Der Honigkotten*) immediately display a proximity to the 'Arbeiterdichtung' of the Twenties in their tendency to mythologise or demonise, rather than describe realistically, everyday life in a mining community. The initial programme of Gruppe 61 stressed concern with the earlier literature, and indeed the bulk of the early writing was poetry indistinguishable from what had gone before. The group's avowed literary aim was not realism, but 'literarisch-künstlerische Auseinandersetzung' with the industrial world, with 'die Wahl der Themen, der Gestaltungsmittel und Ausdrucksformen' being left to the individual writer.[29] For some time there was a rift between the older members of the group, who had their roots in the established local tradition, and younger writers who joined the group and who were indeed anxious to create a socially critical realist literature; eventually this was to lead to the break-up of the Dortmunder Gruppe 61. During its latter years, in the wake of the Student Movement, it aroused considerable interest, but initially it was ignored by critics and scholars alike, receiving attention only in the GDR and the local press. The breakthrough to a wider audience and public interest was the achievement of Max von der Grün, whose *Irrlicht und Feuer* (1963) benefited from a subsequent court case; indeed, the novel of the 'Arbeitswelt' in West Germany then as now

29. 'Programm der Gruppe 61', Dortmund, 1964/7.

is synonymous with the name of von der Grün. However, many contributions to the *Almanach* were short prose pieces close to reportage and it contained one of Günter Wallraff's earliest 'Industriereportagen'; this tendency was to increase and to lead to the demise of the group in 1970.

It was really only in the second half of the Sixties, coinciding with an increasing demand for socially engaged literature that constituted part of the contemporary politicisation of culture, that Gruppe 61 figured in major literary debates. Nevertheless there were one or two earlier pointers to a growing unease about the major tendencies of West German literature of the day — inwardness, satire and the grotesque, the avant-garde. In 1964 Martin Walser delivered a speech to the German *Germanistentag* (and elsewhere), in which he attacked the rejection of realism as 'von Idealisten gemacht und immer noch im Bann einer historischen Abbildungsideologie'; this had the (intended) effect of reducing it 'für immer auf sekundäre Merkmale . . . , auf Oberflächenähnlichkeit und eine eher dümmliche Art Psychologie'.[30] Walser rightly stressed that realism was rather, 'immer zuerst eine Auffassungsart und dann erst eine Art der Darstellung'. But a close reading of his ideas on 'Realismus X', as he called it, reveals a great affinity with those who attacked realism and supported literature of the avant-garde and the examples he gave of writers who exemplified his notion of 'Realismus X' — Adamov, Ionesco and Beckett, its 'Kirchenvater' — indicate his continued closeness to the ideas of Walter Jens, and other leading theoreticians of Gruppe 47.

The only literary critic of any stature who at that time rejected both the old idealist literary tradition and the avant-garde in favour of realism was Marcel Reich-Ranicki. In an otherwise very critical analysis of Walter Höllerer's own rather idiosyncratic ideas for a so-called 'new realism' (as a turning away from the avant-garde) he stressed that they were to be seen as part of an 'eindeutigen Hinwendung zum Konkreten, zum Stoff, zum greifbaren Gedanken, zur Wirklichkeit, zur Gegenwart, zu unserer tatsächlichen Umwelt' [31] that he also noticed in other contemporaries (1965). He praised the newcomers Peter Bichsel, Günter Seuren and Günter Herburger as representatives of an undogmatic realism free of 'jeglicher programmatischen Festlegung' which marked a 'Rückkehr zum Erzählen, zur Fabel, zur Darstellung realer Bereiche und konkreter gesell-

---

30. Walser, 'Imitation oder Realismus?' in *Erfahrungen und Leseerfahrungen*, Frankfurt, 1964, pp. 91–2.

31. 'Die Avantgarde ist tot — es lebe die Veränderung' in *Literarisches Leben in Deutschland*, Munich, 1965, p. 281.

schaftlicher Milieus' and the portrayal 'des kleinen Mannes auf dem Hintergrund seines Alltags'. While Reich-Ranicki's formulations betray ideas on realism close to those of the late Forties and early Fifties, especially in his suspicion of ideology and his pronouncements were somewhat premature, he had rightly sensed that a number of young writers — whose work he called the 'Literatur der kleinen Schritte' — wished to go in this direction, the most important of these being Alexander Kluge. Marcel Reich-Ranicki was, however, still very much a lone voice; his ideas about realism provoked a hostile response from the supporters of 'abstract' literature. In a bitter criticism of him, Hermann Peter Piwitt totally rejected what he called the 'animistisch abgesättigte Dingwelt eines überkommenen Realismus'; for Piwitt 'gegenwartsnah schreiben' was in no way dependent on 'realistischen Mitteln'. Countering the writers named by Reich-Ranicki, he lined up Ror Wolf and H.C. Artmann, before whose 'Kräftespiels der Begriff des "Realismus"' paled, he maintained, 'zur abgegriffenen Münze'.[32] The prominent position then accorded by literary critics to these two writers and the vehemence of an attack by someone clearly speaking for a major grouping within Gruppe 47 are further indications that in the mid-Sixties the hostility to realism, which had so long dominated West German literary life, was still strong.

---

32. 'Landschaft des Gedächtnisses und "Augenblick"', *Sprache im technischen Zeitalter*, 14, 1965, pp. 1187–9.

3

The Struggle for Realism: Literary Debates 1965–80

The German novel for much of the Sixties was dominated by various manifestations of what Walter Jens had called 'abstract' literature; the two major trends were the literary exploration of the theme of identity, in a manner that had little to do with the relationship between the individual and society, and a whole series of neo-picaresque novels inspired by the success of Grass's *Die Blechtrommel*. The dominant style of prose writing, in the short story as in the novel, was the use of the grotesque.[1] Not surprisingly, therefore, the target for anyone wishing to argue in favour of realist writing was Günter Grass, seen as the figurehead of the anti-realist movement. Ingeborg Drewitz fired the first shots in this skirmish in an article published in *Merkur* in 1965, in which she sought to draw attention to the 'Gefahren, die mit der Intellektualisierung der in der Absurdität gipfelnden grotesken Mitteln verbunden sind', citing Grass as the arch-practitioner of grotesque literature.[2] Later in the same year Dieter Wellershoff also attacked 'die manieristische und groteske Literatur, deren Prototyp die Romane von Günter Grass sind', the intent of which, he believed, was merely to achieve 'das Extravagante, Aparte, Auffällige, den bizarren Effekt'.[3] This salvo was the beginning of a conscious campaign by Wellershoff for recognition of the merits of realist writing, both in his various essays and in his capacity as a *Lektor* for the publishers Kiepenheuer & Witsch; his sponsorship of several young writers (Brinkmann, Born, Herburger, Steffens) led to his being seen as the leader of the so-called 'Kölner Realismus' school of writing. Wellershoff himself has always rejected that label and role, stressing, indeed, that his use of the term 'Realismus' was initially meant as a 'grober Unterscheidungsbegriff' to distinguish a then rather vague idea from both

1. Cf. in this connection W. van der Will, *Pikaro heute*, Stuttgart, 1967, and R. Hinton Thomas and W. van der Will, *Deutsche Literatur in der Wohlstandsgesellschaft*, Stuttgart, 1969.
2. *Merkur*, 19, Heft 4, 1965, p. 346.
3. *Die Kiepe*, 13, 1965, Nr. 1.

grotesque and 'metaphysical' literature.[4] But his very use of the term 'Realismus' provoked vehement criticism, which, in his view, clearly revealed a rigidly narrow and negative attitude, so that, in connection with realism, people automatically thought 'an erstarrte Konzepte . . . , etwa an die oberflächliche Milieutreue und die schablonenhafte Psychologie, wie sie zum Beispiel heute im Kriminalroman üblich ist. Sicher war der Begriff in Deutschland auch durch die Nachbarschaft des sozialistischen Realismus tabuisiert' (LuV, 64).

Initially Wellershoff used the term 'new realism' only to try and distance it from the associations he mentions above. However, it is clear — as he himself was to realise only later — that his ideas have nothing in common with what is known as 'deutscher Realismus' (of the nineteenth century), but that they start from more fundamental epistemological concerns. In 1980, for example, he was anxious to stress 'daß Realismus für mich nichts inhaltlich Bestimmtes ist und auch nicht festgelegt werden kann auf eine bestimmte Schreibweise. Ich verstehe unter diesem Begriff das Erkenntnisinteresse der Literatur . . . ' (WL, 82). The starting-point of his view of contemporary realism, not that far removed from ideas of Brecht, Kahler and Adorno examined earlier, is that the increasing complexity of modern society has rendered it impossible for the writer to produce a 'Realitätsabschnitt, . . . eingebettet im größeren Horizont des Allgemeinen':

> Wenn die Wirkungszusammenhänge von Industrie, Verwaltung, Geldwirtschaft und Politik so weitläufig, indirekt und abstrakt geworden sind, daß sie sich der Anschauung, Kompetenz und den Einfluß jedes einzelnen entziehen, ist nicht mehr der Handelnde exemplarisch für die Gesellschaft, sondern der Betroffene, der nicht einmal weiß, wie, warum und wovon er bestimmt wird, der den gesellschaftlichen Druck als Privatsituation erfährt und mehr oder minder glücklich individuell zu verarbeiten sucht. So kann auch der Schriftsteller kaum noch ein konkretes Gesamtpanorama der Gesellschaft schreiben. Er weiß zu wenig dazu. (LuV, 32)

Wellershoff does not, however, conclude that literature can only respond to this situation by being thrown in on itself; for him, literature (he is not here talking about the German literary tradition) can continue to be realistic, in the sense of remaining true to its

4. All references in the texts to Wellershoff's theoretical pronouncements are taken from the following works: *Literatur und Veränderung* (1969), Munich, 1971 (LuV); *Literatur und Lustprinzip*, Cologne, 1973 (LuL); and *Die Wahrheit der Literatur*, Munich, 1980 (WL).

epistemological intent, i.e. 'die Darstellung des gesellschaftlichen und des individuellen Lebens, die Darstellung der Kämpfe und Irrtümer des Menschen bei der Gestaltung ihres Lebens' (WL, 76), but only if the writer takes full account of the changed nature of modern experience. Only by portraying life in quite specific sectors of society or, even, in 'abseitigen Situationen', can the writer hope 'daß man in ihnen auch etwas über die ganze Gesellschaft erfährt' (WL, 142). Above all the writer must recognise that there are no easy solutions for him as cognitive subject; realism is directly related to the extent to which 'wir darauf verzichten, bei der Wahrnehmung des Lebens auf vereinfachende und tröstende Schemata zu verzichten' (WL, 96). He must recognise that our experience of reality is completely individual, things are perceived as 'augenblickshaft, ungeordnet und subjectiv', and yet at the same time the highly specialised division of labour has led to 'die funktionell verarmte Privatsphäre' becoming the 'Müllabladeplatz der technologischen Rationalität' (LuV, 29–31). For Wellershoff the literary concomitant of the total subjectivisation of experience is the total subjectivisation of narration as expression of the isolation of the (now) unrepresentative individual. One way of achieving this is the perspectivisation of narration that Wellershoff demonstrated in his first novel *Ein schöner Tag* (1966), another — derived in part from modern filmic narrative techniques — lies for him in the 'nouveau roman' of Claude Simon and Alain Robbe-Grillet:

> Realistisch . . . wäre eine bewegte, subjektive Optik, die durch Zeitdehnung und Zeitraffung und den Wechsel zwischen Totale und Detail, Nähe und Ferne, Schärfe und Verschwommenheit des Blickfelds, Bewegung und Stillstand, langer und kurzer Einstellung und den Wechsel von Innen- und Außenwelt die konventionelle Ansicht eines bekannten Vorgangs und einer bekannten Situation so auflöst und verändert, daß eine neue Erfahrung entsteht. Die subjektive Blickführung, verwandt den Kamerabewegungen des Films, demontiert die konventionellen Sinneinheiten, zerlegt und verzerrt sie, . . . zeigt das Fremde, das Ungesehene im scheinbar Bekannten und fügt neue ungewöhnliche Komplexe zusammen.(LuV, 67)

The idea of the need for a 'new' realism as a response to the growing complexity of modern society is, however, constantly contradicted by Wellershoff's simultaneous stressing of its being determined by the impenetrability of reality as such. In this view, realism is understood as a 'neue Annäherung an eine nie ganz faßbare, nie ganz ausschöpfbare Sache . . . , die wir umfassend die Realität nennen' and he talks of a 'grundsätzlich unausschöpfbaren Wirklichkeit'

(LuV, 66–7). In Wellershoff's first volume of essays, *Literatur und Veränderung* (1969) the concept of the 'Dichte, Vielfalt und Unausschöpfbarkeit des Realen', based initially on ideas of Arnold Gehlen, seems slowly to gain the upper hand and, although he never abandons his other notion of reality, still stressing in 1980 the factor of increasing social complexity on realism, the second volume, *Literatur und Lustprinzip* (1973), confirms the impression of the first. Drawing not only on Gehlen, but later on Freud and the existential psychiatry of R.D. Laing, Wellershoff brings to the fore a view of reality far deeper and more complex than the surface suggests, with social conventions obscuring and even suppressing its richness; the job of 'die eigentliche Literatur' is to try to open this up: 'Unter Routine und schablonenhafter Informiertheit verschwindet die Realität. . . . Realistisches Schreiben wäre die Gegenbewegung, also der Versuch, der Welt die konventionelle Bekanntheit zu nehmen und etwas von ihrer ursprünglichen Fremdheit und Dichte zurückzugewinnen, den Wirklichkeitsdruck wieder zu verstärken, anstatt von ihm zu entlasten' (LuV, 66).

Whilst Wellershoff sees prevalent literary forms as tending 'die Realität durch Abstraktion und Stilisierung radikal zu vereinfachen und zu ordnen', the realism he seeks questions given attitudes, in order 'neue, bisher verbannte Erfahrungen zu ermöglichen'. A greater degree of realism — in the sense of penetrating beyond misleading surface reality — can be obtained, he asserts, by radically challenging traditional linear narration through the 'Technik der Dissoziation, Isolierung und Häufung der Realitätselemente', or by perspektivised narration (LuV, 65–8). Originally Wellershoff could see the collage as fitting into his ideas, but, as the element of change, as an essential dimension of realist literature, is ever more stressed, he comes to reject this technique as one 'die sich einer verändernden Behandlung [widersetzt]', making a literary work 'zum bloßen Anführungszeichen ihres Erscheinens'. The degree of irritation necessary to deprive the reader of 'die Sicherheit seiner Vorurteile und gewohnten Handlungsweisen' (LuV, 19) is better achieved by the stressing of everday details, the precise description 'des gegenwärtigen alltäglichen Lebens in einem begrenzten Bereich' (giving as an example his protégé Rolf Dieter Brinkmann's *Keiner weiß mehr*, 1968) (LuV, 65). Later, though, he was to revise certain aspects of this theory, dropping the accentuation of the everyday and substituting for it 'die Abweichung und Brechung vom normalen Verhalten' and the need for special attention to be paid to subjective experiences, to the individual's thought-processes and to 'die Dunkelzonen des Vorbewußten und der Körperreaktionen oder . . . die flüssigen und flackernden Gestalten des Tagtraums' (LuV, 22). Since 'die eigentliche Literatur' has passed the 'alte Funktion der Verhaltenssteuerung im Sinne gelternder Normen . . . an den Trivialroman' (LuV, 20), it is now concerned with the demonstration of latent human faculties, hitherto suppressed by society, and the release of which will lead to a change in our regulated mode of living.

These formulations demonstrate how quickly Wellershoff left behind his early realist fundamentalism and moved far beyond the traditional claims of the realist method. Literature is not to be 'Mimesis der gesellschaftlichen Praxis' but 'ein der Lebenspraxis beigeordneter Simulationsraum', a 'Spielfeld für ein fiktives Handeln, in dem man als Autor und als Leser die Grenzen seiner praktischen Erfahrungen und Routinen überschreitet, ohne ein wirkliches Risiko dabei einzugehen' (LuV, 18). Central to this concept of literature is his instrumentalisation of Freud's idea of the sublimation of human drives, desires and true potential through culture. In literature this sublimation expresses itself, says Wellershoff, through conventional mimetic styles of writing that reproduce a known world and thereby serve to confirm it, as well as through 'das scheinbar progressive Gegenteil', modern techniques such as collage and concrete poetry. Although born of 'oppositioneller Phantasie', these 'neutral' methods reproduce 'die Logik des gesellschaftlichen Produktionsprozesses unbefragt . . . und in deren seriellen Mustern [kommt] das abgedrängte Leben nicht mehr zu Wort' (LuV, 45). These criticisms of Max Bense and Helmut Heißenbüttel reveal how important is the concept of 'das abgedrängte Leben' to Wellershoff's 'new realism', the major function of which is to expose the 'gesperrten und verstümmelten Kapazitäten des Menschen' and to reveal through the portrayal of dreams and 'abweichendem und gestörtem Verhalten' 'den Preis der herrschenden Praxis und . . . das Potential möglicher Veränderung'. It is not the development of modern technological society, but the nature of Western culture which demands that literature, as a bastion of utopian ideas, should now concentrate its attention on alternative experiences, on unknown risks, new social structures and the liberation of man's suppressed potential, with the aim of constituting social reality anew. Whereas, in the traditional novel of the nineteenth century, the author presented the reader with more or less representative life histories, Wellershoff now sees it as his task to define literature as a 'vor- oder nebenpraktische[n] Bereich, in dem praktisch unbeherrschte Komplexität der Erfahrung zugänglich gemacht wird, wo also auch die fremden, gefährlichen, abweichenden oder auch, wie

Robbe-Grillet sagt, die falschen Möglichkeiten durchgespielt werden' (LuL, 140). In his imaginative writing, which is a more or less
direct putting into practice of the theory, the non-normative presentation of material is, as already mentioned, initially achieved by
stylistic means; increasingly, though, perspectivisation or fragmen-
tation of the narration is allied to a critical treatment of individual
neuroses and ontological crises, in order to bring out both the social
means of repression and what is repressed. Ultimately, in his theory,
in the 'Hörspiele', the novels and the novella *Die Sirene* (1980), we
are left with a psychological realism — based on Freudian and, to a
lesser extent, Laingian ideas.

Although the initial stimulus for Wellershoff's development of
theories on realism arose from his disquiet about the prominence of
the grotesque in West German literature, it is clear that the essays of
the late Sixties are directed more and more against the increasingly
strong case being made for experimental literature, particularly by
Helmut Heißenbüttel. Wellershoff not only revised his ideas on
collage, but also criticised 'die Konzentration der Literatur auf
Schreibtechnik und Methodik, ihr Rückzug auf eine nicht mehr
über sich hinaus greifende Selbstreflexion, die sich als Basis der
Textherstellung verabsolutiert' (LuV, 44). Not surprisingly, the
strongest rejection of his ideas came from Heißenbüttel's close
associates; years later Wellershoff himself said that he was attacked
by those who shared 'die gängige Auffassung, Literatur müsse vor
allem sich selbst und ihr Medium, die Sprache, reflektieren' (WL,
69).

The most thoroughgoing criticism came from Heinrich Vormweg, over the years Heißenbüttel's greatest champion.[5] Vormweg
reproaches Wellershoff for taking full account of the latest
findings in physiology, psychology and sociology, 'ohne jedoch auch
die Sprache zum Gegenstand der Sprache zu machen'. In addition
he has not, Vormweg maintains, thought through the consequences
of the changed nature of modern existence as they affect individual
perception: 'der grundsätzlich veränderte Zustand humaner Existenz in der Epoche der Wissenschaft kommt gar nicht zum Bewußtsein. Der Schriftsteller ist derselbe geblieben, verändert haben sich
nur sein Instrumentarium, seine Themen und Stoffe, die Reichweite
seiner Aktion'. The position Wellershoff ascribes to the author
merely continues the old aesthetic notion of the writer creating a
mirror-image of reality, his position is 'noch immer gegründet auf

---

5. Cf. 'Die Theorie Dieter Wellershoffs' in *Eine andere Leseart*, Neuwied & Berlin,
1972, pp. 101–5.

dem Begriff eines weiterhin autonomen Subjekts, das weiterhin fähig erscheint, den Inhalt Welt direkt, wenn auch nur partiell zu greifen'. The writer's use of contemporary thinking derived from the social sciences remains a 'Scheinwissenschaftlichkeit' until he recognises that it is 'unerläßlich, dieses Denken zunächst auch auf den Benutzer, auf sein Bewußtsein und seine Wahrnehmung und auf sein Verständigungsmittel, die Sprache, auszudehnen'.

Here, at the beginning of the Seventies, is an exemplary theoretical collision: Vormweg, following on the ideas of Adorno, takes the view that narration as such is impossible and, turning to notions first put forward in the Fifties by the proponents of concrete literature, sees the focus on language as the way out of the literary cul-de-sac, while Wellershoff, far more influenced by models from other literatures, is unable to understand the blanket rejection of realist writing. For him, as he was to put it later, the 'Grundsituation, daß ein Mensch in der Welt lebt und darauf reagieren kann, indem er sie darstellt und darüber spricht, ist unangefochten, kann ja gar nicht angefochten werden' (WL, 141). He does admit, though, that the relationship of the individual to an increasingly complex society is becoming ever more problematical, that the writer has lost his representative status, that the information industries have changed people's relationship to language and that the flood of material from the media and non-fiction has changed the attitude of the reader to fiction and has had an impact on the writer's choice of subject matter. The author is increasingly just one more individual, rather than the mouthpiece of a definable reference-group and he, like everyone else, feels the impact of change: nevertheless, argues Wellershoff, he is still in the position of describing the individual experience of reality, the ultimate intention of all realist writing.

In 1969 Wellershoff received the *Kritikerpreis* for *Literatur und Veränderung*, but there can be little doubt that far greater attention was paid at the time to the theories emanating from the proponents of experimental writing, particularly Heißenbüttel and Vormweg. In their *Briefwechsel über Literatur*,[6] their starting-point, as with all recent theories of realism, is the change in the nature of society since the middle of the last century. Heißenbüttel, in terms occasionally reminiscent of the Naturalists, stresses that our consciousness is determined by the spirit of the technological age: 'Tatsächlich stellen wir uns, wenn wir uns nicht mit Relikten herumplagen, heute Wirklichkeit wissenschaftlich-statistisch vor' (BüL, 65). Mere sensitive awareness is no longer able 'sinngebend und ordnend in die

---

6. Neuwied & Berlin, 1969 (BüL).

Welt einzudringen . . . , es sei denn im Sinne der spezial-wissen-schaftlichen Statistik oder der Fotographie' (BüL, 29). The problem for the individual in this situation, according to Vormweg, is 'sich innerhalb von Wahrnehmungs- und Informationsabläufen zurecht-zufinden, die allgemeingültiger Entscheidungsmuster entbehren'.[7] Relatively traditional literature is unable to help the reader who turns to it for guidance; it is not possible merely to update literary techniques in order to describe 'eine faktisch und dem Bewußtsein nach veränderte Welt'. Instead, realist literature should respond by making use of 'ready-mades' and collage, so that it can objectify the impenetrability of reality: 'Wenn außersprachliche Vorstellung von Menschenwelt wissenschaftlich aufgesplittert und kaleidoskopiert ist, kann die Literatur nicht unmittelbar Spiegelbilder liefern. Sie muß das Spiegelbild sozusagen aus den Mitteln der Sprache erst entwickeln'. This means that it must attempt 'die Welt und Sachen im abgelösten Sprachzitat zu verdoppeln', in order, 'indem wir den im Wort gespeicherten Sprachbezug zitieren, . . . dem zu nähern, was man außerhalb der Sprache Welt nennen könnte' (BüL, 29).

The concept of a reality beyond the confines of the language of the individual cognitive subject, clearly based on a reading of Wittgen-stein, rests ultimately on the idea that, while formerly there was a straightforward relationship between experience and reality, in re-cent times human consciousness has been fundamentally changed and has lost contact with 'einem scheinbar vorgegebenen gültigen Allgemeinen'.[8] In this situation the traditional presupposition of literature, that 'sie könne Wirklichkeit, Leben, Sein direkt, komplex, anschauend und anschaulich, gleichsam erlösend vermitteln, . . . in einer problemlösenden Handlung', loses all validity. The gulf be-tween external reality and individual consciousness is now such that it cannot be bridged by language 'als weitgehend neutraler Bedeu-tungsträger', since this now mediates 'inhaltlich schon vorgerich-tetes Material'. For the writer, the consequence of all this has to be radical mistrust not only of established literary forms as a means of shaping the mediation of experience, but also of language itself. Only a 'Literatur, die aus der Konzentration auf Sprache und aus der Destruktion etablierter sprachlicher Formen resultiert, läßt sich interpretieren als eine Literatur, die ihrer tatsächlichen gesell-schaftlichen Relation in dieser Epoche bewußt geworden ist'. Ex-perimental literature, in the form of a collage or montage of

---

7. Heinrich Vormweg, 'Literatur und Lebenshilfe, neue Version', *Merkur*, 26, 1970, p. 785.
8. Cf. in this connection Vormweg, *Eine andere Leseart*, pp. 85–8.

'ready-mades', would alone appear acceptable as contemporary realism.

This literary theory presupposes a past age in which language was neutral and untarnished and in which literature was an expression of the identification with his society of the individual as author. The former condition can only have applied in somewhat primitive civilisations and certainly not since the invention of the printing press. The second presupposition, seen in, for example, Lucien Goldmann's study of the sociology of the novel, has a certain usefulness if applied as an ideal-type, but becomes absurd if asserted as empirical truth. Heißenbüttel and other advocates of experimental writing, such as Jürgen Becker, have, for example, a dangerously oversimplified understanding of the relationship between society and literary forms. Becker regards genres as such as 'historische Phänomene, die durch bestimmte äußere gesellschaftliche, soziale Umstände bestimmt sind'; this is to some extent true, but becomes nonsense when he claims that the novel has to be seen exclusively as an 'Ausdruck des Bürgertums des neunzehnten Jahrhunderts. Im Roman sah dieses Bürgertum sich selber in einer Art von Selbsterklärung, einer Art von Interpretation jener Welt, in der dieses Bürgertum mehr oder weniger geschlossen lebte'.[9] He therefore concludes that, given subsequent social change, the novel is now out of date. Such an undifferentiated appropriation of otherwise useful ideas from the sociology of literature leads here to the ludicrous concept of the novel as an historically delimited phenomenon; this is to ignore the pre-bourgeois novel, the achievements of the essentially aristocratic Russian novel of the nineteenth century and the entire development of the genre in the twentieth century. Moreover, as shown in Chapter 1, such ideas cannot be applied without a considerable degree of differentiation to the German novel of the nineteenth century.

In looking back from the mid-Eighties on the vast body of West German realist novels in the Seventies, the weight of support for the experimental 'Text', rather than the novel, seems astonishing. The shorter prose form, as produced by Heißenbüttel, Becker, Ror Wolf, Wolf Wondratschek and others, rapidly revealed its limitations and soon showed a tendency to formalistic repetition. The shortcomings in the theoretical pronouncements are today obvious to Heinrich Vormweg. He now qualifies Heißenbüttel's then position by seeing it as a polemical stance against the still prevalent ideas on realism

9. 'Jürgen Becker im Gespräch mit Reinhard Lettau' in Werner Koch (ed.), *Selbstanzeige*, Frankfurt, 1971, pp. 77–8.

from the early days of Gruppe 47, against the 'Bestseller-Realismus' of Lenz, Simmel and Willi Heinrich and post-war 'magischer Realismus', but he himself now considers the attempt 'die Welt individuell zu verstehen' to be 'ein menschliches Bedürfnis'.[10] While still condemning the uncritical application of the forms of traditional realism as producing a cosy and reassuring, but distorted picture of reality, Vormweg now accepts the legitimacy of newer forms of realist writing, such as the more or less immediate reflection of experience in the autobiographical novel. The important thing here is that the individual experience should not carry any claim to totality. In his view, the aim of a contemporary realist novel should be not objectivity, but subjectivity, in the sense of the mediation of the personal response to interaction with reality.

There is no doubt that this sort of realist writing, which is not all that far removed from certain aspects of Wellershoff's early theory, came to play an increasingly important role in the novel of the Seventies. Nevertheless the most crucial influence on the breakthrough of the realist novel at the turn of the decade came, in fact, from quite the opposite direction — from a literary movement based on a claim to objectivity: the documentary. While there had been a strong documentary movement in the Twenties (Piscator, Kisch, the 'Bund proletarisch-revolutionärer Schriftsteller', etc.) and a number of personal accounts of wartime experience had been published in the Forties and Fifties (such as Erich Kuby's *Nur noch rauchende Trümmer* and Plievier's *Stalingrad*), there is no doubt that the documentary prose works of the late Sixties, which, like documentary drama, try to authenticate a polemical point of view by the use of 'authentic' material, represent the emergence of a form of realism new in the post-war context.

The immediate non-literary influences on the development of documentary literature in general in the Sixties were the Eichmann Trial in Jerusalem and the Frankfurt Auschwitz Trials. These led to an evaluation of the question of war-guilt amongst a younger generation of writers, and this was quite different from the highly personal so-called 'Bewältigung der Vergangenheit' and the war memories of the Fifties. The first manifestations of this new, highly critical position were in the drama, the obvious examples being Hochhuth's *Der Stellvertreter*, Heinar Kipphardt's *Joel Brand* and Peter Weiss's *Die Ermittlung*. In prose the first major documetary examinations of the National Socialist past came from Alexander Kluge. The starting-point of his major work of the Sixties, *Schlachtbeschreibung* (1964),

---

10. In conversation with the author, Cologne, 3.12.1980.

which can legitimately be considered the precursor of the Seventies' documentary novel, was that a disaster on the scale of the battle for Stalingrad cannot be dealt with through recollections of eye-witnesses alone. Instead he assembles a montage of material from a range of different sources (including some fictional matter) to show, on the one hand, how an event of this magnitude can be viewed in a number of different ways, and, on the other hand, how it can be distorted systematically by official sources in the way in which they 'inform' troops and public. In *Schlachtbeschreibung*, we are confronted with an undoubtedly more accurate, much more complex re-construction of 'Informationsabläufen . . . , die allgemeingültiger Entscheidungsmuster entbehren' (Heinrich Vormweg); at the same time the work represents a literary response to the inability of the individual to come fully to terms with an increasingly impenetrable external reality. In this it anticipates Heißenbüttel's later propaga-tion of the use of 'ready-mades' within a montage, but, significantly, within the epic form. Moreover, the simultaneity achieved in Kluge's narration through the complex co-existence of the various strands represents very much the formal correlative to Heißenbüttel's later assertion: 'Das, was Realität, Faktizität heißt, einschließlich der gesellschaftlichen und physiologischen Bedingungen, unter denen es erscheint, ist außer Reichweite selbst der simplifizierendsten Ideolo-gie (oder gerade dieser) geraten'.[11]

In the context of the increasing politicisation of West German literature such apparently un- or anti-political pronouncements were sharply attacked: Karl Markus Michel, in the famous *Kursbuch* 15, asserted that Heißenbüttel did nothing more than 'die Welt im Zitat zu verdoppeln, ohne irgend etwas zu verändern', whilst others reproached him for his 'Gefühl der Ohnmacht' or 'Statik'.[12] Ironi-cally, though, it was the thrust to politicise literature that took up Heißenbüttel's techniques and other forms of documentary writing to make this the outstanding literary form at the turn of the decade. The initial impetus generated by the Nazi trials had in the mean-time been complemented by a number of further burning issues, particularly the Third World (including Vietnam), the proposed 'Notstandsgesetze', the Grand Coalition of 1966–9 and the econ-omic recession of 1966–7, as well as by the catalyst of the Student Movement. These various factors wrought a radical change in the nature of West German literature and their consequences can still be observed today. They accelerated, at the very least, the demise of

11. *Briefwechsel über Literatur*, p. 93.
12. Cf. Karl Markus Michel, 'Ein Kranz für die Literatur', *Kursbuch*, 15, 1968, p. 183 and Renate Matthaei (ed.), *Grenzverschiebung*, Cologne, 1970, pp. 22ff.

Gruppe 47, helped to bring to an end the dominance of 'abstract' literature (cf. Chapter 2), and unleashed a fundamental debate on the social function of literature that led, or so it seemed for a time, to it being thrown overboard in favour of direct political action. The problems at home and abroad were felt to be such that neither the continued autonomy of the writer nor what was felt to be 'ivory tower', 'bourgeois' literature could any longer be justified. The literary and political development of such leading writers as Martin Walser, Peter Weiss and Hans Magnus Enzensberger at this time shows just how radical were the changes in the consciousness of the writers and, ultimately, in the practice of literature. In the context of the novel the position of Martin Walser is particularly revealing.

Most of the socially critical writers of the early Sixties, Walser included, had been 'nie besonders politisch und nie besonders links . . . ; sie waren [alle] Moralisten'.[13] At that time, any involvement of Walser's in public protest of one sort or another was essentially moral in nature and, indeed, the socio-critical element in his work had weakened in intensity over the years. The problems posed for the individual by the increasing pressure of the 'Leistungsgesellschaft', that he first takes up in *Ehen in Philippsburg*, are admittedly still the central theme of *Halbzeit* and *Das Einhorn*, the first two parts of the Anselm Kristlein trilogy, but the pluralism forced on the individual personality is seen increasingly positively and the whole pattern of narration becomes ever more playful; a motif determined by social forces turns into a literary device. It was no surprise that in his essay 'Imitation oder Realismus' (1964) he rejects any 'exklusiven Erklärungsversuch' in literature and that his 'Realismus X' was to aim for 'das ideologische Minimum'.[14] But Walser's position was soon to change. In his case it was above all the Vietnam War that transformed moral into outright political protest, his politicisation leading ultimately to a position on the fringes of the DKP. His campaign against the acquiescence of the Federal government in US policy soon came to involve a critical re-evaluation of his view of literature and of his earlier writing. He came to feel that the bourgeois literature of which he was part, and which had once played a not insignificant part in a movement for emancipation, had become merely affirmative, such that it could be afforded 'der gewährte Spielraum, die genau garantierte Narrenfreiheit, die kühn aufgemachten Sprach-Expeditionen in elegante oder attaktiv üble Sackgassen . . . , ins modern Überirdische. Ins Absurde. Ins pure

13. Karl Heinz Bohrer, *Die gefährdete Phantasie, oder Surrealismus und Terror*, Munich, 1970, p. 90.
14. *Erfahrungen und Leseerfahrungen*, Frankfurt, 1964, pp. 84, 89.

Sprachspiel'.[15] The self-criticism inherent in such a statement, which could certainly be applied to some of the more extravagantly virtuoso passages in *Das Einhorn*, turned in Walser's case into politicisation at the point where he felt that those artistic skills so highly rated by literary experts not only served to provide the middle classes with self-congratulatory 'Ausstattung', but had acquired the function of legitimising established authority by omitting all mention of uncomfortable aspects of society. The problems of the lower-middle and working classes, in particular, were hardly touched upon, and then far from adequately, in the established literary tradition

It is very much to Walser's credit that he showed himself to be aware of the limits of his own 'Überblick über die Gesellschaft und über uns selber'. He found it, for example, quite laughable to expect of writers that they could 'mit Hilfe . . . der sogenannten schöpferischen Begabung Arbeiter-Dasein im Kunstaggregat imitieren oder gar zur Sprache bringen'.[16] His short-term answer to the question of restoring the emancipatory dimension to literature and of finding a real alternative to existing aesthetic codes — and for him, as one of the leading practitioners of the anti-realist 'abstract' novel, these presented grave problems — was to cease writing himself and to persuade those with direct experience of life outside the middle classes to document their experiences. Casting doubt on the authenticity of the products of the creative imagination led to the belief in the authenticity of the direct statement of 'real' people; the first literary results were Erika Runge's *Bottroper Protokolle* and Ursula Trauberg's *Vorleben*. Not only did this 'Literatur der Nicht-Autoren', as Reinhard Baumgart called it, symbolise for Walser the attempt 'dem überaffirmativen bürgerlichen Bewußtsein Bestätigung zu entziehen', by treating in literature pressing social problems, he also saw in it the possible means of regenerating the novel, which he felt had in the preceding 150 years 'uns den Geschmack an Lebensläufen fast verdorben'. In Ursula Trauberg's autobiographical account, which followed entirely 'dem Diktat der Erinnerung', 'entstehe . . . eine Glaubwürdigkeit, die man nur erreichen kann, wenn man sie nicht beabsichtigt', and which was quite different from the pseudo-credibility of those writers 'die aus ästhetischer Verlegenheit ihre Fiktionen "Bericht" nennen . . .'. In *Vorleben*, he claimed, 'wird endlich einmal berichtet, nichts als berichtet . . .'.[17]

The stress laid by Walser on the life story and other accounts of

15. 'Freiübungen', ibid., p. 97.
16. Preface to Erika Runge, *Bottroper Protokolle*, Frankfurt, 1968, p. 9.
17. Afterword to Ursula Trauberg, *Vorleben*, Frankfurt, 1968, pp. 269–70.

personal experience clearly shows how far he was now intent on getting back to the first principles of realist narration. It was not only a matter of the injection of new material into literature that would by its nature press for change, but of a radical challenge to what he now felt to be the sophisms of the German novel tradition and of a return to a more immediate form of narration, long since lost by bourgeois novelists. The solution lay in the more or less direct presentation of individual experience by ordinary people. (What Walser was proposing was by no means new, but it should be remembered that earlier works of this kind, such as Ludwig Turek's *Ein Prolet erzählt* and Willi Bredel's *Maschinenfabrik N & K* were hardly known at the time, only being rediscovered during the Student Movement.) In reality, though, the various texts that Walser and others published were highly problematical; the mentors of the non-authors found themselves forced to intervene and 'edit' or even 'correct' works that were meant to appeal in part through their authenticity. Moreover, the style of *Vorleben* and Wolfgang Werner's *Vom Waisenhaus ins Zuchthaus*, another volume sponsored by Walser, revealed the influence of the mass media, the yellow press and the 'Groschenroman' to be so negative as to call into question the notion of the naïve immediacy of their reports.

This impact of the entertainment industry on the self-expression and, therefore, the growth of self-awareness in Walser's protégés ultimately provides the most informative aspect of the documentary works in question. Their social criticism, clearly affected by the linguistic limitation of the 'authors', lacks the clarity and class-conscious aggression of the essentially similar autobiographical novel *Ein Prolet erzählt* (republished in 1972). At the same time the clichéd use of language and the considerable degree of linguistic unevenness shows the limitations on such literature as a model for the regeneration of the German novel and the establishment of a new realism.

One reason for these life-stories failing to meet Walser's expectations is undoubtedly that he was asking too much of them. They were, on the one hand, to open up a way out of the literary impasse in which he found himself and which he saw applying also to the German novel in general and, at the same time, to expose 'historische und streng gesellschaftliche Bedingungen'.[18] A few years earlier the first 'Reportagen' of Günter Wallraff (*Wir brauchen Dich*, 1966) had shown the limitations of fairly primitive style in

18. Martin Walser, 'Über die Neueste Stimmung im Westen', *Kursbuch 20*, 1970, p. 39.

persuading those in another part of the political spectrum of the need for social reform. In his second volume, *13 unerwünschte Reportagen* (1969), Wallraff retreated as narrator and operated instead as the compiler and organiser of other people's statements and further forms of material. Quite independently of Heißenbüttel he had come to an awareness of how efficient a montage of 'ready-mades' could be in exposing the modern world in its complexities and contradictions. Heißenbüttel's own creative writing had persuaded critics that this technique could not be used in a politically engaged way, and Walser had described it as merely a new form of playful formalism, but Wallraff's socio-critical documentary literature of the late Sixties, which went beyond 'die bloße Wiedergabe von zufälligen Realitätsausschnitten' (Wallraff), had a significant influence (denied to other documentary prose) on the realist novel of the Seventies.

The extent of the 'basisorientierten Wirksamkeit' (Peter Kühne) achieved by Wallraff's reportages, particularly compared with the minimal response to the writing of Gruppe 61 (with the significant exception of Max von der Grün), was such that he seemed the obvious model for the documentary literature proposed by the theoreticians of the Werkkreis Literatur der Arbeitswelt at its founding in 1970. They rejected the increasingly 'bürgerlich-literarisch' tendency of Gruppe 61 in favour of a straightforward realism taking a 'politisch-emanzipatorisch' line. The task of the Werkkreis should be generated, according to Erasmus Schöfer, 'nicht von den Erfordernissen der Literatur her, sondern aus den Erfordernissen der Arbeiterbewegung' and prevailing social conditions. The crucial criterion for literature (in the sense of 'Basisliteratur') produced by the new organisation was 'Brauchbarkeit' of the kind achieved by Wallraff. However, the problems of generating such texts soon revealed themselves here as well. Schöfer, in the early years the leading theorist of the Werkkreis, had to complain of a 'Trend zur Literarisierung' and in a review of the first publications Heinz Ludwig Arnold noted a rather pathetic 'Literatur-machen-Wollen' and a 'klischierende Behandlung' of the material; only in the very few documentary texts inspired by Wallraff were the didactic aims of the group in any way fulfilled.[19] In one sense this initially disappointing result is not entirely surprising, given the programme's general formulations with regard to literary form, presumably designed to accommodate disparate views amongst the founding members: 'Informationen, Dokumentationen, beschreibende und gestaltende

19. H. L. Arnold, 'Wenn ich dat allet aufschreibe . . .', *Die Zeit*, 1.10.1971.

Arbeiten', using all 'erprobten und neuen Formen realistischer Gestaltung' were considered appropriate to the aim of the organisation, namely, the 'kritische und schöpferische Auseinandersetzung mit den Arbeits- und Alltagsverhältnissen'.[20] While those close to Schöfer thought this possible only in reportage, Martin Walser, for a little while involved in the work of the Werkkreis and demonstrating that he had drawn his conclusions from his published works, was pleasantly surprised that the 'Werkkreis-Aufforderung zu berichten' had had no great success, while he sensed that truly 'modern' authors were to be found amongst the membership, 'eine wirkliche Avantgarde'. Peter Schütt, like Walser, recommended a 'literary' path, which for both meant linking up again with the literature of the BPRS. (It should here be said that the realism discussions in the Seventies, and not merely in the Werkkreis, were at times strongly influenced by the rediscovery of these novels, the literary debates in *Die Linkskurve* and the 'Expressionismusdebatte' of the Thirties, all of which were republished and widely discussed in the early Seventies.) Not only can the Werkkreis be, therefore, to some extent considered the heir of the BPRS, the internal disputes that have taken place in it also mirror those in its predecessor.[21] There are those who consider realism as that which 'gibt gesellschaftliche Wirklichkeit nachvollziehbar, d.h. verbindlich wieder', corresponding to the position of Willi Bredel, while others understand it as the presentation of both 'der tatsächlichen Realität' and 'der möglichen und der erwünschten Realität', which is closer to Georg Lukács. But the Werkkreis has shown itself capable of accommodating both views, indeed the tension produced has led to the idea that the literary form it adopts should depend in part on the target group. There is, for example, a threefold treatment of a strike in a foundry in Pierburg (Neuß) — a full-scale documentation intended essentially for internal use, a reportage (included in the volume *Dieser Betrieb wird bestreikt*) aimed at a wider audience, and Hermann Spix's novel *Elephteria oder die Reise ins Paradies*. According to Peter Fischbach, another leading member, the documentation was intended to provide 'ein weitaus umfassenderes Bild der komplexen Zusammenhänge' than the other two, but its length clearly militates against its reaching outside the organisation. The reportage is a sensible compromise between the full documentation and the novel, while the novel, still essentially documentary in nature, narrates

20. 'Programm des Werkkreises Literatur der Arbeitswelt', 7.3.1970.
21. Cf. here the detailed description of the first years of the Werkkreis by Peter Fischbach and Maria Meyer-Puschner in Manfred Brauneck (ed.), *Der deutsche Roman im 20. Jahrhundert*, Bamberg, 1976, pp. 301–27.

events from the perspective of one of the participants, a Greek 'Gastarbeiterin', so that the eventual focus is much more on the human consequences of poor conditions in the foundry (cf. Part II). The satisfactory fusion of personal experiences and documentary evidence, through the use of montage, results in extreme credibility; it is by no means the only example from the Seventies of the successful blending of more conventional narrative techniques with the documentary.

Another important feature of the debates in the Werkkreis was the participation of Martin Walser, who, as already noted, played a prominent role in the early years. It is somewhat difficult to follow fully the path of Walser in the early Seventies; at times seemingly despairing he lurches from one position to another both in the novels (*Fiction, Die Gallistl'sche Krankheit* and *Der Sturz*) and in his theoretical pronouncements. His pleasure at detecting the existence of a literary avant-garde amongst Werkkreis members seemed to indicate a lessening of political commitment, but his speech to the convention of 1972, 'Wie und wovon handelt Literatur?', evinces a deeper political conviction that is very close to Marxism and contains a reassertion of the important social role of realist literature. He holds up the group's work as an expression of human rights and the unjust suffering borne by the writers in their daily work; the 'realistische Ausdruckspraxis' is for him only justified when it is such an 'Ausdruck eines historischen Moments'.[22] Realistic literature is, therefore, inherently critical; it shows 'was wirklich geschieht, und fordert dadurch, was geschehen muß'. At this point Walser's position seems perfectly reconcilable with his definition of realism from the early Sixties, but he has added to it the 'marxistische Erkenntnis darüber, daß das Wichtigste am Realismus seine nie zum Schema . . . erstarrende Fähigkeit sein muß, den historischen Prozeß durch die Verdinglichungen zu erkennen und darzustellen'. The crucial quality of realist literature is now its 'Brauchbarkeit'. A further indication of the redefition of his earlier position is the stress he lays here on the need to take up the threads of the interrupted realism discussions of the Twenties and Thirties. He is, however, concerned at the close affinity of the theoretical views of leading Werkkreis spokesmen to Lukács' ideas on 'Gestaltung'. Realism is for him not an 'unveränderlicher Spiegel . . . , der über die Realität schwebt, um sie einzufangen'; like Brecht, to whose ideas he moves ever closer at this time, Walser believes that such writing rapidly ossifies into 'Manierismus' (= Brecht's 'Formalis-

---

22. Martin Walser, *Wie und wovon handelt Literatur?*, Frankfurt, 1973, pp. 119–39.

mus'), becoming increasingly 'erfahrungsunabhängiger'. The writer then 'läßt seine Sensibilität auf einen beliebigen Wirklichkeitsausschnitt reagieren und führt vor, was sie dabei, bzw. was er alles in dieser Wirklichkeit entdeckt'. In order to avoid the degeneration of his writing into 'autonome Kunst' the realist should always respond 'auf das aktuelle Stadium der realistischen Ausdruckspraxis'. Consequently, as with Brecht, there is no firm notion of style.

Outside the Werkkreis, which has always been a somewhat special case, the essential stimuli to the realism debates resulted from the effects of the 'Studentenbewegung'. In literary scholarship and theory there was, for a time at least, a radical rejection of the hegemony of established ('werkimmanent') approaches and of the view of literature as autonomous 'schöner Schein'. Suddenly materialist aesthetics were to the fore, with particular attention being paid to the Frankfurt School and the writings of Georg Lukács.

The most influential figure, whose impact can be seen on such critics as Heißenbüttel, Vormweg and Lüdke, was Theodor Adorno, whose works of the Fifties and earlier were extensively republished in the course of the student unrest. He it was who was responsible for a number of prominent critics of a new generation continuing the German tradition of anti-realism, although it should be said, in fairness, that this was in part the result of a reading of Adorno that was either oversimplified or consciously selective. His essay 'Der Standort des Erzählers im zeitgenössischen Roman' (1954)[23] put forward ideas on the modern novel, familiar to us from, amongst others, Brecht, Kahler and Broch, that were widely taken up. For Adorno 'die Oberfläche des gesellschaftlichen Lebensprozesses' has become increasingly impenetrable in modern society, so that it 'als Schleier das Wesen verhüllt'. In this situation Adorno saw it necessary for the realist novel to be redefined: if it were to *'seinem realistischen Erbe treu bleiben und sagen, wie es wirklich ist, so muß er auf einen Realismus verzichten, der, indem er die Fassade reproduziert, nur dieser bei ihrem Täuschungsgeschäft hilft* [italicised in original, KB]'. The realist novel, which he compares to the conventional stage with proscenium arch, is incapable of reflecting 'die universale Entfremdung und Selbstentfremdung'. Moreover, it has lost its traditional function of informative narration to reportage and other modern media, while the writer's intuitive insights into character have been overtaken by modern psychology. The new novel, responding to new social conditions, is characterised by 'ein anti-realistisches Moment . . .

---

23. *Noten zur Literatur I*, Frankfurt, 1969, pp. 61–8. All quotations from this edition.

[eine] metaphysische Dimension' and its aesthetic tools are to be alienation itself. Realism, on the other hand, is dismissed as a 'Gestus kunstgewerblicher Imitation', as 'Kitsch vom Schlag der Heimatkunst'.

A reading of these and other pronouncements by Adorno on the novel is complicated somewhat by the need to realise that, in a very German way, he is using the term 'Realismus' in an historically specific sense — as applying to the nineteenth century. His main point, which emerges clearly from his 'redefinition' of the novel quoted above, is that the modern realist novel has to respond to a changed social reality. Unfortunately, too many writers and theoreticians pounced uncritically on his ideas, wielding their reading of Adorno like a sword to rout realism. This is seen very clearly in the collection of essays *Realismus — welcher?* (1976). The most extreme example here is the contribution by Lother Baier. Taking his cue from the editor of the volume, Peter Laemmle, who puts forward a similar statement, also without any justification in terms of social or historical analysis, Baier claims that 'weil die gesellschaftliche Organisation so unüberschaubar geworden ist, ist ihr Porträt in einem Roman handelüblicher Lange nicht mehr unterzubringen'.[24] Over and above this the 'Grad der Spezialisierung und der Perfektionierung wissenschaftlicher Aussagen über die Welt' has become so extreme, 'daß die Literatur mit ihrem Anspruch auf *Realismus* hoffnungslos ins Hintertreffen geraten müsse'. In this situation the means of literary production have not remained untouched: 'der Zeichenvorrat, aus dem die Literatur schöpfen kann, hat sich in viele Einzelordnungen aufgelöst, die kaum mehr integrierbar sind'. The basic premise in this post-Adorno theory of the novel, as with the experimental writers like Heißenbüttel and Becker, is that the novelist of the nineteenth century portrayed a world in which he felt at home and which he could comprehend in its totality (i.e. it was 'überschaubar'). As already demonstrated, this was far from the case with Fontane and Raabe, but it must also be stressed that — as Jan Myrdal has shown so decisively [25] — neither was it true of Balzac, who is invariably cited as the prime example of this elusive nineteenth-century novelist: his mature works are an expression of his sense that the property-owning class was endangered, and are as conscious a defence of the known and cherished in the face of a threatening, far from transparent reality as are the 'Condition of

24. Lothar Baier, '"Kinder, seid doch einmal realistisch!"', in Peter Laemmle (ed.), *Realismus — welcher?*, Munich, 1976, pp. 117–26.

25. Jan Myrdal, 'Zum "Triumph des Realismus"', *Akzente*, Heft 6, 1975, pp. 539–59.

England' novels. The sweeping description of the nineteenth-century novel given by both the experimental writers and the disciples of Adorno is pure myth, a rhetorical falsification of a far more complicated relationship between writer and society, used with the intent of discrediting any form of modern realism and enthroning experimental literature.

Baier's conclusion from his reading of the situation of the novel is proof enough of this: 'der Realitätsbezug der Kunst muß auf der Ebene der Art des künstlerischen Verfahrens gesucht werden', he proclaims, going on to approve montage and collage, 'ready-made' poems and the 'Neues Hörspiel'. These, instead of merely reproducing reality, hold up to it 'die negative Utopie eines vollkommen künstlichen, also fiktiven Universums'. While this seemed perfectly plausible in the early phase of experimental literature, we would here tend to share the criticisms of Walser and Wellershoff, amongst others, as to the danger of a drift into empty formalism. Despite his anti-realism, however, Baier's statement reveals that his ultimate criterion in the evaluation of types of writing is the utopian dimension, a position which he shares with the generation of writers and critics springing from the Student Movement. Whilst there were those who,, following to some extent the ideas of Adorno, used this yardstick to reject realism, another group, agreeing with Michel's view of experimental writing as quietistic, accordingly turned to a modern realism in an attempt to reintroduce the utopian element into West German literature. Justifying this, they make an important point: that the modern writer, given that the rapid general social change of the nineteenth century has slowed down (despite intense change in specific areas), is able to grasp the overall nature of (Western, modern capitalist, technological) society and identify what areas are obscured and by what institutions. He can thus address his writing to the demonstration of ways in which life in this society baulks the free development of the individual. In this, the group in question see themselves as the heirs of the novelists of the nineteenth century who, as they rightly point out, did not merely create a mimetic reproduction of reality, but who, at their best, always pointed to social inadequacies and made an implicit utopian plea for change. In this sense Hans Christoph Buch claims: 'Ich halte überhaupt nur eine Literatur für realistisch, . . . die nicht nur das darstellt, was ist, sondern die die utopischen Möglichkeiten zeigt, die in der täglichen Wirklichkeit ersticken und verkümmern'.[26]

26. Buch, 'Das Hervortreten des Ichs aus den Wörtern', in Laemmle, *Realismus*, p. 40.

The first German writer to lay stress on the utopian element as a crucial component of realism was Bertolt Brecht. He was the most outspoken and subsequently the best-known adversary of Georg Lukács in the 'Expressionismusdebatte' of the Thirties — with the result that Jörg Drews and others have felt able to cite Brecht as an ally in their campaign against recent realist ideas. Nevertheless, a close reading of his views on realism reveals that he opposed only uncritical and, in the modern age, inappropriate championing of nineteenth-century realism as a still viable model. Brecht makes it quite clear that realism was for him not a matter of form or style, but was ultimately dependent on the simultaneous presence in literature of epistemological and utopian dimensions: '*Realistisch* heißt: den gesellschaftlichen Kausalkomplex aufdeckend/ die herrschenden Gesichtspunkte als die Gesichtspunkte der Herrschenden entlarvend/ vom Standpunkt der Klasse aus schreibend, welche für die dringendsten Schwierigkeiten, in denen die menschliche Gesellschaft steckt, die breitesten Lösungen bereithält/ das Moment der Entwicklung betonend/ konkret und das Abstrahieren ermöglichend'.[27] Although Georg Lukács, wrongly in our view, sets great store by the example set for modern writers by the great realist novels· of the nineteenth century, his thinking in this respect is very similar to Brecht's. Despite a recent tendency to see Lukács's theoretical writing as propounding merely a somewhat primitive idea of mimesis (which in turn amounts to a trivialising of the achievements of last century's outstanding writers), what he commends is anything but a crude naturalism; 'die Aufgabe der Kunst' is for him 'die treue und wahre Darstellung des Ganzen der Wirklichkeit . . . ; die Kunst ist geradeso weit entfernt von dem photographischen Kopieren wie von der — letzten Endes — leeren Spielerei mit abstrakten Formen'.[28] Art represents for him, in terms much the same as those used by Engels to Miss Harkness, 'ein Ganzes des menschlichen Lebens . . . , es in seiner Bewegung, Entwicklung, Entfaltung gestaltend',[29] pointing to a better life than the known. He is not concerned with merely accurate reproduction of an aspect of social life — this is what he rejects about the Naturalist movement — but with a 'Realismus des künstlerisch versinnbildlichten Lebens' that 'den gesellschaftlichen Prozeß zur Bewußtheit erhebt'.[30]

Brecht's position on realism came to the attention of a new

27. Bertolt Brecht, *Über Realismus*, Leipzig, 1968, p. 123.
28. Georg Lukács, 'Einführung in die ästhetischen Schriften von Marx und Engels', *Probleme der Ästhetik*' (Werke, Bd. 10), Neuwied & Berlin, 1969, p. 219.
29. Ibid,. p. 220.
30. Ibid., p. 223.

generation during the rediscovery of the Expressionism debate during and after the Student Revolt. Dieter Wellershoff's ideas, too, while not betokening a particular political stance, brought to the fore at much the same time the notion of the crucial implicit plea for change in realist writing. The thoughts of Brecht and Wellershoff together went a considerable way towards rescuing realism from its rigid categorisation as belonging to an earlier age (which, incidentally, was only assisted by the tremendous attention paid to Lukács's contribution to the debates within the BPRS). Further impetus was added to this shift by Heinrich Vormweg's *Eine andere Leseart* (1972) and Christa Wolf's volume of essays, *Lesen und Schreiben* published in the Federal Republic in the same year; the service to the cause of realism in West Germany of Christa Wolf's exemplary development away from the constraints of Socialist Realism and the consequent removal of a major stigma attached to the realist novel in the last decade or so should also be emphasised here.

For Christa Wolf the dilemma of the realist author today lies not so much in the dominance of life by science and technology, as in the way in which so-called reality, which is 'phantastischer als jedes "Phantasieprodukt"', turns against the writer: 'Ihre Grausamkeit und ihre Wunderbarkeit sind durch Erfindung nicht zu übertreffen. Wer also "die Wahrheit" lesen will, das heißt: wie es wirklich ist, der greift zu Tatsachenberichten, Biographien, Dokumentensammlungen, Tagebüchern, Memoiren' (189).[31] She states that she 'kenne und schätze und teile' the demands of the age for documentary writing, but — and here her position is crucially different from Adorno and Jens, who had earlier made not dissimilar general points — she is also aware of the limitations of such literature. The scientific age will 'nicht sein, was es sein könnte und sein muß, . . . wenn nicht die Kunst sich dazu aufschwingt, dem Zeitgenossen, den vielen einzelnen, an die sie sich wendet, große Fragen zu stellen, nicht locker zu lassen in ihren Forderungen an ihn. Ihn zu ermutigen, er selbst zu werden' (79). The uncritical adoption of scientific methods by the writer of imaginative literature may well help in the striving for accurate reproduction of external reality, but such writing lacks what is for her the crucial utopian thrust: 'Prosa kann die Grenzen unseres Wissens über uns selbst weiter hinausschieben. Sie hält die Erinnerung an die Zukunft in uns wach, von der wir uns bei Strafe unseres Untergangs nicht lossagen dürfen' (220). Implicitly Christa Wolf resists the questioning of the power of artistic

---

31. All quotations from Christa Wolf, *Lesen und Schreiben*, Darmstadt & Neuwied, 1972.

creativity at the heart of experimental literature. Not only does she believe in the existence of a world 'jenseits der wichtigen Welt der Fakten' that cannot be attained by any sort of scientific method, but she is convinced that the truly creative role of the writer lies in the ability to explore those important dimensions of human existence that lie behind the facade of facticity. He or she can learn from and use the results of scientific research, 'aber was er selbst auf der Suche nach der Natur des gesellschaftlich lebenden Menschen entdecke, dürfe wohl als "wahr" gelten, ohne daß der Nachweis der "Richtigkeit" erforderlich wäre, den jeder naturwissenschaftliche Schluß verlangt' (209). The vital tool of the writer that can in no way be replaced by scientific advance is *experience*; to write a piece of narrative prose is for her, wahrheitsgetreu zu erfinden auf Grund eigener Erfahrung' (199), and thereby to mediate 'zwischen der objektiven Realität und dem Subjekt Autor'. Here once again is the notion of the realistic author as cognitive subject, whose job it is to represent 'gesellschaftlich bedeutsame Erfahrung' of social life, with the ultimate intent of changing it for the better.

Christa Wolf's renewed stress on this central aspect of, as we would see it, all realist writing was of great influence on a particular group of younger writers which emerged from the Studentenbewegung: the Autoren-Edition. They were tired of all 'established' literature — be it the later Gruppe 47 or Peter Handke — as it seemed to them in no way to address itself to social questions, and at the same time they were unable to accept the political quietism that they, like others, detected in experimental literature. Accordingly, these writers (going some way towards realising one of the key demands of the Student Movement for the 'democratisation' of literature) established a publishing venture based on a consciously provocatively formulated programme of realism. 'Angestrebt', they announced, 'wird eine realistische Schreibweise. Nicht die Schreibschwierigkeiten des Autors angesichts einer widersprüchlichen Realität, sondern die Realität selber ist das Thema der Autoren-Edition'. The books produced by the Autoren-Edition range from Engelmann's 'Tatsachenromane' (which have, as the author himself admitted, a 'dürftige Groschenheft-Handlung') to Kipphardt's *März* and *Traumprotokolle*; they cannot, therefore, be seen as reflecting a tightly unified programme, but are, rather, a variety of works having in common a rejection of formalism on the one hand and a desire to create a body of realist literature on the other. According to Horst Holzer, the overall aim was, 'die Widerspiegelung der herrschenden gesellschaftlichen Realität und die Durchbrechung des dieser Realität konvergierenden Alltagsbewußtseins mit spezifisch ästhetischen Mitteln'.[32] Realism is understood — and again the influence of Christa Wolf may be sensed here — as an aesthetic code that 'durch sozusagen "*sinnlich*" zugängliche Sprache *allgemeine* ('gesetzesartige') Erkenntnisse von Natur und Gesellschaft an *subjektiv-individuell* sich vollziehende und nachvollziehbare Zuständlichkeiten und Entwicklungen rückbindet und damit zu einer gleichermaßen *subjektiven* wie *subjektzentrierten* Rekonstruktion gesellschaftlicher Totalitat gelangt . . .'(140).

The counter-position to that of the Autoren-Edition was taken up by Jörg Drews, who launched into a bitter attack on the new group, 'Wider einen neuen Realismus', which shows both the influence of Adorno at this time and the continued strength of the anti-realist sentiment amongst leading West German critics in the mid-Seventies.[33] The starting-point of Drews' polemic is, inevitably, his sweeping dismissal of realism as a style rooted in the last century. He then argues that, whereas Balzac's characters could still be 'plastische Gestalten', their modern equivalents yield virtually nothing 'an sinnlicher Anschaulichkeit, an unverwechselbarer Individualität, as 'die modllhaft Bedeutung exemplifizierende Erzählung' has become very problematical; it can now portray nothing more than 'ein zufälliges Einzelschicksal' in Balzac's day the natural and the social sciences, not to mention psychology, had 'schon so weit in die Bereiche des Unanschaulichen vorgestoßen, hatten jenen Komplexitäts- und Abstraktheitsgrad erreicht, der heute den Begriff der Realität so schwierig macht'. From this Drews concludes that reality today is inaccessible to any form of '*unmittelbarer* literarischer Darstellung'. Those who today work on the assumption that society is 'noch nicht so total und unangreifbar, daß sie völlig hinter dem Rücken des Individuums als ein übermächtiges Abstraktum regieren würde' are blind to the nature of modern reality. Today, 'die sinnliche Anschauung ist täuschend vordergründig', the essence of reality cannot be conveyed in the form of a piece of narrative prose concerned with aspects of individual lives. This is all the more true, since the novelist as intuitive reader of the human psyche has long ago been overtaken by the modern science of psychological analysis. The language of the realist novel can only reproduce clichés, since 'Erkenntnisse' are today only formulated in 'Fach- und Spezialsprachen'.

We are dealing here with a dexterous command of German that

32. 'Die realistische Literatur und ihr gesellschaftlisches Subjekt' in Uwe Timm & Gerd Fuchs (eds.), *Kontext 1*, Munich, 1976, pp. 134–40.
33. The dispute between Drews and Timm is contained in 'Für und wider einen neuen Realismus', Laemmle, *Realismus*, pp. 139–83.

can, on the one hand, dismiss with questionable sleight of hand (what on earth, it might be asked, is 'täuschend vordergründig' about 'sinnliche Anschauung'?), but which also constitutes a dangerous mythologisation that invalidates any common-sense empirical enquiry about the causality of social phenomena. The world of specialised skills is elevated to the status of an all-powerful but anonymous fate that has the effect of negating all attempts — not merely literary ones — at getting to grips with the new world over which expertise seems to hold sway. The ignoring here by someone otherwise so sensitive to language of the obfuscating function of specialist jargon is particularly astounding. The argumentation is surprisingly thin, but Drews, as if he had sensed this, conscripts Brecht as the 'classic' supporter of his position, in a manner reminiscent of the nineteenth-century Germanist's use of Goethe quotations to disarm criticism: indeed, it may be recalled at this point that his essay opens with a (highly obscure) Brecht quotation that seems to dismiss realist writing out of hand. But a closer look at it reveals that — in keeping with his general attitude to realism, referred to earlier — Brecht merely rejects the attempted 'einfache Wiedergabe der Realität' in literature, not realism as such. Nevertheless, Drews tries to present Brecht as a confirmed anti-realist and claims to be advancing Brechtian argument in stating that literature needs today 'abstrakter Verfahren, um die konkrete Wahrheit sichtbar zu machen, die vergleichweise naiven Verfahren wie denen des Realismus gar nicht mehr zugänglich ist'. Not only does Drews here contradict himself, by stating that reality can be illuminated through literature, he yet again distorts the position of Brecht, who did indeed criticise rigid (and what he saw as formalist) notions of realism, but nevertheless stood for the 'Weite und Breite der realistischen Schreibweise'.

The tone of Drews' argument, as the description of realism as a 'naïve technique' indicates, is essentially one of contempt. It is, he tells us, merely 'ein photographisches Abbild . . . ein bloßes Abziehbild der Wirklichkeit' and any attempt to create a modern realism amounts to the 'Wunsch nach einer Entlastung von der ganzen Bürde der Erkenntnisse' which make 'das naive Erzählen immer schwieriger'. For the writer of such primitive stuff literature is understood as 'ein Bereich des Unmittelbaren . . . , der komplikationslosen Kommunikation'. There are, Drews admits, critics of repute like Buch and Wellershoff, who have tried to embody in their concept of realist writing a full awareness of the nature of the relationship between the writer and reality, but realism 'so verstanden' becomes 'sinnlos'. It is clear, however, that his real target is not these revisionist critics, as they might be called; modern realism is ultimately the desire that 'bei bestimmten literarischen Gruppierungen . . . nach einer Rückkehr zu den bewährten, scheinbar so handfesten realistischen Schreibweisen immer wieder auftaucht, wie sie im Osten durch die sozialistische Kulturindustrie dekretiert worden sind'. The consequences, Drews goes on, of the 'bürokratischen Abschaffung der Phantasie und die Installation einer realistischen Literatur in der Sowjektunion und . . . in der DDR' should, for all of us in the West, 'eine Warnung sein'. He reverts, therefore, to a crude, politically coloured dismissal of realism as a more or less treasonable Red import. This would have been extreme at the height of the cold war, and, at a time of real advances in the East German novel, is all the more amazing.

Drews' anti-realist ideas are not without their further contradictions. He argues, on the one hand, that reality is unfathomable, that modern society is an anomymous, all-powerful abstract force, yet claims, on the other: 'Erst durch das begriffliche Schauen, erst durch die "Theorie" der Wissenschaft wird die Sicht auf die Erscheinungen der Wirklichkeit zur Einsicht in die Konstituenten'. It is, in other words, possible after all to penetrate below the surface and to comprehend reality. Moreover, Drews then holds up Günter Wallraff as a model writer, lauding him for turning his back on realist, 'Trivialformen ausnützende Romane' and developing instead a form of writing 'die konsequenterweise auf den *Kunst*-Charakter absolut pfeift'. But this example is beset with problems: Wallraff's work from *Der Aufmacher* through to his recent *Ganz unten* (1985) has indeed become increasingly less literary and more straightforwardly journalistic in style and method, but in the early Seventies his use of the montage technique (as in *Neue Reportagen*, 1972) was in a major stream of literary thinking and much admired by, for example, Heißenbüttel. More important still, in this context, is that Wallraff is an empirical researcher, believing that the individual, through direct experience, can come to an understanding of social reality and can highlight aspects of that reality critically in literature: that the individual is able to show that what is portrayed 'keine Einzelfälle sind, keine so einfach wegzuretuschierenden Mißstände, vielmehr systemimmanente Zustände'.[34]

Jörg Drews seems ultimately to have sensed the weaknesses in his arguments, as he descends, in the last part of his article, into almost despairingly scornful mockery of any sort of realism, which has

---

34. Günter Wallraff, 'Wirkungen in der Praxis' in Thomas Rother (ed.), *Schrauben haben Rechtsgewinde*, Düsseldorf, 1971, p. 15.

become 'ein lachhafter Anachronismus'. Reality has become so complex, 'daß der Griff derer, die da *realistisch* schreiben wollen, fast zum Gespött werden muß'. Realism today can only be 'Bestseller-Schinken' in the style of the nineteenth century or a 'neue Einfachheit', the 'Re-Simplifizierung der Literatur'. Such cheap comments from a Professor of Literary Criticism indicate the continued strength of feeling at that time against realist writing in German academic circles and were sufficiently provocative to evoke a response from the novelist Uwe Timm, leading to a full-blown public argument between the two that still stands as an exemplary clash between the realist and anti-realist camps.

Timm, then one of the co-editors of the Autoren-Edition, which had been Drews' particular butt, immediately rejects the idea that realism (of any merit) is merely 'eine platte naturalistische Abschilderung der bestehenden Verhältnisse'. Moreover, it is not a canonised style outdated to the point of total inappropriateness, but a critical method. Despite the false claims attributed to it by Drews, realism aims 'nichts primär auf Gegenständlichkeit, sondern auf die Entwicklung der Gegenstände, mehr aber noch auf die Entwicklung von Menschen u.a. in ihrem Verhältnis zu anderen Menschen und zu den Gegenständen'. It is by no means content with portraying — in Drews' phrase — what is 'täuschend vordergründig'; its purpose is, rather, 'das Wesen einer Gesellschaftsform, das heißt der Wirklichkeit, aus deren Erscheinungsform heraus darzustellen', and an avowedly political realism is concerned to show thereby 'Wirklichkeit als gesellschaftlich bedingt und als veränderbar', hoping to contribute to 'eine bewußte Veränderung dieser Gesellschaft'.

Timm considers it 'selbstverständlich' that 'die Schwierigkeiten beim Beschreiben einer widersprüchlichen komplizierten Wirklichkeit sich auch in der realistichen Literatur niederschlagen müssen, will sie nicht simplifizieren'. But he rightly identifies the flaw in the arguments of Drews and other followers of Adorno, when they baldly assert that the novel of the nineteenth century was written at a time when the 'Antriebskräfte und Organisationsformen der Gesellschaft' had not yet become abstract. In reality, these forms had certainly changed by the time Fontane was writing (i.e. the transition from post-feudalism to advanced capitalism had been accomplished, KB). For Timm the example of Fontane shows that realism — admittedly changed — is possible in the modern capitalist era; it also demonstrates how such writing, in showing the human need for existing society to change, continues the utopian element, so central to realism. In constrast, anti-realist literary theories, such as those of Jörg Drews, posit 'die Mystifikation und den Grad der Entfremdung' as being so absolute, 'daß die Wirklichkeit nicht mehr erkennbar und damit nicht darstellbar ist', with the result that reality cannot be shown as being in need of change and as changeable. The anti-realist school understands it, rather, as being 'von einem alles durchwaltenden Abstraktum bestimmt', whereas Timm views reality as 'eine gesellschaftliche, von handelnden Menschen bewirkt, die wiederum von dieser gesellschaftlichen Wirklichkeit geprägt werden'. His premise is, therefore that the essence of an admittedly ever more complex external world can indeed be comprehended by the individual, if he draws on a range of possible information; realism, the literary method appropriate to the aim of 'Wirklichkeit erkennbar beschreiben', must, though, go beyond merely 'Befindlichkeiten niederschreiben' and attempt at all times 'gesellschaftliche Bedingungen durch und in der Sprache transparent zu machen'.

As with Wellershoff, the crucial thing about realism is the epistemological claim that it makes. While the anti-realists have an almost Hegelian, idealist view of reality, whereby — since it is determined by abstract ideas — the experiences of an individual reveal nothing of its true nature, the realist is a materialist, attempting by means of 'modellhafte Einzelschicksale' to represent the 'Schein der Wirklichkeit auf ihr Wesen hin'. Timm, like Brecht, is concerned 'daß das Einzelne, Individuelle auf sein gesellschaftliches Wesen, auf den allgemeinen Charakter der ganzen Bewegung transparent gemacht wird, daß im Besonderen das Allgemeine aufscheint'. Unlike his forebears, today's writer cannot rely on intuition alone to do this, he is required 'sich zugleich um wissenschaftliche, insbesondere um gesellschaftswissenschaftliche Erkenntnisse[zu] bemühen'. But for Timm, as for Christa Wolf, such material has its limitations: 'die Naturwissenschaften können das Verhältnis Mensch/Gesellschaft nicht befragen', i.e. they tell us nothing about the actual *experience* of reality. The realist novel can provide such information through its treatment of aspects of the life of individuals, complementing this with relevant external material; Timm lays here particular stress on the need to integrate the historical dimension into the novel. It is important that individual experience is seen as being influenced not by abstract forces — such as history, portrayed as immutable fate, or an anonymous state — but by socially determined causes that conform to certain patterns; the apparently isolated event affecting an individual is to be shown as part of such general tendencies.

An important part of the changed nature of modern experience for Timm is the degree of 'Verdinglichung durch Sprache', and the writer has to adopt a style that reflects this if realism is to be more than 'das naïve Abpinseln bestimmter Oberflächenphänomene'. At the same time he feels that the extreme 'Reflexion auf sprachliche Phänomene', as represented by writers of concrete and other experimental literature, can easily become a '*Metasprache*'. Such works can nevertheless be 'wichtig und nützlich, weil sie bestimmte Phänomene der Sprache, des Bewußtseins reflektieren, aber sie liefern als Techniken nur einen begrenzten Ausschnitt der *ganzen gesellschaftlichen Bewegung*'. In order to show this, it is important that in the 'Mittelpunkt einer realistischen Literatur . . . konkrete Menschen stehen und keine linguistischen Sprechblasen', while at the same time, so that the modern problem of language is reflected adequately, modern realism will 'sich von der experimentellen Literatur holen, was sie braucht'. While, however, this latter writing tends towards formalism, the modern realist novel will become 'so radikal experimentell . . ., daß sie jenen Kunstcharakter, der Literatur in dieser Gessellschaft als reine Kunst von der Wirklichkeit abtrennt, zu durchbrechen sucht, indem sie auf eine zu verändernde Wirklichkeit zielt, und zwar mit allen künstlerischen Mitteln'.

Yet again we are brought back here to the charge of quietism made against experimental literature. Timm and other modern realists do not share Jörg Drews vague assertion — seemingly derived from Adorno's concept of 'Engagement' — that all imaginative literature 'die etwas taught' is 'implizit ein Plädoyer für die Freiheit des Menschen'. This is particularly not the case in works that present individuals as 'metaphysische Marionetten' or some other sort of abstract figure. Only by portraying real people and their experiences can the element of 'Veränderung, sowohl thematisch als auch formal, als Handlung' be brought into literature; it can then be shown 'inhaltlich an den dargestellten Figuren . . . , als Veränderung ihres Bewußtseins, ihrer Sensibilität und schließlich ihrer Praxis'. This crucial utopian dimension, which, we would argue, is central to the great novels of the last century, including those of Fontane and Raabe, represents for Timm — through suggestion, implication or direct criticism — 'einen Gegenbereich und Gegenentwurf zur Wirklichkeit', opening up perspectives 'die über das Bestehende hinausgehen, indem sie dieses als veränderbar darstell[en] oder doch darauf insistier[en], daß es verändert werden muß'. This humanising function, the contribution of literature to a continuing process of man's shaping of his social environment, extends 'bis in den Rezeptionsvorgang und konstituiert ein *neues* Einverständnis über gesellschaftliche Wirklichkeit'. Modern realism, which was to produce such a body of novels in the Seventies, is to be seen, therefore, as an attempt to break with the anti-realist novel tradition that has dominated German literature since the beginning of the nineteenth century and to establish thereby a relationship between literature and reading public that has rarely existed in Germany. As Lucien Goldmann has said of the mainstream nineteenth-century novel, that relationship is characterised by 'a process of the structuration of a collective consciousness . . . , which the writer transposes on to the plane of conceptual thought or creative imagination, pushing it at the same time to a very advanced degree of coherence'. Such a realism does not view literature as existing in, and adding to, a world of 'schöner Schein', but rather, over and above the sense of aesthetic pleasure it can generate, as contributing to a process which helps readers 'to gain awareness of themselves and of their emotional, intellectual and practical aspirations'.[35]

Despite the volume of recent realist novels corresponding more or less to Uwe Timm's notion of realism, German literary criticism has continued to be dominated by the anti-realist lobby. There has been no further public debate as such, but the tenor of reviews and articles in the leading literary periodicals reinforces this reading of the situation. A revealing example is provided by the reception of Heinrich Böll's penultimate novel *Fürsorgliche Belagerung* (1979). While we should allow for the factor of familiarity breeding contempt here, the swiftly unanimous dismissal of a carefully crafted novel (cf. Chapter 6) is astonishing. Marcel Reich-Ranicki called it 'ein schwaches und fragwürdiges, streckenweise ein geradezu fatales Buch',[36] while Wolfram Schütte condemned it as 'desaströs gescheitert': Böll's rendering of colloquial German in the dialogues was 'fast naturalistisch reproduziert' and he had quite clearly intended to give 'das Bild einer "epischen Totalität" und "Objektivität" (wie Georg Lukács gesagt hätte)'.[37] The old negative clichés are thus reproduced yet again. To this pattern of reception in the *feuilletons* can be added further ones: the award of literary prizes mainly to experimental writers and the places occupied by such writers in the monthly 'Bestenliste' produced by the leading critics for the Südwestfunk's 'Literaturmagazin' programme. All pointers indicate,

---

35. Lucien Goldmann, *La création culturelle dans la société moderne*, Paris, 1971, pp. 97–8; in the absence of an acceptable alternative, this is my translation. The relevant passages in the original are as follows: 'un processus de structuration d'une conscience collective à l'intérieur duquel transpose sur le plan de la pensée conceptuelle ou de la création imaginaire, en les poussant à un degré de cohérence très avancé, l'ensemble catégorial en cours de constitution'; ' . . . à prendre conscience d'euxmêmes et de leurs propres aspirations affectives, intellectuelles et pratiques'.

36. 'Nette Kapitalisten und nette Terroristen', *Frankfurter Allgemeine Zeitung*, 4.8.1979.

37. 'Lauter nette Menschen', *Frankfurter Rundschau*, 4.8.1979.

then, an antagonism to realism continuing into the Eighties. Against this, though, may be observed the considerable success, in terms of readership, of such realist authors as Böll, Lenz, Walzer, Kempowski and Härtling, as well as of foreign authors like Marquez, V.S. Naipaul and Doris Lessing. In addition, a whole series of documentary, biographical and autobiographical novels, as well as those of so-called 'Neue Subjektivität', achieved remarkably high sales (cf. Part II). This does not necessarily mean, as some critics would have us think, that the Seventies represent the breakthrough of 'bessere Trivialliteratur'.[38] It would seem, rather, that the success of this literature represents (by no means for the first time in the history of German literature since 1800) something of a revolt by the educated reader against the dictates of the cultural critics. The evaluation of the reasons for this development cannot be examined in detail within the context of this work, but it would seem very likely that it is due, if only in part, to an identification with the portrayal of individual experience in such works, as affording insights into the problems of modern social life. Given the rapid changes in contemporary society emanating from ongoing technological progress, its threat to the environment, the shadow of nuclear disaster and the beginnings of a computerisation that can only lead to an increased gulf between the individual and the forces that determine people's lives, it is hardly surprising that there is a sense of need for help in self-orientation. This is one of the crucial functions of realist writing, and so the recent successes of realism in West Germany, where awareness of these modern problems seems to be particularly acute, ought not to be that surprising. In the second part of this volume the range of realist writing produced since the end of the Sixties will be examined with a particular eye as to how far it meets this human need.

38. Cf. here, in addition to numerous articles and reviews by Jörg Drews, W. Martin Lüdke, 'Der stetig steigende Unterhaltungswert der späten Prosa Martin Walsers' (a lecture given in the context of the Deutsch–Englisches Germanistentreffen of the DAAD, Berlin 1982), K. Bullivant and H.J. Althof (eds.), *Subjektivität — Innerlichkeit — Abkehr vom Politischen?* Bonn, 1986.

PART II

The Contemporary Realist Novel

4

The Novel of So-called 'Sprachrealismus'

The main characteristics of concrete literature, which achieved a general critical breakthrough in West Germany in the late Sixties (although much was written substantially earlier), were on the one hand an understanding of language as an autonomous system of signs, on the other the element of linguistic play so reminiscent of Dada and as exemplified at its most extreme in the sound poems ('Lautgedichte') of Gerhard Rühm and Ernst Jandl. This latter aspect, in particular, makes it easy to overlook the claim made by a number of the writers for some of their experimental literature to be seen as a conscious act of cognition of the world through reflection on its mediation through language; the writer starts from the premise that he 'kann nicht Realität aufs Papier bringen, sondern nur, was es zur Realität zu sagen gibt, was es über die Realität zu erzählen gibt'.[1] Such literature has, quite reasonably, been called 'Sprachrealismus', in that it aims not at the depiction of reality through language, but at the critical treatment in literature of language as a crucial mediator of reality. The role of the writer is very different from the traditional one: he is not called upon to demonstrate 'imagination' or 'linguistic creativity', he has, in fact, no 'eigene Sprache', but 'übernimmt Sprache ... als etwas Vorgegebenes nämlich, so, wie heute mündlich und vor allem schriftlich vorkommt und verkommt'.[2] The 'Sprachrealist' does not operate with a language 'die von der Wirklichkeit losgelöst ist', but with 'einer sprachlichen Wirklichkeit',[3] whereas in concrete poetry proper language '[weist] nicht auf eine wie sehr auch fingierte Wirklichkeit außerhalb der Sprache, sondern auf sich selbst'.[4] Thus for Max

---

1. Peter Bichsel, 'Die Geschichte soll auf dem Papier geschehn', *Akzente*, 15, 1968, p. 409. Cf. in this general connection U.K. Eggers, *Aspekte zeitgenössischer Romantheorie*, Bonn, 1976. Eggers was, to our knowledge, the first to use the term 'Sprachrealismus'.

2. Reinhard Baumgart, *Aussichten des Romans oder Hat Literatur Zukunft?* (1968), Munich, 1970, pp. 51–2.

3. Bichsel, p. 409.

4. Christoph Wagenknecht, *Konkrete Poesie II*, Munich, 1971, p. 7.

Bense, one of the leading theoreticians of concrete poetry, the '"*Außenwelt*", die ein Text beschreibt', is not 'das Medium der Zeichen, sondern gerade die *Eigenwelt*, in der er sich bildet, also die Materialität der Sprache'.[5] He is concerned ultimately with the creation of a 'vom sprachlichen Sinn losgelöste Schönheit'. Franz Mon, one of the foremost practitioners, has a similar view of literature as autonomous art, as a means of creating a completely independent, 'vielleicht nur in diesem künstlerisch-künstlichen Medium erreichbren Welt'.[6] Mon even goes so far as to call into question the validity of what we call reality, since for him 'real ist, was formuliert ist', nothing more.

And yet in Mon such notions of literature as the only reality are seen to be contradicted by formulations that point clearly in the direction of 'Sprachrealismus': literature operates 'mit den Brocken aus der nur zu bekannten Realität' and through control of language in it 'wird Realität geordnet, werden ihre Zusammenhänge aufgedeckt'. As an example of such writing, he cites Döblin's *Berlin Alexanderplatz*, which should indeed be considered the most significant precursor of recent 'linguistic' realism; for Mon, Döblin's achievement is the way in which the montages and collages of 'ready-mades' are used to erode the 'Erzählgemütlichkeit' of the novel and to jolt the reader 'aus der angenehmen Fiktion auf die eigene banale Realität'. Through this deconstruction of conventional narrative flow an otherwise autonomous fictional world, contained in the story of Franz Biberkopf, is brought into direct relationship with the reader's experience of reality.

The inconsistency both in theory and in literary practice is by no means peculiar to Mon. We find, for example, that Helmut Heißenbüttel, so energetic in his rejection of realism — as conventionally understood —, can nevertheless countenance it in a modern, language-orientated form. He asserts, as seen earlier, that the complexity of the modern world is such as to deny us empirical understanding of it; insight into its nature is only possible through modern scientific analysis (which includes, somewhat surprisingly, Marxism, which he considers 'wissenschaftlich und theologiefrei').[7] The real problem now is, 'wie wir das von der Wissenschaft Erlernbare literarisch verwenden können' (BüL, 46). Heißenbüttel admits here that he has no clear answer, other than that, since 'außersprachliche Vorstellung

---

5. Bense, *Bestandteile des Vorüber*, Cologne, 1961, p. 117.

6. 'Collagetexte und Sprachcollagen' in *Texte über Texte*, Neuwied & Berlin, 1970, pp. 116–35, here: pp. 123, 130. Cf. also 'Text als Prozeß' in the same volume, pp. 86–101, esp. 93–4.

7. Heißenbüttel/Vormweg, *Briefwechsel über Literatur* (BüL), p. 46.

von Menschenwelt wissenschaftlich aufgesplittert und kaleidoskopiert ist', literature cannot 'unmittelbar Spiegelbilder liefern. Sie
muß das Spiegelbild sozusagen aus den Mitteln der Sprache erst
entwickeln' (BüL, 65). Although a good number of the texts in the
Textbücher demonstrate in their playfulness a closeness to concrete
poetry, there are others which, in these terms, are realist in intent.
By the organisation of ready-made material in collages according to
mechanical, i.e. non-subjective principles (the sequence in 'Deutschland 1944' was dictated, he says by dealing cards), he attempts
'aus der Sprache herauszuholen, herauszulocken, was als Reali-
tätsspur darin aufbewahrt ist . . .'.[8] He rejects traditional narration
of an exemplary story in favour of a decoding of language, the
isolation of those elements of reality it conveys, elements normally
obscured, so serving to obfuscate our perception of the world around
us. The primary task of this contemporary realism is to demonstrate
'den unauflösbaren Zusammenhang . . . zwischen der faktisch veränderten Welt und der Unmöglichkeit, diese Veränderung direkt und
unreflektiert zu benennen' (BüL, 28).

Heißenbüttel's concern here with the problems of the modern
writer, above all the doubt he casts on the power of language in the
hands of the creative author to reflect external reality, has a certain
tradition within German literature of the twentieth century. Such
questioning of language is fundamental to much of the writing of, for
example, Rilke, Musil and Broch, and finds its most cogent expression in Hofmannsthal's famous 'Chandos-Brief'. Round about the
turn of the century writers for the first time became aware that, in
rapidly changing social conditions, the self-awareness of the individual, essentially determined by established linguistic patterns, was
being undermined by a growing gulf between the self and an
increasingly alien world. This new environment was both shaped by
science and technology and reflected in new metalanguages, generated by those forces, that were more or less incomprehensible to the
average person. Even in areas still apparently accessible to individual experience, discoveries in psychology and psychoanalysis were
calling into question the tools of everyday language as an adequate
means of expression. All these factors impinge very much on Heißenbüttel's thinking, but they are seen by writers today in a different
light. The crisis depicted in the 'Chandos-Brief' has to be perceived
as a highly sensitive response to the changed material conditions of
literature from an author schooled in an aesthetic code that required
of him a creative relationship to language: the contemporary writer,

8. Heißenbüttel, *Zur Tradition der Moderne*, Neuwied & Berlin, 1972, p. 51.

however, if he is at all sensitive to these problems, has accepted the limitations on his awareness of reality, on the language at his disposal and the effect of that acceptance on his work. To this extent, the position of Heißenbüttel, Mon and others should not be seen as one of linguistic scepticism, but rather of a critical attitude to language, the ultimate aim of which is its regeneration.

These radical changes in the relationship of the writer to the outside world and to language fundamentally undermine the old concept of the writer as 'Mundstück der Götter', whose pronouncements on the nature of social experience have particular force. Wittgenstein has confirmed what Kant and Humboldt had felt before him, namely, that the limitations of language define the limitations of the world experienced by the individual as subject; as a result the writer is not able to convey an objective reality, but only his subjective impression of it. For some this has led to a fundamental change in the nature of the creative process: 'Da in einer Welt der Trugbilder und subjektiven Täuschungen dem Dichter die objektive Realität unerkennbar und unbeschreibbar bleibt, wird er zum bewußten Hersteller von Fiktionen und Unwahrheiten, während er früher meinte, Realität zu erfassen'.[9] Such a reaction is, however, overhasty and wrong in its absurd denunciation — as 'lies' — of literature written from a consciously subjective point of view. The writer has undoubtedly lost any claim to objectivity he once had (assuming for the moment that, outside the realms of ideal-type analysis, he ever had any such thing), but the mediation of personal experience has long been a legitimate part of literature, especially in lyric poetry. Even the so-called objective picture of society given by Balzac is, we would argue, highly personal, and even the most 'consequential' Naturalists like Zola and Holz showed themselves fully aware of the importance of the subjective element in literature. The novel, after the turn of the century, displays its most sensitive and productive reaction to the sensed shift in the relationship of writer to external reality in its conscious stressing of the subjective perspective by means of first-person narration, stream of consciousness, interior monologue etc.; these techniques, which make clear the absence of any claim by the writer to be telling the 'objective' truth, have, in the main, dominated the twentieth-century novel. It is only since 1945 that writers have become familiar with Wittgenstein's ideas of 'Sprachspiel' (in the sense of the manipulation in literature of linguistic material) and, drawing on the pioneering example of the 'Wiener Gruppe', have attempted to put these into

9. C.A.M. Noble, *Sprachskepsis über Dichtung der Moderne*, Munich, 1978, p. 11.

literary practice.

Awareness of the consequences of social change for language, and thus for writing, has been accompanied in recent literary theory by a questioning of the continued viability of the major genres, especially the novel. While, as argued above, it is an oversimplification to view the novel as the central instrumental work of art of nineteenth-century bourgeoisie, there can be little doubt that Jürgen Becker is right in declaring: 'Unsere gesellschaftlichen Formen sind heute offen, diese Welt ist anders, und ein Roman, glaube ich, ist da nicht mehr imstande, diese Gesellschaft, die so aufgestückelt ist in Einzelheiten, so zu repräsentieren, wie das im neunzehnten Jahrhundert möglich gewesen ist'.[10] In any of the ways already listed and others, the serious novel has developed away from the classic form, with only the popular novel (the so-called 'Trivialroman') adhering to it. Heißenbüttel, however, goes so far as to call into question even the appropriateness of the consciously subjective representation of social experience in the novel; the 'gesellschaftliche Grund der neuen Literatur' is found, he maintains 'in der Auflösung des subjektiven Bezugspunktes'.[11] The example of Rolf-Dieter Brinkmann's *Keiner weiß mehr* proves to him that whoever 'sich an das Authentische des Persönlichen, Privaten hält, erzählt nicht autobiographisch, er häuft das Unverständliche und Uneinsehbare als bloß reproduzierten Stoff an' (BüL, 54). Such novels do not afford insights into the workings of society, but merely reproduce the façade of an inscrutable reality.

This querying of traditional genres, together with the intense concentration on language, would appear to rule out the epic prose-form for the 'Sprachrealisten' and, indeed, the bulk of their major literary production consists of shorter 'texts' or 'Hörspiele'; where a longer piece of prose, such as Ror Wolf's *Fortsetzung des Berichts*, is actually written, the 'Kontinuität des traditionellen Erzählens' is merely 'vorgetäuscht' in a highly self-conscious 'ironisch-spielerische[n] Umgang mit den Techniken des konventionellen Romans'. In this work 'die Komposition tritt an die Stelle der durchgehenden Handlung';[12] it is as radical a questioning of the conventional form as Wolf Wondratschek's 'Roman', where, as with most of his prose work, extreme concentration on the individual sentence represents the total renunciation of 'jene letzten bürger-

---

10. In Werner Koch (ed.), *Selbstanzeige*, Frankfurt, 1971, p. 78.
11. *Über Literatur*, Olten, 1966, p. 202.
12. Ror Wolf, 'Meine Voraussetzungen' in Lothar Baier (ed.), *Über Ror Wolf*, Frankfurt, 1972, p. 11.

lichen Extravaganzen, die man Geschichten nennt'.[13] Despite all this, there exists a number of lengthy prose works, essentially composed with documentary material of one sort or another, which can be described as 'sprachrealistische Montageromane'.

The first of these, which actually predates the coming to prominence of the views we have been examining, is Alexander Kluge's *Schlachtbeschreibung* (1964). Kluge made his literary debut with a volume of shorter prose texts, *Lebensläufe* (1962), in which he first developed a literary technique that, in its essentials, anticipates the criteria for modern realism generated by Helmut Heißenbüttel in *Briefwechsel über Literatur*. Through constrastive arrangement of the available material, Kluge presents fascinating human situations that cannot be rounded off neatly, as a conventional story demands; instead the reader is confronted with open-ended incidents, enigmas and contradictions, in keeping with Kluge's intention of avoiding the distortions inherent in existing cultural forms: 'Alle Ausdrucks-formen der bürgerlichen Öffentlichkeit . . . zerschneiden aber ge-rade die Komplexität der Wahrnehmung, die eigentlich die Grund-form der Sinne ist'.[14] Whereas for Wilhelm Meister the world was 'ein Versuchslabor', which he as subject confronted, for someone like Franz Biberkopf it is so impenetrable, that he 'gar nicht mehr sagen [könnte], was in seinem Kopf subjektiv und was darin frei-flottierende Objektpartikel sind' (205–6). Because of this develop-ment, mimetic realism cannot be anything but 'eine Real-Ordnung, die das chaotische Ganze nicht faßt. In Wirklichkeit ist dieses Verfahren Raubbau' (207). True realism is for him neither reflection nor 'Bestätigung der Wirklichkeit, sondern Protest' (216), and can take one of three forms — 'radikale Nachahmung', in the sense of a highly conscious imitating of reality, 'Ausweichen vor dem Druck der Realität' through dreams, negation, distortion or utopian vi-sions, and 'Angriff', primarily in the sense of aggressive use of montage. These forms of 'Realismus der Arbeitsweise des menschli-chen Wahrnehmungsapparates', as subjective experience, are com-plemented by the objective side of things, i.e. the 'Vermittlung der gegenständlichen Situation', but the difficulty here is that a 'gegen-ständliche Situation für sich, also die bloße Momentaufnahme' does not contain within it 'das organisierende Element, das sie konkret macht' and which has to be produced by the artist constructively and reductively through 'analytische und synthetische Arbeit' (217–18).

13. Wolf Wondratschek, *Ein Bauer zeugt mit einer Bäuerin einen Bäuernjungen, der unbedingt Knecht werden will*, Munich, 1970, p. 15.
14. *Gelegenheitsarbeit einer Sklavin. Zur realistischen Methode*, Frankfurt, 1975, p. 222. All subsequent quotations from this edition.

Kluge's second and, in the context of this analysis, most important book, *Schlachtbeschreibung* (1964) deals with the 'organisatorischen Aufbau eines Unglücks', as the author puts it. It is a clear example of his attacking realism in the form of an aggressive montage of both subjective and objective material, compiled from archives and other official records, survivors' testimony and answers to Kluge's questions, adding up to a multi-perspectival treatment of the incredibly complicated phenomenon that was the battle for Stalingrad. In accordance with his theoretical position, Kluge does not try to prove a private theory about the ultimate causes of the disaster (and this is what, essentially, distinguishes it from documentary literature proper): rather, the book documents the impossibility of coming to an unambiguous understanding of what happened, even though — or perhaps just because — there exists a vast body of evidence. The information available about the Soviet High Command's decision-making process is shown to be limited and even detailed reports from the German side are often contradictory; one doctor talks of good working conditions and an absence of vitamin deficiency among the troops, another of unshakable evidence of death by starvation. The montage technique builds up an enormous but incomplete jigsaw puzzle that includes an examination of the social world of the officer corps (which might well have shed light on aspects of the tragedy), on daily records, even guidelines for winter warfare, which certainly show the inadequate preparation of the German army. But the major focus of examination is language — the language of the army's upper echelons and military chaplains, that used in evaluation reports, that of press briefing and coverage relating to the progress and outcome of the battle. The contrastive technique used in assembling the material clearly brings out the obfuscation, then and now, engendered by the language of the various parts of the battle machine, how those involved in the struggle for survival and the German people as a whole were deceived all along as to the course and likely outcome of the battle. The panorama built up amounts to a far more detailed picture of the various aspects of the whole than would have been possible in any narrative account. Nevertheless, it is still not an exhaustive analysis, nor was it intended to be one; Kluge's aim was, rather, the objectification of the impossibility, despite the marshalling of a vast body of information, including eye-witness accounts, of doing so. Kluge's aim, therefore, is to create 'ein Gitter, an das sich die Phantasie des Lesers anklammern kann, wenn sie sich in Richtung Stalingrad bewegt' (237) and, at the same time, to document the impossibility of making complex phenomena in the modern world 'understandable', to show that the modern realist writer should not attempt to shape ('formen') them, but should, instead, release the imagination of the reader, the vehicle 'des Realismus des auf die Wirklichkeit umformend reagierenden menschlichen Hirns' (218).[15]

For several years, *Schlachtbeschreibung* was either ignored or regarded as an isolated curiosity, undoubtedly because it was published some time before the onset of the wave of documentary prose, with which it has much in common (it was republished in 1968). A somewhat different fate befell Hubert Fichte's *Die Palette* (1968), reflecting the changed literary situation, including the then prevalent fascination with the 'pop' world, in which so much of the novel takes place. It is the second volume of a quartet (the others being *Das Waisenhaus*, 1965, *Detlevs Imitationen 'Grünspan'*, 1971 and *Versuch über die Pubertät*, 1974) and shares with the other volumes a series of motifs — wartime, especially the bombing of Hamburg, life in an orphanage, the world of homosexuality, literature, language and life in the 'underground'. In structural terms the series represents the consequences for literary composition of Jäcki's statement (in *Die Palette*) that 'jede bekannte Form schriftstellerischer Synthese . . . aber eben gerade all das Inkohärente, Doppelzüngige, Alberne, Vielbewußte und die gleichzeitigen eingeschränkten Bewußtheiten aus[klammerte]'.[16] All the varied layers of his experience cannot be organised into one linear narrative pattern, as any attempt to produce a coherent analysis of them 'würde sich ins Uferlose verlieren'. *Die Palette* is, therefore, the representation of the impossibility of rounding Jäcki's experiences into a literary synthesis; each novel could have been extended ad lib, as could the quartet as a whole, given that the material, particularly Jäcki's continuous reflection in language on experience and on the use of language itself, is seemingly inexhaustible. A particular source of linguistic richness is the 'argot' developed in the pub scene and the homosexual underground in Hamburg and its playing-off against the 'straight' language of the petty bourgeoisie. This slang is so obscure, so inaccessible to the outsider, that we are given a Palette 'dictionary' and two 'Paletten-ABCs', which in turn bring out how much this alternative scene lives in language. While Gerd Fuchs' novel *Beringer oder die lange Wut* (1973), set in a similar Hamburg milieu, operates with the same slang within a conventional novel, as an exotic component of a more or less naturalistic portrayal of events, the

---

15. Alexander Kluge, *Schlachtbeschreibung* (1964), Frankfurt, 1968 ('überarbeitete Ausgabe' in Fischer Bücherei),.
16. Hubert Fichte, *Die Palette* (1968), Reinbek, 1970, p. 31.

clash of the various linguistic levels in *Die Palette* brings out the coexistence and yet irreconcilability of these differing types of experience, particularly as combined in the fragmented and often contradictory experiences and life style of Jäcki. Here, as in the other novels of the quartet, Fichte tries, by means of a strongly autobiographical first-person narrator and the implementation of linguistic 'langsam zur Oberfläche geschwemmtes Material', to penetrate through 'zu den verborgenen frühen Bewußtseinsschichten, zu jenen verschütteten Zonen des Unbewußten und Infantilen . . . , die die ganze komplexe Widersprüchlichkeit seiner Biografie bedingen'.[17]

The most significant 'sprachrealistisch' novel, in that it is the realisation of his theoretical views, is Heißenbüttel's *D'Alemberts Ende* (1970), his 'Projekt Nr. 1'. His continual stress on the need to duplicate external, impenetrable reality by means of quotations and his rejection of the importance of linguistic creativity and literary imagination in the writing process seems at times to point towards the documentary 'Literatur der Nicht-Autoren' (indeed, in the *Briefwechsel über Literatur* he speaks positively about the authenticity this technique achieves). But he also stresses the impossibility of mediating experience directly in literature, since we can 'nur darüber reden', and the 'Einheit des subjektiven Selbstbewußtseins' has, anyway, been exposed 'als eine Fiktion'.[18] For Heinrich Vormweg, Heißenbüttel's discussion partner, the *Bottroper Protokolle*, for example, are in no way a satisfactory response to the changed situation of literature, but 'die Verlagerung der traditionellen Über-Ich-Idee auf für deren Ansprüche nun völlig ungeeignete Träger' and in fact had been charged with rescuing 'eine Weltvorstellung, (= Gültigkeit allgemeiner Verbindlichkeit) die sich totgelaufen hat' (BüL, 79). Direct quotation in such works is not the duplication desired by Heißenbüttel, but 'eine Methode, einer Aussage eine allgemeine Verbindlichkeit und Bedeutung wohlbekannter Art zuzusprechen. Sie [the *Bottroper Protokolle*, KB] transportieren eine Absicht, und das merkt man' (79). Thus, while at that time Martin Walser saw this documentary prose as representing the way out of a crisis of narration, Heißenbüttel thought the way forward lay in the capacity of language 'so etwas wie einen Sprachraum herzustellen, wie es am einfachsten etwa in Jargonsprachen geschieht' (56). Through the creation of such language areas it ought to be possible to duplicate the way in which language both contains elements of reality and, at the same time, obscures the nature of reality, thus making it possible

---

17. Peter Bekes, 'Hubert Fichte' in *Kritisches Lexikon der deutschsprachigen Gegenwartsliteratur* (KLG), Munich, 1978, p. 2.
18. Heißenbüttel, *Über Literatur*, p. 202.

in literature to express both the lack of generally valid patterns of orientation and also the true character of the area under consideration. In this way, 'synthetische Halluzinationen' can be created, in order 'rückwärts an ihnen zu spiegeln, was ist' (56). Modern realist writing should at all times show 'daß Literatur im Grund problematisch ist und daß ich zum Beispiel aus dieser Problematik heraus versuche, Literatur zu machen . . . als radikale Aufklärung'.[19]

Both these conditions are fulfilled in *D'Alemberts Ende*;[20] it is an ironisation of the traditional novel form and its conventions (in the relationship established with *Die Wahlverwandschaften*) and a stylistic reflection on the validity of the continued uncritical use of established literary genres. At the same time, its concentration on the activities of a circle of Hamburg friends on one specific day, 26 July 1968, is intended to establish a confined language area enabling Heißenbüttel to carry out a critical portrayal of the group and its ritualised conversations through the use of the montage technique. The reporters and radio correspondents in this circle meet in bars, conduct conversations in their offices about various current projects and in the evening foregather in a flat to discuss the events of the day. Later d'Alembert is found dead, but he is not wearing his toupee; the cause of death cannot be established, but the toupee is eventually found on the revolving turntable of a record-player. This story outline is, however, not of great importance: 'Was an Story erkennbar geworden ist, hat verknüpfende Funktion, keine Bedeutung' (387). The real focal point of this 'anti-novel' is neither the events nor the central character — indeed, the very title is itself an ironic reference to the conventions of the novel — but the linguistic 'fixing', as it might be called (by analogy with photography), of a particular group's social life. In the process, the reader is presented with a broad and detailed picture of the various component parts of this existence. This, however, is incidental to the real aim of the 'project' and not to be confused with conventional depiction of milieu — as may be seen, for instance, by reference to 'Versuch der Rekonstruktion eines Datums: 26.7.1968', where, in a manner reminiscent of *Berlin Alexanderplatz*, Heißenbüttel merges advertisements, press and radio announcements, film programmes and other aspects of metropolitan life, including the activities of members of the group during the day:

---

19. Heißenbüttel, *Zur Tradition der Moderne*, p. 382.
20. *Projekt Nr. 1: D'Alemberts Ende*, Neuwied & Berlin, 1970. All quotations from this edition.

Bildungspolitik: Ostberlin reformiert die Hochschulen. Engere Zusammenarbeit zwischen Wissenschaft und Praxis ist das Ziel. Biafra wartet auf die ersten Hilfesendungen. Dahrendorf kündigt präzises Programm seiner Partei an. Dem Ruhrgebiet droht Überalterung. Die Kulturrevolution in China ist zersplittert. Eberhard Müller: Den Mut haben, heiße Eisen anzufassen. Wagnerfestspiele in Bayreuth eröffnet. Bundesaußenminister Willy Brandt von Autogrammjägern umlagert. Spielplan der Filmtheater am 26.7.1968: Unterm Holunderbusch; Zur Sache Schätzchen; Ich habe Lust; Mit allen Wassern gewaschen; Alle Herrlichkeit auf Erden; Engel — gibt's die? Donald Duck als Sonntagsjäger. . . . Dies alles ist an einem einzigen Tag passiert oder wurde an diesem Tag der Öffentlichkeit mitgeteilt. Von dem, was gleichzeitig Ottilie Wildermuth, d'Alembert, die Schildkröte, Eduard und in gewisser Weise auch Frau d'Alembert, Dr. Johnson und Andie Wildermuth am meisten beschäftigte: die 4. Dokumenta in Kassel, war an diesem Tag in der Öffentlichkeit keine Rede. . . .(111–16)

This piling up of information does not contribute to a precise portrayal of the specific social world of d'Alembert and his friends, but brings out, through the fusion of various component parts of the vast public domain with the private, the insignificance and ultimate irrelevance of individual experience for the outer, public world, as was also the case with *Berlin Alexanderplatz*. But Heißenbüttel goes much further than Döblin in his attitude towards the individual. In *Über Literatur* he puts forward the idea that the individual subject has been reduced in modern society to a 'Bündel Redegewohnheiten'; this is worked out in *D'Alemberts Ende*. The characters do not exist as authentic personalities (as can be seen clearly in 'Drittes Quergespräch. Demaskierung'), but as the utterers of quotations and participants in ritual conversations, all of which form the real substance of the work.

From the perspective of the mid-Eighties, several sections provide a fascinating word-picture of the left-wing or 'progressive' world of the young intellectuals of the time. 'Gespräch über bürgerliche Moral und verwandte Gegenstände' contains, for example, a whole range of — then — fashionable and, indeed, new attitudes towards sexual taboos, together with references to various widely read authors on the subject, such as Henryk Broder, Reiche, Reich and Marcuse, as well as the influence of certain Anglo-Saxon pop artists in helping to break down former barriers: 'Frau d'Alembert fragte, ob Lustbefriedigung tatsächlich nur unter geschichtlichen Bedingungen gesehen werden könne, wozu dann auch ihr Reflex in der Musik der Rolling Stones, der Fugs, der Mothers of Invention . . . oder Leonard Cohen gehöre. Bedeutet Sexrevolution nicht zugleich Destruktion der gegebenen geschichtlichen, das heißt gesellschaftlichen Bedingungen? Und

was dann? Alle befriedigt, aber nichts funktioniert?' (244). Such conversations are not merely rituals, in the sense that those then involved in this social scene could have written the 'score' of such conversations without difficulty, but this particular quality is brought out in the structure of the sections by identical formulations being used by different characters. The individual speaker and the sequence of statements (in the form of quotation) are completely interchangeable; there is no real exchange of ideas taking place, merely automatic responses within what only appears to be a discussion. The once-creative individual now demonstrates but a 'synthetische Authentizität' in what has been degraded into 'chatter' ('Gerede', in Heidegger's sense). A sort of creativity can be achieved in parasitic conversations, but the participants are, as has been seen, interchangeable and what is ultimately created is not authentic culture, but endless sterile prattling; even quotations used in such exchanges, from Marcuse, Benjamin, Freud, Reich and others, are themselves merely comments on culture, there is no direct relationship to it as such. This is a highly persuasive argument, but the difficulty with Heißenbüttel's attempt to create a language area from such jargonistic rituals is that the reader has to be able to recognise the quotations as such, in order to be aware of the nature of the linguistic game being played. If unfamiliar with the particular area under examination, the reader will fail to identify many of the statements as quotations, while there is also the danger that for others Heißenbüttel's technique can provoke another game — that of trying to 'spot the quote' — rather than leading to contemplation of his real point. Both these effects, therefore, weaken the critical intent. In 'Gespräch über Studenten und verwandte Gegenstände' we read, for example, that both Frau d'Alembert and Eduard find 'nicht das Bild einer nackten Frau, die ihre Schamhaare entblößt, obszön, sondern das eines Generals, der seine Orden zur Schau stellt'; a little later Ottilie Wildermuth responds 'endlich mit einem Zitat von Herbert Marcuse' and even 'Dr. Johnson zitiert nun Herbert Marcuse' (226–30). But not only is this entire conversation based on Marcuse's ideas, the notion of obscenity, ostensibly attributed to the d'Alemberts, is in fact a quotation from his 'Essay on Liberation'. Something similar happens in 'Gespräch über die eigene Lage': the various references by the 'Schildkröte' to the 'sprachlose Intelligenz' originate in a series of articles by Karl Markus Michel, called 'Die sprachlose Intelligenz' (in *Kursbuch 1, 4* and *9*); a large part of the dialogue in what seems to be a discussion on the individual and the masses, illuminated by quotations from E.T.A. Hoffmann, Poe and Lichtenberg's 'London im Jahre 1759', is taken more or less directly from Walter Benjamin's *Baudelaire. Ein Lyriker im Zeitalter des Hochka-*

pitalismus, without any indication of the fact. Even if Heißenbüttel in 1969 assumed that all his readers were aware of this, he is, consciously or unconsciously, intensifying the element of play in the book and, from our present perspective, the likelihood of these conversations being misread is all the greater, so that the didactic point may be almost entirely missed.

One possible response to such criticism might be that Heißenbüttel is not turning his use of quotation into a game, but is concerned, rather, to expose the social ritual underlying many conversations, particularly the empty, repetitive jargon of people in the media circles. This was undoubtedly his specific intent here, but the examples given show that his method, as applied in much of *D'Alemberts Ende*, is too sophisticated, even elitist, for him to achieve it; he demands familiarity with a broad range of imaginative literature, the sociology of literature and progressive intellectual essays, not to mention English and American pop-song lyrics. For the reader of today who was not immersed in this scene the book is almost impenetrable. These weaknesses, which, together with the extreme length, are more likely to produce irritation than critical insights, condemn *D'Alemberts Ende* to a failure caused ultimately by a starting-point that could only lead the author into a blind alley. He proceeds here, as in the first two of the *Textbuch* series, from Wittgenstein's pronouncement that 'alle Sätze sind gleichwertig', attempting to expose the 'fußlosen Gedanken' as being 'Gesichtspunkte ohne wirklichen Standpunkt'; the 'noch zu Sagende besteht jetzt einzig in der enzyklopädischen Registration des vorgefundenen Formelrepertoires'.[21] The lack of sharp focus in *D'Alemberts Ende* — a 'Satire auf den Überbau. Durchgeführt am Beispiel Bundesrepublik Juli 1968' — leads to what seems to be totally arbitrary length, to an apparently random and often rather pointless piling-up of quotations and a perceptible lack of a real shaping principle. A somewhat earlier and shorter prose text shows, however, that Heißenbüttel's basic literary technique, if applied without this Wittgensteinian perspective, can indeed promote linguistically critical realist literature. 'Deutschland 1944', a collage of speeches, military orders, reports, right-wing literature, a newspaper article on atomic fission and extracts from the diary of an unnamed observer, reproduces a horrendous world in which there co-exist propaganda, racial hatred, the agony of the death-camps and work on ever more terrifying weapons. By taking phrases out of their normal syntax and context, and then contrasting them within the structure of his collage,

21. Otto Lorenz, 'Helmut Heißenbüttel', *KLG*, p. 2.

Heißenbüttel achieves an amazingly economical and yet highly evocative word-picture of the range of horror that was Nazi Germany, showing clearly the way in which it was all contained in the language of the time.

'Deutschland 1944', like Kluge's *Schlachtbeschreibung*, proves the point that this type of writing works best when applied to a clearly defined subject area. It would be wrong, however, to regard *D'Alemberts Ende*, Heißenbüttel's only attempt at a lengthy prose work, as being merely a failed curiosity. There can be no doubt that his ideas on the nature of modern realism, including this unsuccessful experiment, greatly influenced a great number of novelists in the Seventies; the adoption of the contrastive and critical use of quotations and other material evidence in the documentary montage-novel of the Seventies, as exemplified by Urs Jaeggi's *Brandeis*, Uwe Timm's *Morenga* and, above all, Manfred Franke's *Mordverläufe*, realises the full potential of techniques pioneered by the 'Sprachrealisten'.

5

The Novel and Documentary Literature

Despite the publication in the first half of the Sixties of Alexander Kluge's *Lebensläufe* and *Schlachtbeschreibung* (both having considerable affinity with what was later called documentary literature), despite the example of Günter Wallraff's early reportages (*Wir brauchen Dich*, 1966) and of the impact of the socially engaged documentary drama, the real origins of the documentary prose of the late Sixties and beyond lay not so much in the politicisation of the writer as in a growing concern about the problems of artistic creativity in the modern age. In the case of some authors, it is true, the two did to some extent go hand in hand, but the hope for an emancipatory role for documentary prose, even with such an increasingly political animal as Martin Walser, was still less important than its potential, as he saw it, to escape from an established literature that had degenerated 'ins pure Sprachspiel' and in which narration was no longer possible. His support for Ursula Trauberg and Wolfgang Werner is essentially the expression of his doubt as to the authenticity of the products of the writer's creative imagination, although Walser, like so many others at the time, had also come to question the aura of the writer and his role as expert; he too felt the need to democratise a literature which had increasingly functioned within bourgeois society as a repressive 'Struktur- und Ordnungsbegriff'. The socio-critical impact of the books which he sponsored was, however, severely reduced by weaknesses indicated above, one major problem being the unreflected transference to their authors of the traditional role of the bourgeois writer as the authentic mediator of experience, in a modern situation that renders such a role impossible. In his 'Anmerkungen zur dokumentarischen Literatur' Michael Scharang draws attention to the difficulty with such expectations: 'wie man etwas erzählen oder beschreiben kann, hängt nicht bloß vom subjecktiven Willen dessen ab, der das tun will oder tut, sondern vor allem in der objektiven Beschaffenheit der Dinge, die erzählt oder beschrieben sein wollen. Die Frage nach der Erzählbarkeit oder Beschreibbarkeit ist eine geschichtliche und

gesellschaftliche Frage'.[1] For Scharang the 'Hauptmoment der einfachen Erfahrung ist das subjektive Erleben und dessen sprachliche Darstellung', but modern society has rendered this basis of traditional narration impossible, so that serious writing today is only possible as concrete literature or, for those who wish to be realists — in Brecht's terms — in some form of the documentary. Scharang understands this, in a way that is close to Heißenbüttel, as the use of already existing linguistic material, since the mediation by the individual of his or her own subjective experience communicates nothing of general relevance to others. He does, however, admit the possibility of writers using diary material as a means of writing 'je nach Klassenzugehörigkeit . . . füreinander', and a means, therefore, of identifying problems common to a social class. In this sense the books Walser helped to produce, which provoked only short-term interest on the literary scene and had no real effect on the practice of writing, could have achieved a certain usefulness if they had been aimed at the underprivileged groups from which the 'non-authors' themselves came. This was undoubtedly the intention behind a number of such life-stories published within the Werkkreis and which have indeed had the important function of promoting the exchange of information and experience, and helping to create the political group consciousness so necessary to political action. Outside the particular context of the organisation, however, such personal confessions are condemned to the same fate as those of Walser's protégés; they may have a certain curiosity value, but are inappropriate within mainstream realist literature, as they offer no aesthetic solution to the problems of writing in a complex modern society. There do seem to be similarities with the autobiographical novels so central to the literature of the Seventies, but the crucial difference is that the latter consisted essentially of the working-out of personal experience in an effort to grapple with problems of identity, as opposed to the portrayal of such experience with the intent of establishing common ground and thus helping to promote political solidarity.

Although the debates, at times energetic, provoked by this kind of documentary literature were ultimately to be of only short-term importance, they played a not inconsiderable role in keeping attention focused on the question of documentary writing at the end of the Sixties and the beginning of the Seventies. Other factors to be mentioned in this context are the renewed interest in the documentary of the Weimar period, brought about by the Student Move-

---

1. *Einer muß immer parieren*, Darmstadt & Neuwied, 1973, p. 7.

ment, and the impact of Wallraff's reportages on a wider audience at a time when doubt was increasingly cast on imaginative literature, as irreconcilable with political activism. In the famous fifteenth number of *Kursbuch*, Wallraff's texts were cited as positive examples of those few 'begrenzte[n], aber nutzbringende[n] Beschäftigungen' that remained to the writer. Over and above this, as a result of the influence of Marcuse and others, the traditional roles of writer and literature were increasingly called into question, coupled, in particular, with pressure for the desublimation of literature; what was needed was a literature that could be used as a weapon against bourgeois authority and repression. The perpetuation of traditional forms of literary expression therefore only served, as Herbert Achternbusch put it, 'dem blockhaften politischen System', with the novel in particular representing a realm divorced from the real world of experience; it was now important to recognise that reality was 'der Kunst überlegen'.[2] Finally, in this connection, mention must be made of the boom in the West German non-fiction (*Sachbuch*) market towards the turn of the decade, undoubtedly assisted by the television feature, and the influential success of documentary works by foreign writers at this time, notably Truman Capote's much discussed *In Cold Blood* (1965) and Norman Mailer's *Miami and the Siege of Chicago* (1968) and *A Fire on the Moon* (1970).

There was, it has to be said, a very swift counter-movement to the pressure in favour of documentary literature. As early as 1969 Rolf Dieter Brinkmann was announcing in the anthology *ACID* that he wanted to have nothing to do with art 'mit politischem Inhalt', as 'dieses Thema nicht die Relevanz besitzt, wie es das Klischee wahrhaben möchte' and in 1970 Reinhard Baumgart came to much the same conclusion. He felt that 'schöne Literatur' would soon loose its sense of aesthetic shame and turn once again to the forces of 'Phantasie und Sinnlichkeit'. Even in *Kursbuch*, where the 'death of literature' had been proclaimed in 1968, a change of mood had become obvious by *Nr. 20* (1970), particularly in influential articles by Peter Schneider ('Die Phantasie im Spätkapitalismus und die Kulturrevolution') and Hans Christoph Buch ('Von der möglichen Funktion der Literatur'). Nevertheless, the stylistic influence of the documentary was very noticeable in the novels of the early Seventies; it has indeed been argued that, as Walser had sensed, time it helped a number of established writers out of a stylistic impasse at this time.

A typical feature of the novel of the early Seventies is the blending

2. Herbert Achternbusch, *Die Alexanderschlacht*, Frankfurt, 1971, p. 34.

of conventional narrative with documentary elements. While the four volumes of Uwe Johnson's *Jahrestage* cannot be considered truly documentary, the frequent quoting from the *New York Times* plays an important part in the blend of past and present in the novel and at the same time lends some apparent authenticity to the fictional parts. The same is very much true of Günter Grass's *Aus dem Tagebuch einer Schnecke* (1972), which is a more complex mix of the two elements on a number of levels.[3] The most important narrative thread is constituted by the life story of Hermann Ott, known as Dr Zweifel, describing his activities amongst the Jewish community in Danzig, followed, after the mass emigration of the Jews to Palestine, by his concealment in Stomma's cellar, where he carries out research into snails. This part of the Ott/Zweifel story spawns a whole mass of symbolism based on the snail and this permeates the whole book: on the one hand it releases that playful, imaginative element that is so central to the Danzig Trilogy, *Der Butt* and *Die Rättin*, and reaching here its grotesque height in the portrayal of the sexual healing of Lisbeth Stomma by a snail; it is also used as a means of self-ironisation and of linguistic criticism (as, for example, in the context of the discussion during the visit to Schnecklingen). The snail is depicted as the embodiment of moderation, of 'Stillstand im Fortschritt', of the anti-extremist political philosophy that Grass has clung to over the years. Closely linked to this body of symbolism is the leitmotif of melancholy; the novel contains a number of Grass's musings on Dürer's 'Melancholia I' and parts of the public lecture he gave during the Dürer anniversary celebrations in 1971. Just as Ott/Zweifel's investigations are an endeavour 'in der Substanz der Schnecken ein Mittel gegen die Zeit zu finden' (157), the diary is conceived of as a corrective 'Sudelbuch' in Lichtenberg's sense, i.e. one attempts 'mit leichter Hand gegen die Zeit [zu] schreiben'. It is intended to relieve any possible depression that Grass may have ('Niezwurz*sud*' was reputedly a cure for the black bile, i.e. melancholia, KB) and at the same time to be a highly differentiated personal statement on the dangers of intolerance and political extremism of all kinds. The metaphorical treatment of this particular theme is then widened and deepened by the documentary strands of the novel, the most important being the detailed account of anti-Semitism in Danzig and the mass exodus of the Jewish inhabitants in the latter Thirties. The life and sufferings of the Danzig Jews are not, however, viewed as the collective fate of one group of people in one place at a particular time; by contrastive

3. Neuwied & Darmstadt, 1972. All references to this edition.

documentation or other associative techniques — such as Grass telling of the intolerance he saw in his own childhood, in order to warn his children of the dangers of similar excesses today — this strand is constantly presented as having relevance far beyond its time: 'Damit, Kinder, beginnt es: Die Juden sind. Die Fremdarbeiter wollen. Die Sozialdemokraten haben. Jeder Kleinbürger ist. Die Neger. Die Linken. Der Klassenfeind. Die Chinesen und die Sachsen glauben haben denken sind . . . ' (20). The story of the fate of the Danzig Jews and their emigration is also followed through into the present by means of Grass's account of two visits he made to Israel and of his interviews there with survivors. The same principle of historical documentation and simultaneous reference to the present is applied in other episodes. A visit to Bohemia provokes a chain of thought that brings together Theresienstadt, Vietnam, the Kronstadt mutiny of 1921 and the Russian invasion of Czechoslovakia as other examples of political intolerance. The somewhat baffling suicide of the SS soldier Manfred Angst is also brought into a relationship with the present day through the activities of Angst's son, a member of the SDS, who, like his fanatical father, knows 'keine Kompromisse'. Over and above these more detailed parallels, the interrelationship of past and present is continually underlined by the insertion of references to recent happenings — the revaluation of the D-Mark, the Defregger case, Apollo 11's moon landing — and to incidental aspects of the day-to-day life of the Grass family and Günter's own professional activities. These are by no means mannered insertions, but, rather, carefully constructed equations, through which the moral chronicler Grass forces us at all times to relate the excesses of the past to the dangers inherent in the present; throughout, the description of Grass's own activities — including his general 'redenreden für die espede' and his involvement in the campaign on behalf of the SPD in 1969 — emphasises this and pleads for our concern.

This narrative and documentary circling round a basic theme fuses the apparently disparate thematic strands, time levels and styles of *Aus dem Tagebuch einer Schnecke* into a remarkably satisfying whole, realising the potential of the hybrid form to present otherwise seemingly totally private experiences in a much wider social and historical context. Grass, like Böll in *Gruppenbild mit Dame* (1971) responded to the crisis of the novel by integrating documentary material into the work of literature and was thus able to make a general socio-political comment on the nature of society in a way no longer attainable in the conventional realist novel. The success of the new mixed form in Böll's case was such as to convince even a committed opponent of narrative prose like Helmut Heißenbüttel of the virtues of the quasi-documentary novel: 'Der dokumentarische Antistil der Erzählung dient der Versachlichung. Nicht subjektive Regungen und Beweggründe sind Thema dieser Erzählung von Heinrich Böll, sondern objektiv erfaßbare soziologische Relationen. . . . Dieses Subjekt aber wird . . . nicht in ihren subjektiven Beweggründen dargestellt, nicht in ihrer Emotionalität, allenfalls in ihrer sexuellen Verhaltensweise — dieses Subjekt Leni Pfeiffer wird gezeigt als das Muster sozialer Verhaltensweise'.[4]

For Heißenbüttel, one important feature of this novel is its rejection of a traditional authorial stance, a particular source of objectivity, which leads to Böll narrating 'wie die Dokumentar-Autoren Günter Wallraff, Erika Runge oder Per Olaf Enquist'. These are astonishing claims; Böll is in no way presenting here an objective picture of socially determined behaviour, but — at least in the first instance — he is using the pseudo-documentary form of the novel (no use is made, in fact, of truly evidential material) to achieve yet another variation on the theme of woman as Madonna, which runs through so many of his works. The range of testimony, often contradictory, here serves to bring out, with a clarity not achieved before, the fact that the impulses of the central character Leni — whose spiritual life, *pace* Heißenbüttel, is the major focus of the novel — cannot be elucidated fully, even by the most wide-ranging examination. In her emotional make-up may be observed a number of traits that we associate with other similar figures: a modest but genuine sensuality, spontaneity, faithfulness, devoted service to loved ones, lack of regret for impulsive action and strong moral rectitude. Yet such features do not, as with so many other Böll novels and stories, remain merely metaphors or emotional tags: a vast number of statements are collected by the 'Verf.' in his research into the character of Leni, and these ultimately cloud, rather than illuminate, our understanding of her. The real achievement of this somewhat problematical novel is that it does just the opposite of what Heißenbüttel claims for it: the patiently assembled statements, documents, newspaper reports and other material that the 'Verf.' puts before the reader show, rather, that the modern writer, if he attempts to go beyond the examination of a very specific social problem, of the type found in the work of Günter Wallraff, is confronted with 'eine sehr komplexe, in sich widersprüchliche und psychologisch aufgefächerte "wirkliche" Wirklichkeit . . . , kaum aber *die* Wahrheit, auf die doch die "Dokumentarliteratur" so treuherzig

4. 'Wie man dokumentarisch erzählen kann', *Merkur*, 25, 1971, pp. 912–13.

zusteuert'.[5] On the other hand, the documentation of the enigmatic nature of Leni is extremely lengthy — comparison with the later *Die verlorene Ehre der Katharina Blum* shows that the same effect can be achieved far more economically — and eventually becomes somewhat pointless, merely confirming our previous knowledge. In addition, the simulated documentary style is somewhat irritating, with the continual and highly self-conscious interventions of the 'Verf.', recalling the behaviour of the first-person narrator in Siegfried Lenz's *Heimatmuseum*, giving the impression of a mannered and laboured attempt at pseudo-authenticity. We must, of course, consider seriously Heißenbüttel's claim that 'diese dokumentarische und antistilistische Schreibweise nicht Selbstzweck [ist]', with Böll endeavouring to satirise certain 'Anregungen, die an der Wende zu den siebziger Jahren unseres Jahrhunderts in der Luft liegen'.[6] This may well have been Böll's intention, but the frequent and often lengthy reflections on the narrative perspective in the text serve to indicate that the quasi-documentary style becomes much more than the means to an end; it has itself become a major strand of the novel, but does not really get us very far. Perhaps because of this distraction, *Gruppenbild mit Dame* fails to place the experiences of Leni Pfeiffer in a wider context; while a considerable amount of social and historical information is incidentally gleaned, the major focus remains firmly on the enigmatic personality of Leni. Comparing the novel with Böll's early ones, we clearly see the superfluity of the documentary method; it is, as Michael Scharang has put it, merely an 'Ersatz für die alte Konstruktion'.[7]

These examples of the hybrid, the pseudo-documentary novel, have, in terms of authorial intent, little in common with the documentary literature of the late Sixties, in which the demonstrable authenticity of the material was seen as a means of regaining an objectivity and a representative stature lost both by traditional literary forms and by writers. In *Gruppenbild mit Dame*, however, the 'Verf.' confronts us with a strongly subjective authorial voice, and in *Aus dem Tagebuch einer Schnecke* — although Grass succeeds, through his bold mix of narrative and the documentary, in placing subjective experience in a much wider context — the very style of the novel sets before us, as in no other of the author's works, the person of Günter Grass. Nevertheless, a distinction should be made between the claims made for documentary and the reality; behind the façade of objectivity there is always a high degree of subjectivity, which led to

5. Hans Schwab-Felisch, *Merkur*, 25, 1971, p. 915.
6. Heißenbüttel, 'Wie man dokumentarisch erzählen kann', p. 912.
7. 'Zur Technik der Dokumentation', *Einer muß immer parieren*, p. 21.

considerable weaknesses in the works promoted by Martin Walser. The case of Günter Wallraff, the most prominent exponent of such writing, is particularly interesting here. After the highly personal initial industrial reportages he developed an apparently much more neutral technique which made use of montage. This received considerable attention from writers and critics in the early Seventies and was, we would argue, not without its influence on the novel of the time. Since then Wallraff has returned to the much more subjective reporting style of his earlier period and, interestingly enough, achieved far more of a general impact with his reports on working for the Springer Verlag (*Der Aufmacher*, 1974) and on his range of menial jobs while disguised as a Turkish immigrant worker (*Ganz unten*, 1985).

In the novel in general the fusion of the documentary style, for which such objectivity has been claimed, and the subjective authorial position was, for a time at least, a productive one. Apart from the examples already given, mention should be made here of Dieter Wellershoff's outstanding *Einladung an alle* (1972), which has never received the critical acclaim it deserves. Although Wellershoff's novel, unlike those of Grass and Böll, operates with truly authentic and extensively verifiable source material and is, therefore, more 'documentary' than its contemporaries, there is no pretence of objectivity. In his theory, it should be remembered, Wellershoff claims that the real creative force in modern realist writing is the subjectivity of the author and, in keeping with this view, his novel represents a cautious, but highly personal reading of the case of Bruno Findeisen (i.e. Bruno Fabeyer, the so-called Moors Murderer and most-wanted criminal of the mid-Sixties in West Germany). In addition Wellershoff is anxious to work into the structure his rejection of the conventional crime novel, which for him consists in the 'glatte Wiederherstellung der vorübergehend gestörten Ordnung', following the tendency of all conservative literature, 'die Realität durch Abstraktion und Stilisierung radikal zu vereinfachen und zu ordnen'.[8] In his 'Antikrimi' Wellershoff is intent, rather, on 'die Unterwanderung dieses Realitätsprinzips durch die Erzähltechnik . . . , bei der das ständige Infragestellen unseres Wahrnehmungsvermögens als strukturelles Prinzip fungiert'.[9] He aims to portray the 'true' reality that lies behind the simplifying façade erected by, in part, the conventional narratorial position and therefore rejects any pretence of omniscience, making instead 'die hand-

---

8. Dieter Wellershoff, *Literatur und Veränderung*, Munich, 1971 (dtv), p. 65.

9. Stephen Lamb, 'Einladung an alle — Dokumentation und Wirklichkeit', R.H. Thomas (ed.), *Der Schriftsteller Dieter Wellershoff*, Cologne, 1975, p. 68.

feste Recherche zu einem Moment des Schreibens'.[10] The central figure, Bruno Findeisen, is not seen as existing as an empirically verifiable entity, but 'in Bewußtseinsaugenblicken verschiedener Individuen', i.e. those who come into contact with him, and there is no attempt to structure the novel so as to produce a reassuring and neat conclusion. The reader, like anyone else trying to investigate the case, is presented with a mass of often contradictory material which, far from giving a clear perception of what happened, can at best provide us with a number of theoretical approaches, of possible ways of 'reading' events.

The main source of documentary evidence was the material prepared by the State and made available by the court to Bruno's defending counsel for the trial, in which 'die genaue Lebensgeschichte von Bruno Fabeyer, der Tatverlauf mëhrerer Einbrüche und der beiden Gewalttaten, wie sie von Polizei und Untersuchungsrichter und später vom Gericht rekonstruiert worden sind'; their accuracy was later confirmed by Fabeyer when Wellershoff visited him in prison.[11] In addition, the author had access to the findings of the police investigations, such as witnesses' testimony, post-mortem reports and the official psychological report on Fabeyer, as well as details of what was found in his various caches and other pieces of material evidence, the charges laid by the victims or their next of kin and day-to-day instructions to the police units involved in the case. There is no doubt that, had he so wished, Wellershoff could have produced a full non-fictional account of the case of the Moors Murderer. In the novel, however, the documentary material is used at all stages, but precisely not to recreate verisimilitude; the book is structured in such a way as to prevent our treading a clear path through the events and creates instead a confusion that must correspond much more to the experiences of those directly involved in the case as it developed. Instead of Wellershoff distilling, for example, a clear picture of events from the statements made by the Bentrups, the family of the first murder victim, he puts together extracts from these in a montage that, linguistically and structurally, confronts us with an unclear and highly emotional scene which contrasts with the preceding matter-of-fact account of the official reports and is then, in turn, juxtaposed with the sober language of a scientific pronouncement:

Was tun, er starb. Das war aber doch nicht möglich, das durften sie doch

10. Heinrich Vormweg, 'Einladung an alle', *Jahresring*, 1973, p. 248.
11. Wellershoff in an unpublished letter to Stephen Lamb of 28.7.1974.

nicht zulassen. Nein nein nein, sagten sie zu ihm, sie wischten ihm die
Stirn ab, das war doch schrecklich, so schlaff wie er da lag, und immer
mehr blutend.... Der Mann hier verblutet, wenn der Arzt nicht
kommt.
Unter Schock versteht man ein Versagen des Kreislaufs. Die Blutmenge,
die pro Minute vom Herzen in den Kreislauf gepumpt wird, ist kritisch
vermindert. Symptome des Schocks.... (38, 42f.)[12]

The passage continues with a report on Bentrup's death, particularly focused on the effects of shock and loss of blood, which is
dispassionate and strictly factual, in a way reminiscent of the
account of Hanno's death from typhus in *Buddenbrooks*. In a later
scene, dealing with the death of Police Officer Weidemann, a very
similar effect is achieved by the text-book description of the impact
of a bullet on tissue and the bureaucratic language of the post-
mortem. Any suggestion of a pretence at scientific objectivity is,
however, nullified by the simultaneous presence throughout of a
range of other information of a different kind, often emotional and
highly contradictory in nature, that makes us see such dry factual
material as but one part of the whole.

Another area of documentary material drawn on by Wellershoff is
that of press reports and headlines on the case, which add the
important dimension of public reaction to events and to Fabeyer/
Findeisen. Here the author admits that he has 'mit den Dokumenten
frei umgegangen'; he has, for example, 'Zeitungszitate verkürzt
oder aus zwei verschiedenen Quellen zusammengestellt, wenn es
die Ökonomie des Romans erforderte'.[13] Even less documentary, in
the strict sense of the word, are the passages recreating Findeisen's
thoughts and dreams, based on Wellershoff's unrecorded conversations with Fabeyer. Although there seems little real difference here
from the method Capote used in *In Cold Blood*, in this case account
has to be taken of the way in which — as became obvious during
cross-questioning in court — the confused murderer increasingly
came to accept and to identify in his formulations with the newspaper accounts of events. Above all, the remarks and comments in
between the documentary sections are very much to be understood
as the subjective ideas of a narrator who is but one observer amongst
many others, as Wellershoff himself stresses: 'Ich belebe die Fakten
mit meinen Vorstellungsmöglichkeiten. Ich erprobe meine Vorstellungsmöglichkeiten an den Fakten .... Und natürlich überschreitet der Roman auch die Grenze zum Subjektiven'.[14] In no way

12. *Einladung an alle*, Cologne 1972. All references to this edition.
13. Letter to Lamb.
14. Dieter Wellershoff & Christian Lindner, 'Jagd auf Verbrecher als Massenun-

does he intend to conduct a retrial of Fabeyer based on new information, but he is concerned to show, precisely through dealing with a case on which the public is already very well informed, 'daß der Roman wirklichkeitsmächtiger als das Sachbuch sein kann, wenn er die Tatsachenforschung in sein eigenes vielfältigeres Methodenarsenal übernimmt'.[15] The power of the novel to mediate reality is for him so much greater than that of any report, 'weil man innere und äußere Vorgänge sinnlich aktualisieren kann, die im dokumentarischen Material nur angedeutet sind oder überhaupt nicht erscheinen'.[16] Quite apart from the material that, it would seem, Wellershoff alone elicited from Fabeyer about what was going on in his mind at the time, none of the other sources to which he had access revealed anything of the emotional response of those involved in some way in the consequences of Bruno's actions; as a result the author had to add or invent 'was sich nicht recherchieren ließ: die innere Realität des äußeren Geschehens'.[17] Since Wellershoff — and here again his position differs from that of Capote — was not so much interested in the Fabeyer case as such, as in its 'exemplarische Bedeutung', a strictly documentary approach would not have given him adequate material to bring out those wider aspects of the case that had attracted him. He therefore allowed himself 'immer die Lizenz zur schriftstellerischen Gestaltung, z.B. auch der Bewußtseinsvorgänge . . . (Beispiel, der Polizist während der Verfolgung und sein Sterben)'.[18] In this particular case, the death of Police Officer Weidemann, his major concern was to work out his hypothesis as to the way in which Weidemann, the highly trained policeman, was possibly disorientated in his routine, programmed behaviour by the intuitive actions of the murderer.

This consciously personal interpretation of certain aspects of the case distinguishes the approach of the author from the analytical methods of the policeman in charge, Kriminaloberrat Bernhard. Bernhard's view is that the 'sachliche Gestaltung von Berichten folgt den Methoden, die für das kriminalistische Denken typisch sind: Scharfe Trennung der festgestellten Tatsachen von allen subjektiven Erwägungen' (26). If an investigating officer does not work in this way, he maintains, within a few days he will no longer know 'was er selbst festgestellt hat und was Hypothesen sind, was Zeugen aus eigener Wahrnehmung oder was sie nach Hörensagen mitgeteilt

terhaltung — ein Gespräch', *Kölner Stadt-Anzeiger*, 11/12.5.1972.
15. Ibid.
16. Letter to Lamb.
17. Wolfgang Werth, 'Jagdszenen aus Niedersachsen', *Die Zeit*, 29.9.1972.
18. Letter to Lamb.

haben und was schließlich unqualifizierte Mutmaßungen sind' (26). Wellershoff, on the other hand, is interested precisely in 'die Kontraste . . . zwischen den von mir ausgeschriebenen Parteien und den Dokumenten, zwischen der Sprache der subjektiven Erfahrung, der inneren Beteiligung und der Sprache des Sachbuchs, der Reportage, der Wissenchaft, der Polizei oder der Justiz'.[19] These subjective additions to the documentary material are in turn complemented by a number of theoretical approaches to the understanding of Findeisen's psychological make-up.

In the 'Bausteine zu einer Theorie des Verbrechens' bourgeois society is viewed as a body which represses 'aggressive und destruktive Triebe', so that by and large it is only by pursuing criminals that the conformist member of the corporate whole can give vent to the aggressions locked in his unconscious. At the same time, according to Robert Merton, it is a society with an intense competition ethos and so, since 'Menschen mit ungleichen Chancen werden nach denselben Standards gemessen', this leads 'zu Frustrationen und . . . [der] Erfahrung des Versagens'. This problem can, apparently, be solved either by 'dropping out' of the social game or by provoking 'die Autoritätspersonen zu übermäßiger Strenge', so that they, in effect, lose that authority. The ego gains a 'freie Hand, den Tendenzen seines Unbewußten nachzugeben', there is a consequent 'Auflösung der Hemmungsinstanzen' and the individual can then live 'jetzt für sich nach ganz eigenen Gesetzen' (160–6). The 'Bausteine zu einer Theorie der Konformität' effectively continue this chain of thought: human society is seen as repressive, as defending itself 'gegen das Traumbild einer Welt . . . , die frei sein könnte' and in the process reducing us to machines (233). Criminality and conformism are two sides of the same coin; society presents man from realising his human potential and casts aside the weak, like Bruno Findeisen, who can, though, once beyond the pale, have brief access to a world of hitherto unknown sensations and experiences.

These theoretical excursuses point to the novel's reflecting the concept, so central to Wellershoff's theory, of literature as a simulator, in which basic human qualities (identified primarily from the work of Freud and Laing) that are suppressed in existing literary forms, can surface and help to change the individual — and thus, in the long run, society itself. While traditional realism now tends to affirm normative behaviour, accepting and reflecting a cosy (but oversimplified) interpretation of the world, a more intense realism is

19. Ibid.

attainable through the 'möglich werdende Verzicht auf schützende Wirklichkeitsverkennung'. This true realism, as part of a 'permanente Erkenntnisbewegung' has the task of revealing 'die Tiefe der menschlichen Erfahrung' and of penetrating 'das Schablonenhafte des Lebens'.[20] If we then apply such a notion of realism to *Einladung an alle* there are, however, considerable problems. The range of material in the novel certainly tells us far more about the relevance of Findeisen's past to the present than the brief and somewhat cynical entry in police records ('Das Vorleben war entsprechend. Man hätte es also erwarten können', 63); through Bruno's daydreams we come to realise how a number of past events — his father's suicide, the execution of his brother Fritz, his own ill-treatment in a home and later internment in a concentration camp — still weigh on his mind. These are all factors that made the drift into a life of habitual petty crime seem virtually unavoidable; nevertheless there is no sign in Findeisen's past of a part that might have been played by social pressures of a conformist kind. Then, although Bruno is not so surprised that he has shot a man ('Es kam ihm so vor, als sei das schon immer so gewesen oder habe schon festgestanden, und er habe jetzt nur nachgeholt', 49), the attack on Bentrup comes over more as the unavoidable consequence of a chance encounter than as the unconscious (i.e. subliminally desired) provocation of authority into strong action. Above all, though, Findeisen's subsequent life on the run, his movements curtailed by the glare of public interest in the case, does not evince any sign of liberation from social constraints, of his having crossed the threshold into a freer existence. He does dream of 'die große Beute' that will enable him to flee to South America and start a new life there, but this is simply a clichéd vision he has picked up from some thriller or other. In fact, he loses that — admittedly illusory — sense of freedom he had as a mere petty criminal; he now runs blindly until he can see no way out, other than to allow himself to be captured. Nothing in this full and rich treatment of the life of a social deviant confronts us with 'ungenutzte und verdorbene Kapazitäten des Menschen' in a way that forces us to re-evaluate our own lives. Wellershoff's novel does awaken our sympathy for the criminal and alerts us to the factor of social deprivation in his development, as well as confronting us vividly with scenes beyond our normal experience. The hunt for Findeisen, as conducted by Bernhard, and the death of Wiedemann are episodes that demonstrate most plausibly Wellershoff's hypothesis as to the limits of rational thought and

20. In conversation with the author, Cologne, 11.12.1980.

of bureaucratic training when confronted with an unusual situation. Yet the novel does not function as the 'Platzhalter einer Utopie', in the sense of evoking a world delightfully free of normative constraints. The sympathy that readers are made to feel for Findeisen is, rather, such as to make them accept gratefully the cosy confines of a familiar existence.

We should not, however, forget that this aspect of realism — the erosion in literature of repressive social mechanisms through the extension of the reader's range of experience — is but one part of Wellershoff's 'Neuer Realismus'. In one of the earliest pronouncements on the subject he stressed the need to reject authorial omniscience in favour of the reflection of 'subjektive, begrenzte, momentane und bewegte Perspektiven' and in *Literatur und Veränderung* he writes of realism as necessitating the literary equivalent of constantly shifting focal lengths of shot in a film. All this seems to point towards the sort of realism that Arno Holz once propounded to Johannes Schlaf, whereby the most exact recreation of a complex reality could only be achieved by integrating into writing the perspectives of all those involved in the particular aspect of reality being described. And, indeed, this is what much of *Einladung an alle* does. The first part ('Spuren') brings together in a montage the various facts and a range of individual speculations about the possible relevance of other facts in a way that persuasively evokes the sense of confusion which must have existed at the time. In this and in other parts of the novel, the most important in this context being the attack on Bentrup ('Ruhe, sonst knallt's'), the death of Wiedemann ('Trifft ein Geschoß auf die Haut') and the various phases of the hunt for Findeisen, the perspectivisation of narration produces a kaleidoscopic impression of the mass of documentary and subjective material — conversations at police headquarters, reports in the press, Bernhard's musings on the case and the thoughts of Findeisen and other participants in the drama — contradicting the simplistic picture given by Bernhard's scientific positivism. The linguistic structure of the novel, with the montage complemented by shifts from the present into the preterite or from reported into free indirect speech, forces the reader into active participation in the enquiry, in the manner of the *nouveau roman*, as opposed to merely sitting back and admiring the skills of the detective. Ironically, the active relationship to the language of the material that is induced brings the novel close to the intentions of the 'Sprachrealismus' so forcefully rejected by Wellershoff.

Compared with the documentary prose of the late Sixties, *Einladung an alle* is marked by an openness of the authorial position and of the narrative style. Wellershoff himself has commented on this, correctly seeing the 'Literatur der Nicht-Autoren' 'als didaktische Informationssammlungen' that are intended to function as the 'Bestätigung einer schon a priori entwickelten Theorie'.[21] While a committed piece of documentary writing need not, in itself, involve the adoption of a constricting form that excludes the active partici- pation of the reader — very different examples that come to mind here are Weiss's *Die Ermittlung*, Kipphardt's *Joel Brand*, Enzensber- ger's *Das Verhör von Habanna* and the reportages of Wallraff's middle period, *Neue Reportagen* — Wellershoff is surely correct in seeing a closed form as indicating a preconceived authorial stance. For him such didactic writing, since it addresses itself only to the 'zweitran- gige relative Funktion' of literature, i.e. 'Informationssammlung', cannot involve the reader in vicarious experiences and thus help to change his consciousness. It is, therefore, inferior literature.

This charge would in no way disturb Bernt Engelmann, author of a number of 'Tatsachenromane', indeed, he has publicly declared his willingness to accept 'die Rüge der Banalität'. His aim in these novels, as in his non-fictional works, is a very specific one that justifies any literary means, even the seemingly trivial — the ex- posure of the political (i.e. Nazi) past of leading figures of the Federal Republic and the subsequent demonstration as to how these 'alte Nazis . . . in der Maske von Biedermännern als reiche und super- reiche Wirtschaftsbosse in der Bundesrepublik Karriere und Politik gemacht haben'.[22] A closely related theme is the involvement of such ex-Nazis with conservative politicians like Franz Josef Strauss and with clandestine right-wing organisations. In *Großes Bundesverdienst- kreuz*, the most sensational — in terms of public impact — of Engelmann's novels, an apparently slight question of inheritance develops into a complex political case that brings about the exposure of the Nazi past of the leading industrialist Fritz Karl Ries (of the Pegulan concern) and that of several other prominent West German manufacturers and public figures. Moreover, apparently charitable organisations in receipt of federal support are unmasked as right- wing groups that have, amongst other activities, organised a smear campaign against Willy Brandt. The novel contains a considerable amount of historical material incorporated into the narrative thread — the justification for this being that Don Hartnell, the American

21. In discussion in the Department of German Studies, University of Warwick, 22.11.1973. Cf. in this connection Wellershoff's essay 'Der Kompetenzzweifel der Schriftsteller', in his *Die Auflösung des Kunstbegriffs*, Frankfurt, 1976, pp. 58–61.
22. Cf. Bernt Engelmann, 'Was ist ein Tatsachenroman?', *Kontext 1*, Munich, 1976, pp. 84–96.

lawyer charged with sorting out the inheritance problem, is totally uninformed about German history and contemporary politics; his function in the novel is similar to that of the initially naïve father in Costa-Gavras's film *Missing*. The innocent Don must therefore be briefed by his interpreter, a trained modern historian of the generation of '68, and he also receives regular reports from his 'ferret', the retired policeman Fretsch, containing a wealth of information — all relevant to the case at issue — about Ries's wartime activities and subsequent career. These in turn give a very unsavoury picture of West German political and industrial life. Despite its thriller form, the novel relies for its impact entirely on the authenticity of the information it puts over, yet at the beginning we are merely informed, through a letter from a New York legal firm, that 'alle von Ihnen zitierten Dokumente echt sind', though the names of employees have been changed in order that 'deren Identität hinlänglich verborgen bleibt'.[23] Only in an appendix to the novel is the accuracy of its material in any way authenticated. We never learn the real name of the law firm or the source of the documents on which Engelmann's case is built; as in Ernst Ottwalt's not dissimilar novel of the Weimar period, *Denn sie wissen was sie tun*, we ultimately have to rely on the author's integrity. Engelmann himself has since excused the shortcomings of his approach by claiming that the vast body of evidence from the records in the West Berlin Document Centre, the Munich Staatsbibliothek and the Library of Congress produced such 'höchst bedeutsamen Kreuz- und Querverbindungen' that they would have been too much even for 'den normalen Leser politischer Dokumentationen';[24] the publishers of the paperback edition also claim that the novel puts over 'Informationen, die sich eine Zusammenstellung von Dokumenten nicht besorgen würden'. There is no doubt that a truly documentary treatment of the material would have been impossible in the novel, but could have been done in non-fiction. Instead, Engelmann — aiming at a larger public than he could ever have reached with a more sober account — attempts to write a political thriller in the style of Frederick Forsyth's *The Odessa File* or *The Day of the Jackal*; he himself admits that his charges and supporting evidence are conveyed within a 'dürftige Groschenhefthandlung'. Even compared with Forsyth it is pretty primitive stuff at times, but the real problem stems from a difference in intent between the two authors. The pseudo-documentary novel, as practised by Forsyth, Len Deighton and

23. *Großes Bundesverdienstkreuz* (1974), Reinbek, 1976, p. 7.
24. 'Was ist ein Tatsachenroman?'.

others is faction (in Norman Mailer's term), in that it is based on researched material, but this serves ultimately to heighten the entertainment value by giving the work added credibility, whereas Engelmann is using the easily digestible form as a means of putting over political information. The facticity, already weakened by the decision not to give sources or real names, is further undermined by deliberate proximity to the existing hybrid, in which proof of a case is not the goal.

However, such criticism of *Großes Bundesverdienstkreuz* ignores the fact that a book of this sort does not depend for its impact on the mere reading of it. The stormy reaction it provoked, including a court case (which went in Engelmann's favour), led to public examinations of the plausibility of his case and these, in the end, supported his interpretation. Although this particular novel enjoyed a *succès de scandale*, we would doubt whether it persuaded the sceptical simply by its evidential value; questions also arise concerning Engelmann's general attitude to his material. His obsession with proving the war guilt and involvement in right-wing organisations of certain leading West German businessmen and politicians leads to a simplistic black-and-white treatment of a complicated chapter of German history. His exposés, he maintains, are designed to demonstrate a correlation between capital and right-wing politics; however, the result is rather that the blame for Nazi excesses and the activities of extremist conservative organisations in the Federal Republic is laid at the door of smart opportunists capable of surviving even the extreme political changes following the collapse of the Third Reich. The shortcomings of such an approach to the understanding of the Nazi past are further exacerbated by the dying-out of the generation involved in it and, above all, the increasing distance from the period. They are illuminated by the contrast of Engelmann's *Großes Bundesverdienstkreuz* and *Die Laufmasche* (1979) with the real insights provided by, for example, Kluge's *Schlachtbeschreibung* and his more recent *Neue Geschichten* (1977), or by Manfred Franke's 'Protokoll von der Angst, von Mißhandlung und Tod, vom Auffinden der Spuren und deren Wiederentdeckung', *Mordverläufe* (1973).

In *Mordverläufe* (subtitled *9/10.XI.1938*),[25] an investigation of the events on the so-called Kristallnacht in one small town in the Rhineland, Manfred Franke set out to examine the question: 'Hat sich die nationalsozialistische Kriegsführung, Judenvernichtung, Besatzungspolitik usw. tatsächlich so abgespielt, wie es unmittelbar nach dem Krieg erst in vagen Umrissen sich abzeichnete? Wer war

---

25. Darmstadt & Neuwied, 1973. All quotations from this edition.

dafür verantwortlich? Einzelne? *Ein* Einzelner? Das System? Wie war es beschaffen?'[26] Those who had experienced living through the Third Reich, he thought, had undergone a learning process, as a result of which 'das unbesehene Hinnehmen von Behauptungen ist zu Recht in Verruf gekommen. Gültige Beweise sind gefordert. Also relevante, überprüfbare Beweise, Beweise, die etwas offen legen, beschreiben und Kenntnis vermehren'.[27] The specific stimulus to his investigations was given by certain vague memories of that night (which he had experienced as a child in Hilden), resulting in a 'bis heute nachwirkende Betroffenheit', and his knowledge that the number of victims in the town was such that it 'weit über den Rahmen des im übrigen Reich Geschehenen hinausgegangen war', as the report of the local criminal police had stated in 1938. *Mordverläufe* is a documentary work in the sense that all the material quoted or in some way used — police records, court findings, newspaper reports, reminiscences and interviews — is authentic; in addition Franke referred to and in some cases, quoted from a number of relevant books (listed at the end of the novel). On the other hand, all names, apart from those of major historical figures, have been changed, 'zum Schutz aller noch lebenden Personen, die als Zeugen ausgesagt haben oder angeklagt und freigesprochen oder angeklagt und verurteilt worden sind' (54). Even street names and other local designations in the town, unnamed in the novel, were altered. The writer is, therefore, in no way concerned to demonstrate the guilt of people involved in the Kristallnacht who have hitherto escaped justice, but rather to examine what he senses could well be an important example of manipulated intolerance towards a minority in a small town.

Franke very quickly realised from his investigations that the material made available to him from official sources gave anything but a clear picture of events, since 'das Ergebnis der Untersuchungen und Verhöre nach dem Krieg, die Urteile im Prozeß offensichtlich fragwürdig waren. Jene Dokumente . . . verdeutlichen nicht zuletzt die Schwierigkeiten, tatsächlich diese selbst, nicht irgendwelche Vorstellungen von ihr noch zu vergegenwärtigen'.[28] He quickly found himself forced to abandon his original project — 'nach den Dokumenten zu erzählen', in the manner of Engelmann — because the 'aus der ersten Niederschrift zu ermittelnden Vorgänge . . . nicht

26. Manfred Franke, 'Vom Umgang mit Dokumenten', lecture held on 4.11.1977 at a conference of the PEN-Club in Celle (unpublished).

27. Ibid.

28. Heinrich Vormweg, 'Realismus als Wahrheitsfindung', *Merkur*, 28, 1974, p. 89 and 'Die übermächtigen Verhältnisse', *Jahresring*, 1974, p. 265.

mehr mit den aus den Dokumenten abzulesenden überein — [stimmten]'. The reader is quickly confronted with a questioning of the notion of clear facticity, the unambiguous attribution of blame, that is central to the cases Engelmann investigates. Whereas the latter is interested in individual guilt, Franke, concerned as he is not to examine the material with prejudice, soon comes to realise that 'die Fakten, um die es hier geht, . . . der handfeste Ausdruck einer zeitbedingten Mentalität und Denkweise [sind], und eben sie sind aufs engste an die überlieferte Sprache gebunden'. Language alone reveals 'was von den Ereignissen über dreißig Jahre später erfahren werden kann. Die *authentischen* Wörter reichen am nächsten an Vergangenes heran. Ob sie eindeutig oder (wie oft in Verhörtexten) bewußt irreführend und ungenau sind, mehr als sie bezeichnen läßt sich nicht mehr recherchieren'.[29] In order to obtain the most complete linguistic representation of the Kristallnacht, Franke went beyond the available public and private written material, and turned to 'Gedächtnisprotokolle', the verbal testimony of people involved directly or indirectly with the events of that night. One witness in the novel, speaking on behalf of the author, goes as far as to claim 'daß Geschichten oder Anekdoten . . . oft mehr über die wirklichen Verhältnisse verrieten als historisch exakte Dokumente' (73). For this reason, a range of such statements play as important a part in the novel as the written accounts.

A further difficulty for Franke, as far as his original intent to deal with the events in the form of a narrative was concerned, was the fact that he, as an eight-year-old child, had been 'ein Zeuge des Mithörens' and still felt 'auch noch nach über dreißig Jahren dafür einstehen zu können, seine Erinnerungen seien verläßlich'. The author Franke, trying to stand back from this instinctive response, was able to recognise that his childish imagination had embraced and embellished the impressions of that night, but that he had long considered these fantasies to be true, 'weil ihm die tatsächlichen Vorfälle vorenthalten blieben' (132–3). Since his childhood impressions can only 'lie', he has to find another compiler of his material about the terrorising of the Jews 'der auskommt ohne Dokumente, oder nur mit solchen, über die er allein verfügt, die nicht festgelegt sind auf eine Perspektive, die noch unbenutzt sind' (65). The adult Franke is well qualified to assume this role, in part because he has grown up in the town and knows his way about, but, above all, since he has recognised from his own recollections just how unreliable memory can be and therefore can stand back and

29. 'Vom Umgang mit Dokumenten'.

look quizzically both at subjective and apparently objective accounts of this chapter of the town's history. His new concern is to assemble the range of information and, by quotation, to present the material to the reader. In coming to terms with 'teils sich ergänzender, teils sich widersprechender Aussagen . . . wird der Leser unmittelbar in den Prozeß der Wahrheitsfindung, in die Ermittlung mit einbezogen'.[30] As with Wellershoff's *Einladung an alle*, the reader takes part in the research process and should, above all, be able to draw his own conclusions from the material presented to him. The quotations assembled into the montage of the novel do not, however, merely reveal the possible course of events, indeed, other aspects of the matter rapidly overtake this in importance. Statements taken in 1938 and by the occupying Allies in 1945 reveal the attitudes that led to the terrible occurrences of that November night; on the other hand, the same statements, having been 'in einen veränderten Zusammenhang gestellt, büßen . . . ihre ursprünglich kriminalistische, beweisebildende und als solche heute historische Qualität ein und konstituieren unter peinlicher Beibehaltung jeder nur möglichen Detailgenauigkeit den Schrecken noch einmal'.[31] As Franke indicates here, we are by no means confronted merely with dry facts about a distant event (indeed, in most cases such facts as do emerge are by no means conclusive): what is ultimately important about the novel is the way in which the assemblage of linguistic material vividly recreates the attitude of many townspeople at the time, the general mood in the town, the brutality of the — still rather shadowy — thugs, the terror of the dying and wounded, the panic of the survivors and the uncertainty of the persecuted minority of those sympathetic to the Jews.

The critical reconstruction of the Kristallnacht and its aftermath is made up of a number of strands, which together go some way towards evoking the horror in its totality. One of the most important of these, which itself is separated into three finer threads, is institutionalised anti-Semitism in the Third Reich. The hatred of the Jews poured out by the Nazi propaganda machine comes out graphically in the local newspaper's bald report on 10 November 1938: 'Zerstörungen in den Wohnungen der hier wohnenden Juden waren *Ausdruck der berechtigten Erregung* [my italics, KB] gegen den jüdischen Meuchelmord' (37). Even more horrific, since it is of relevance for our own everyday existence, is the way in which language is manipulated and used to colour the attitudes of 'normal, decent' people

30. Ibid.
31. Ibid.

through the dissemination of lies and other distorted information designed to fan latent prejudice. The narrator (Franke), in his role as 'der Zeuge' can testify to this by drawing on stories he was told as a child: his mother depicted the circumstances of his grandfather's bankruptcy, stressing above all the difference between his competitors, the Jews Rosenbaum ('die haben immer teurer verkauft') and her father, who — unlike the Rosenbaums — 'wollte immer ein ehrlicher Mann bleiben'. In her version of the fraudulent treatment of her widowed mother, the whole story was structured to lead up to the final cautionary warning: 'Das war ein Jud! Merk dir das!' The final thread of the anti-Semitism of the time, and of more direct relevance to the unleashing of the horrors of the Kristallnacht, is made up by the consequence of Herschel Grynszpan's shooting of Ernst von Rath, a member of the staff of the German Embassy in Paris, on 7 November 1938. This was exploited by the Nazis as the direct 'provocation' that justified the organised attack on the Jews. In purely linguistic terms a chain of causality can be followed through (and is reflected in the novel) from Goebbels' conversations to the reports in the local newspaper, the *Volksstimme*. In the Propaganda Ministry the 'Minister' (i.e. Goebbels) had said: 'der jugendliche Bandit Grynszpan sei von dunklen Hintermännern gekauft; sein Verbrechen werde die schwersten Folgen für die noch in Deutschland ansässigen Juden haben; die Geduld des deutschen Volkes gegenüber den von Juden finanzierten Provokationen sei zu Ende' (122). The formulations used in the leading article in the *Volksstimme* of 9 November reveal the clear influence of these words: 'Das deutsche Volk ist nicht gewillt, noch weiterhin jüdische Provokationen zu dulden. Bisher ist noch zahlreichen Angehörigen der jüdischen Rasse in Deutschland das Gastrecht gewährt worden. Sie mögen sich bei dem Banditen Grynszpan bedanken, wenn wir deren Rassengenossen nicht mehr in den Grenzen unseres Reiches zu sehen wünschen' (123). The central control and manipulation of language could, therefore, prepare and even help to precipitate the crimes of the night of 9–10 November, and on the following day they were then further used to justify what had happened and to draw a veil over the full extent of the horror.

The reconstruction of the likely pattern of events is bedevilled by the 'disappearance' of key areas in the final report made by the local police and dated November 1938, leaving only the later statements of the accused and witnesses. Weyland, the local historian, does, though, grant 'der Zeuge' access to his own records of interviews with witnesses, in which they comment on what they said at the time; the dominant impression of these is the manipulation of these

people through intimidation: 'Die Zeugin Stender sagt: Aus lauter Angst sagte ich damals, daß ich keinen der Täter erkannt hätte, obwohl ich wußte, daß Lindner dabei war. Gefragt wurde ich: Sie haben doch niemanden erkannt? Aus dem Ton dieser Frage schloß die Zeugin: daß ich keinen angeben sollte, und aus Angst tat ich das auch nicht' (38). The truth about the Kristallnacht was further distorted, as far as the official record is concerned, by the way in which the police and local doctors were pressured into changing, in official records, their view as to the nature of offences committed. Gutke, the head of the local CID, is told that he 'könne anscheinend das Politische vom Strafrechtlichen nicht unterscheiden' and has, as a result, wrongly used the term 'Mord' on the charge-sheet instead of 'Totschlag unter Anwendung stumpfer Gegenstände'. Dr Lohmann is threatened with a revolver and made to certify a clear case of murder as suicide, while his colleague Dr Streb initially refuses to sign two previously completed death certificates; eventually, 'auf Ersuchen des Kommissars', he is persuaded to record the cause of death as 'Stumpfe Gewalteinwirkung (Schädelbruch)', rather than as 'murder by . . .'. In this way the official account of the treatment of 'the Jews was sanitised in such a way as to make the task of later investigators all the more difficult.

Fresh efforts were made to unravel matters in July 1945 and in 1948, but the existing difficulties were compounded by the imprecise and often contradictory later testimonies. In extracts from interrogations carried out in these years, most witnesses seem particularly anxious to defend themselves and others by, for example, laying the blame on neighbours killed or missing in the war (cf. 'Nachtrag II: Beginn einer Nacht'). As in a Mafia trial, no one has done, seen or heard anything that might implicate themselves or others still alive. A further complication for Franke's investigations is that, even where there was sufficient proof for the court to come to a clear decision in 1948 as to an individual's complicity, the accused were treated inconsistently, with social status and 'string-pulling' playing a decisive part. Thus Lindner, a minor figure, who had responded over-enthusiastically to the orders of the SA and the SS and had murdered two Jews, cannot cope with the clever questioning of the prosecution and is found guilty. The former Ortsgruppenleiter, now a respected business man, whose fortunes were founded on his astute acquisition of Jewish property and who had, almost certainly, given the decisive orders on the Kristallnacht, is able to afford highly skilled defence counsel. Accordingly — despite evidence assembled by the local SPD indicating his involvement in crimes against humanity and other offences falling under §125 of the penal code —

he is acquitted. Others with apparent heavy responsibility for the attacks on the Jews in 1938 are given minor, almost nominal sentences, whilst Lindner, a social nobody who asks the court, with some justification, 'die damaligen Verhältnisse, Propaganda, Alkoholgenuß und in jedem Falle das Drängen der SA- und SS-Leute bei der Strafzumessung zu berücksichtigen' (325), is initially sentenced to fifteen years imprisonment and, on appeal, to life.

The impression is thus given of three investigations all demonstrating very unsatisfactory judicial handling of the excesses against the Jews. By dexterous linguistic distortion and obfuscation the events are reduced in scale and trivialised, while the material in the hands of the local historian Weyland and the 'Gedächtnisprotokolle' clearly suggest that even long after the war those in the know refused to reveal information compromising to the town and some leading citizens. The result would seem to be that those really responsible for the Kristallnacht in the main escape punishment. This certainly seems to be the conclusion of the narrator; in the last section of the novel, the fictional, and hence highly subjective, 'Beerdigung eines reichen Mannes' (Nohl, the former Ortsgruppenleiter) portrays the final tributes paid by apparently normal, decent citizens, including old comrades, to this war criminal and is the final indication that the guilty have been able to live 'frei und ungehindert' after the war.

The final thread of the novel is the relationship of Franke's own childhood and family memories to all this, which represents in miniature all the problematical aspects of his enquiry. He has the feeling that what he now realises were his mother's unsatisfactory responses to his questions at the time indicate an inability or an unwillingness on her part to see the reality. The Jews are blamed for the economic crisis of 1923–4, his grandfather's business failure and his grandmother's misfortune, while the shop-windows below their flat are smashed in the Kristallnacht 'weil Rosenbaum Jude ist', but at no time could she grasp, he now sees, the 'Zuordnung der vorhergehenden Einzelheiten zueinander, die daraus folgende Tendenz'. Even after the war she clings to the belief that there had been 'doch anständige Menschen, auch unter den Nazis'; the Ortsgruppenführer had not been a 'Bluthund', but a helpful neighbour and Lindner, found guilty of murdering two Jews, is remembered as being 'rücksichtsvoll, ein angenehmer Mieter' (to her own mother), so that, despite the evidence, she still questions his guilt: 'Meinst du, daß er es war? fragt die Mutter. Ist Friedländer nicht die Treppe hinuntergestürzt? Oder von Gäbler umgebracht worden?' Sadly, the adult son has to conclude that she — who has always stressed to him the importance of truthfulness — is unable to see the truth: 'Du hast eine Geschichte erzählt und ziehst die falschen Schlüsse. Und du hast dir ein Bild von Menschen gemacht, dem Genauigkeit fehlt' (267–76). The sorry message here and of the book as a whole is that, despite de-Nazification in the Forties, the so-called *Bewältigung der Vergangenheit* in the Fifties and the show trials in Frankfurt in the Sixties, the sense in West Germany that people had come to terms with National Socialism was illusory — quite apart from criminals escaping justice and, indeed, thriving after the war. That illusion arose because no attention was paid to the effect that twelve years of living in Nazi Germany had exercised on the thinking of the lower middle classes, the group so decisively influenced by the National Socialists.

The fusion of these insights, involving a painful honesty about Franke's family memories, with the various types of written and oral evidence produces a vivid evocation of the horrors in a night which would ultimately lead to Auschwitz, a night which undoubtedly 'enthält mehr, als die Edition der Dokumente hätte verdeutlichen können, er bringt mehr an Wahrheit, in jeder Hinsicht, mehr auch, als ein Enthüllungsbuch hätte bringen können'.[32] Certainly, Engelmann's concentration on the question of individual guilt tends towards a black-and-white picture that tells us nothing about the wider social aspects of National Socialism; his narrow focus makes it difficult to do anything other than accept or reject the case being made. By comparison, the reader of Franke's *Mordverläufe* becomes involved in the actual search for truth. Our reading of the novel does not depend on our being convinced in advance of the honesty or objectivity of the author; the method Franke adopts persuades us of his concern for truth, for 'Wahrheitsfindung und Beglaubigung' of such facts as can be established clearly, while it reveals his inability to come to an unambiguous factual analysis of the Kristallnacht in Hilden as a whole. The disadvantage of the historical approach of, say, Joachim Fest's *Hitler* is that, for all the excellent background research, it merely confirms our existing view of the man and, above all, stresses yet again the important role of an extraordinary individual. Responsibility for events is focused on him in a way that diverts attention away from a complicated range of factors, ultimately providing a rather cosy distortion of the real historical complexity of National Socialism, a part of which emerges so vividly from *Mordverläufe*. The difference in attitude between the self-conscious author anxious to produce a definitive reading of a phenomenon and the modest compiler of documentary evidence is striking; despite the

---

32. Vormweg, 'Realismus als Wahrheitsfindung', p. 91.

seductive interpretability of history propagated by popular historians, historical novelists, film and television, the confusion of Franke's subject-matter prevents its reduction to a neat narrative pattern. The great achievement of *Mordverläufe* as a realist novel is the way in which the open form — as with Wellershoff's *Einladung an alle* — serves to reflect the impossibility of comprehending history and, at the same time, 'dem Publikum etwas zu zeigen, was es bisher nicht wußte. Oder: was es bisher *so* noch nicht wußte'.[33] It also succeeds much better than *D'Alemberts Ende* — which, as Franke has admitted, inspired the technique adopted here — in demonstrating the contribution that implementation of Heißenbüttel's theories can make to the realist novel. The work shows the correctness of Michael Scharang's assertion that language is 'ein Moment der Gesamtrealität, und die Dokumentation, könnte man fordern, habe die Aufgabe, den Stellenwert dieses Moments und dessen Funktion in der Gesamtgesellschaft anzugeben; je mehr sie diese Aufgabe erfüllt, desto mehr Gebrauchswert hat sie'.[34] The usefulness of this, the most important documentary novel of the Seventies, lies both in its examination of its subject and in demonstrating the importance of this dimension to modern realism.

33. 'Vom Umgang mit Dokumenten'.
34. 'Zur Technik der Dokumentation', p. 23.

6

The Novel of Political Realism

In the few surveys of West German literature of the Seventies so far published, it is either portrayed (for example, in the case of Marcel Reich-Ranicki) as characterised by a lack of stylistic and thematic unity [1] or — and this would seem to be the more dominant view — as essentially unpolitical. It was perfectly understandable that the revolutionary impetus of many left-wing intellectuals and writers should quickly fade away after the formation of the SPD–FDP coalition in 1969 and the apparent chance of constitutional change. However, the post-1969 tendency that Johann August Schülein has called the 'Rückzug ins Private' had little to do with satisfied inertia after the collapse of the Grand Coalition or disillusionment about political activity *per se*.[2] Despite the swiftly-coined notion of the 'Tendenzwende' — as betokening a general turning away from politics — the Seventies were a thoroughly political decade, with intellectual life dominated by a range of issues springing from the Student Movement, particularly the most radical product of '68: terrorism. The political climate was increasingly felt to be marked by 'die Einkreisung des Intellektuellen durch modernste staatsapparative Techniken',[3] as well as the issues of 'Berufsverbot' and the negative consequences of the security measures brought on by the wave of terrorist attacks. Testimony to the impact of such concerns, so central to the period, is borne by both non-fiction and imaginative literature; Böll's *Die verlorene Ehre der Katharina Blum*, *Bericht zur Gesinnungslage der Nation* and *Fürsorgliche Belagerung*, Peter Schneider's *. . . schon bist du ein Verfassungsfeind* and *Alte und neue Szenen zum Thema Radikale*, Arnfried Astel's *Ein Lehrer mit Berufsverbot*, Peter O. Chotjewitz's *Die Herren des Morgengrauens*, Franz Josef Degenhardt's *Brandstellen* and *Die Mißhandlung* and F.C. Delius's *Ein Held der inneren Sicherheit* are only the obvious literary examples. In addition to

1. Cf. Marcel Reich-Ranicki, *Entgegnung*, Stuttgart, 1979, p. 35.
2. Cf. 'Von der Studentenrevolte zur Tendenzwende oder der Rückzug ins Private', *Kursbuch 48* ('Zehn Jahre danach'), pp. 101–17.
3. Wilfried van der Will, 'Die literarische Intelligenz und der Staat', in K. Bullivant and H.J. Althof (eds.), *Subjektivität — Innerlichkeit — Abkehr vom Politischen*, Bonn, 1986, p. 15

responses to the surveillance-state, there emerged a feminist literature aiming, particularly in the initial phase, at a radical challenge to established patterns of role-expectation and at promoting group identity and social engagement. Furthermore, in the latter part of the decade, there appeared the 'Väter-Romane', biographical or autobiographical novels constituting a new phase in critical evaluation of the Nazi legacy. The notion that the literature of this peiod was essentially unpolitical also fails to take adequate account of the publication of a whole series of overtly political realist novels, such as Michael Scharang's *Charly Traktor* and *Sohn eines Landarbeiters*, Max von der Grün's *Stellenweise Glatteis* and *Flächenbrand*, August Kühn's chronicle of a Munich working-class family, *Zeit zum Aufstehn*, Chotjewitz's *Der dreißigjährige Friede*, the bulk of the Autoren-Edition publications and, last but not least, Peter Weiss's *Die Ästhetik des Widerstands*. It should also not be forgotten that, contrary to the impression given by a popular, but drastically oversimplified picture of the period, Böll and Scharang did not become politically active until after 1970, while others, like Degenhardt, were far more active in the Seventies than before; in addition, a whole host of younger political writers made their literary débuts during the Seventies.

Amongst middle-class left-wing circles the early Seventies, understandably enough, were very much influenced by the after-effects of the Student Movement and the extra-parliamentary opposition. Despite the sense of disappointment at the lack of political change after the collapse of the Grand Coalition, certain general political aims of 1968 continued to be important, even if activities in support of them were concentrated outside the immediate political arena; this was particularly true of the generation of writers who first began to publish after 1970. Existing society was widely considered to offer no possibility of fulfilling fundamental, 'true' human needs, the concomitant being a drive towards realisation of those needs, rather than the false values of a consumer society dominated by technological rationality. The continued influence of Marx's early writings and of existentialist ideas gleaned from a reading of these and from Hegel and Marcuse can be seen over the range of left-wing groupings. Uwe Timm, for example, writes of the need for social change 'hin zu einer Gesellschaft, in der sich der Mensch frei und allseitig entfalten kann', and in the very formulation of this, as Timm called it, 'auslösenden Moment der Studentenrevolte' the influence of Marx's *The German Ideology* can be identified.[4] While it would be quite wrong

4. 'Sensibilität für wen?', *kürbiskern*, 1976, Heft 1, p. 119.

to deny that the pragmatic politics of the SPD–FDP coalition or reaction against the dogmatic nature of neo-Marxist thought in the political debates of the late Sixties did in some cases induce a resigned withdrawal from activism, politicisation was still a major formative influence in the Seventies, although it frequently had to adopt different forms of expression. Certainly, by 1971–2, when the new government's course and the lack of basic social change had become fairly clear, the 'lange Marsch durch die Institutionen' was seen on many sides as the only realistic possibility of continuing to agitate for the ideals of the Student Movement. In this situation, literature was allotted a new function: after the rediscovery of, in Peter Schneider's phrase, the power of 'Phantasie im Spätkapitalismus', the crude didacticism of agit-prop was rejected in favour of an operative aesthetic code that would call established patterns of consciousness into question and thus play its part in changing human sensibility and, with it, existing society.

The other major starting-point of literary theories amongst the still active student generation was the rejection of established bourgeois literature as politically quietistic. Uwe Timm, who can be considered a representative figure for these authors, sees such literature as a defensive aesthetic code, in that it does not address itself to burning social issues, but to 'das Überzeitliche, das Höhere, das Eigentliche, das Allgemeingültige, das nicht auf das Tagesgeschehen Gerichtete etc'.[5] Timm advances the view that the politically committed author concerned with efficient communication with his audience should turn his back on aesthetic standards that equate quality with exclusivity and should aim to produce literature with a wider appeal. He goes on to argue that popular novels are successful, not only because of the essentially traditional, accessible narrative techniques used, but because of their content, 'in denen geschickt systemkonforme Wünsche mit solchen, die einem echten Bedürfnis entspringen, kombiniert werden. . . . Reproduziert wird eine anheimelnde Unmittelbarkeit'. A didactic popular literature should, on the other hand, endeavour 'diese Unmittelbarkeit als falsch zu entlarven'. Since 'die meisten Genüsse heute noch keine menschlichen, sondern vom Kapital bestimmte sind, daß auch sie den Warencharakter tragen, verdinglichte Genüsse sind', literature should express through the vehicle of the author's imagination 'was den Kapitalismus in Frage stellen könnte'. Literature can evoke a world in which human faculties can develop and thus contrast a potential world with 'der deformierten Wirklichkeit'; it 'würde

5. 'Zwischen Unterhaltung und Aufklärung', *kürbiskern*, 1972, Heft 1, pp. 79–90.

damit eine Utopie artikulieren, die sie zwar nicht vorausnehmen kann, die aber durch "Benennung" Stimulanz wird für die konkrete Arbeit an der Veränderung' — change not only in political consciousness, but also in man's sensual awareness. The portrayal of the attainment of personal fulfilment as a result of such a change can be 'am deutlichsten in der Handlung realisiert. . . . Die Handlung müßte zentrieren um die Problematik Individuum und Gesellschaft'. This is the most appropriately attainable in the epic form, in a negative 'Entwicklungsroman' — concentrating not on the development of extreme individualism, but describing the path of an individual 'das aus seiner bornierten Vereinzelung zu einem kollektiven Bewußtsein gelangt, in einem Kollektiv lebt und arbeitet'. Uwe Timm's first novel, *Heißer Sommer* (1974) is his attempt to put this theory into practice.[6]

Heißer Sommer is clearly intended as the portrayal of the exemplary development of a young student, Ullrich Krause, who progresses from a state of general frustration via an emotionally determined form of political activism to the fringes of the DKP and, above all, to an awareness of the need for concerted, organised political work. Initially, politicisation is no more than a necessary way out of an existential impasse: he has no interest in his thesis on Hölderlin's odes and his efforts to fill the void with girls from the Schwabing 'scene' are unsuccessful. There seems, though, no escape, until one day he hears on the radio news of the shooting in Berlin of a student (clearly Benno Ohnesorg, KB); he literally rises from his lover's bed a changed man. He becomes interested in the situation in Iran, joins in demonstrations and meets people with whom real contact seems possible: 'Ihm war aufgefallen, daß er mit jedem ohne jede Peinlichkeit reden konnte und sie mit ihm' (40). The reader follows Ullrich through a variety of situations, all vividly and accurately recreating the atmosphere of the time. Lectures are interrupted and replaced by discussions, forcing Ullrich to acquire a new vocabulary. He joins the SDS and, in the aftermath of the attack on Rudi Dutschke, takes part in the anti-Springer demonstrations. In keeping with his newfound political awareness, he abandons his work on Hölderlin in favour of a thesis on 'Die Arbeiterliteratur der zwanziger Jahre im Spiegel der Kritik'.

Ullrich's development does not, however, stop here; he soon becomes disaffected with the SDS, rejecting the arid dogmatism of its political discussions: 'Ohne Phantasie vertrocknet man doch, sagte Ullrich. Wie im Keller. Diese Diskussionen. Dieses Gequatsche

---

6. *Heißer Sommer* (1974), Reinbek, 1977. All quotations from this edition.

über die Kategorien des Kapitals. Da trocknet man aus, da verdurstet man. Ohne Phantasie, ohne Spiel, was soll das für eine neue Gesellschaft werden. Lauter vertrocknete Seminarmarxisten. Die Langeweile. Das ist der gessellschaftliche Wärmetod' (154). Now under the influence of the 'Spontis' he comes to feel the need for new experiences; he moves into a 'Wohngemeinschaft', becomes involved in street theatre and takes work in a factory. While one friend joins the terrorist underground and others seem contented with their alternative life style, Ullrich's political consciousness increases to the point where he decides to work together with friends in the DKP, seeing in such activity the possibility of a 'langen organisierten Weg in die Betriebe, in die Schulen, in die Universitäten, in die Wohngebiete. Mit den Arbeitern, für die Arbeiter' (214). In this way there is the hope of bringing about social change, and with it 'ein realisierbares Glück für alle. Eine befriedete Welt, eine Welt ohne Ausbeutung und Unterdrückung' (220).

Heißer Sommer, Gerd Fuchs's *Beringer und die lange Wut* (1973) and Roland Lang's *Ein Hai in der Suppe oder Das Glück des Philipp Ronge* (1975), all three appearing under the Autoren-Edition imprint, show the possibilities and, above all, the limitations of adopting the popular novel form. All are heavily based on the authors' experiences in the Student Movement and so, not surprisingly, are quite successful in portraying events of the time. Particularly in *Heißer Sommer*, in which the first traces of a montage technique can be observed, there is an authentic sense of 'how things were' that will be recognised by those who experienced them at first hand. It is difficult to see, though, who it is that will find it educative. The political activist, possibly having himself followed a similar path, will find Ullrich's development plausible, even convincing, but it is doubtful if the book would convert someone of an unpolitical nature, still less those of a different political persuasion. The psychological dimension of the portrait of Ullrich is exceedingly thin and, from such anecdotal evidence as we do receive, the impression is given that he is motivated, above all, by fear of existential emptiness; once he has been awakened from the state of defensive near-catatonic lethargy this fear expresses itself in the manic projection of hope on to ever-new goals. He is a sort of latter-day Werther, and so it must be doubted whether he can apply himself consistently to political activity. The questionable nature of the ending of the novel is finally compounded by the fact that here, as in the other books mentioned, Ullrich is left on the threshold of a new life; we know that this will be better, but we have no clear idea as to what it will be or how it is to be brought about. We are left with an unconvincing happy ending, as in so many early Socialist-Realist novels from the GDR, which these first novels from the Autoren-Edition basically resemble.

The central character of Uwe Timm's later novel *Kerbels Flucht* (1980; cf. Chapter 8), who is in many ways an extension of the Krause figure, would seem to confirm that the intensity of Ullrich's political engagement was essentially an expression of an instability born of ontological uncertainty. If he is understood in this way, then his eventual closeness to the DKP acquires a certain plausibility as a staging-post on his stumbling way, but not as a definitive conversion. Such an unconvincing utopian ending is typical of a number of other realist novels of a more or less political kind from the early Seventies, including Martin Walser's *Die Gallistl'sche Krankheit* (1972). Josef Gallistl, tired of the struggle for survival in capitalist society, dreams — as Ullrich did for a while — of liberation through manual labour, he has great hopes of a visit to the GDR and intends 'in die Partei ein[zu]treten'. Ultimately, though, the dimension of the weary self-ironisation of the central character saves the ending from falling into the same naïve optimism of the early Autoren-Edition novels and of the best-known fictional treatment of the Student Movement, Peter Schneider's *Lenz* (1973).[7]

Schneider very astutely avoids the dangers inherent in showing us the actual politicisation of Lenz: the novel starts with one of the key phases in Ullrich Krause's development, that of disillusionment with the arid intellectuality of the Student Movement: 'Schon seit einiger Zeit konnte er das weise Marxgesicht über seinem Bett nicht mehr ausstehen', we are told; he loathes 'fertige Sätze' and finds the discussions of his former comrades mere chatter ('Gerede'). He is critical, above all, of the fact that feelings play no part in the students' thinking and he has found an antidote to the emotional barrenness of political activism in his relationship with L., 'einem Mädchen aus dem Volk':

> Zum ersten Mal stößt er auf einen Menschen, der alles direkt und praktisch durchgelebt hat, was in seinem Kopf nur als Wunsch und Vorstellung existierte. Seine Geliebte wird für ihn der Schlüssel zur Welt, er wirft sein ganzes Nachholbedürfnis nach praktischem Leben, seinen Hunger nach Erfahrung in diese Beziehung und beginnt, sie als Sprungbett, die Welt mit den Sinnen zu erobern (45).

Their emotional needs are, however, irreconcilable and Lenz is thrown back on his own resources; he feels ever more alienated from his fellow-students and becomes more and more neurotic (it is here

---

7. Berlin, 1973. All quotations from this edition.

that the real similarity with Büchner's *Lenz* lies and the quotations from the earlier short story that Schneider blends into the work serve to underline this). He abruptly decides to go to Italy and, after an initial encounter with the boring, pseudo-revolutionary chat of the Roman 'scene', discovers amongst workers in Trento 'eine herzliche Humanität des Alltags' (Michael Schneider), which seems to reconcile concepts and feeling. In the course of his political work, the carrying out of 'tatsächliche[n] Pflichten' in Trento, the theoretical knowledge acquired from his involvement in the Student Movement, formerly so hollow-seeming, suddenly appears 'unentbehrlich', since it is no longer applied in a conceptual, impractical vacuum: 'Da er die Bedürfnisse der Studenten und der Arbeiter, die er kennenlernte, jeden Tag offen vor sich sah, zweifelte er nicht an den Begriffen, mit denen er sie ausdrückte' (83). The stay in Italy is short, since Lenz is deported, but he has so much benefited from his experiences that he now feels 'keine Spur von Angst'. He returns to Berlin and, although nothing seems to have changed in his absence, he is filled with new-found energy. While others can only think of getting away, the 'cured' Lenz has a clear purpose: 'Dableiben'. Although it would be wrong not to allow for a different reading of the final scene — with the 'Dableiben' seen as Lenz's self-deception about his immediate future — Schneider, like Timm, Fuchs and Lang, here shrinks from following through and showing us the results of Lenz's change. Moreover, though we are meant to see that change as the start of long-term meaningful activity, its psychological motivation is hardly convincing. In Trento Lenz was, as Michael Schneider observed, merely a 'priviligierter Gast auf Zeit',[8] whose experiences there have as little relevance for his renewed existence in Berlin as a holiday for everyday life. In addition, Schneider's psychological realism, in its portrayal of the character's emotional instability, is sufficiently convincing to call the optimism of the ending seriously into question: two years previously Lenz thought he had found the answer to all his needs in the relationship with L., yet now he sees salvation in an existence apparently unaltered from that which had earlier triggered off his neuroses. The likelihood is, as Hermann Peter Piwitt has said in relation to other novels engendered by the Student Movement, that his 'Bedürfnisse, die ihren politischen Ausdruck nicht finden, . . . sich früher oder später gegen den Bedürftigen selbst [kehren werden]: als Neurose, als Zerstörungswut, als ungelebtes Leben'.[9]

8. Cf. 'Von der Alten Radikalität zur Neuen Sensibilität' in Michael Schneider, *Die lange Wut zum langen Marsch*, Reinbek, 1975, p. 329.
9. Hermann Peter Piwitt, 'Rückblick auf heiße Tage. Die Studentenrevolte in der

Despite the disappointment of the ending, *Lenz* is considerably more realistic than *Heißer Sommer*, in that it mediates the experience of social reality from the perspective of the subject, as opposed to using the central character to put across an oversimplified view of the world. *Heißer Sommer* is essentially the working out in literature of the author's own claim, implicit in the chosen form of the third-person 'Entwicklungsroman', to be reproducing the essence of the totality that is social experience. The lack of reality in this and other novels, above all the totally naïve hope for swift and radical social change, does, incidentally, help to show why there was at the beginning of the Seventies a turning-in on the self and its needs, a sense of disillusionment and stocktaking (the roots of aspects of the 'Neue Subjektivität', to be analysed in Chapter 8). But, inconceivable as it may seem today, many did take the step advocated at the end of *Heißer Sommer* and plunged into political activity 'an der Basis', i.e. outside the major political parties, and so the extra-literary reality has, to some extent, to be set against our reading of the end of the novel. It was really only with the so-called 'deutsche Herbst' of the latter half of the Seventies that hopes of significant social and political change were finally dashed, bringing with it, by and large, the demise of the revived 'Entwicklungsroman'. This time of depression led to a greater degree of resignation and introspection in the novel than was the case earlier in the decade, but, where writers still clung to their hopes of changing society and helping to realise unfulfilled human longings, there may be noted a much more sober awareness of the inbuilt inertia in existing social structures. The situation at that time, reminiscent as it was of that in which Vischer and Ludwig found themselves, induced a significant retreat by a number of writers into the inner world of individual subjectivity. Those who, on the other hand, refused to relinquish the vital ideals of the late Sixties and were anxious to learn from the failures of the Student Movement and their own political engagement, were forced to find new realist techniques to reflect experience in a world, the full complexity of which they were only now able to grasp.

One such novel, dealing fully with the consequences of the experiences of 1968, is Urs Jaeggi's *Brandeis* (1978), which in turn highlights the impossibility of treating these adequately through the form of popular fiction. Jaeggi adopts a montage technique, bringing together autobiographical and documentary material, fictional plots, quotations from a range of sources and diary entries to re-create Brandeis's view of events, as experienced directly and

Literatur', *Literaturmagazin 4*, 1975, p. 329.

through the study of relevant written material; we are confronted with a blend of personal experiences and the individual view of key events on the one hand, and of objective description on the other. Taking due note of the complex reality confronting the individual, it shows one way, 'äußere und innere Veränderungen in einer einzigen Schreibbewegung zu erfassen und dabei die Kluft zwischen theoretischer Analyse und subjektiver Deskription zu überwinden'.[10] This, however, is only a subsidiary aspect of the novel. Its major focus is the emotional breakdown, brought about by social and political factors, of an intellectual sympathetic to the cause of change, but who is, in the last resort, unable to commit himself fully to it. His attitude to events is one of 'resignative Anarchie' (Frank Benseler), with the result that the utopian dimension so crucial to all forms of political realism, the demonstration of the need for, and possibility for, change in existing society, is absent.

This aspect marks off Jaeggi's novel from Otto F. Walter's *Die Verwilderung* (1977), another later novel generated by the Student Movement (the specific influence has been admitted publicly by the author[11]), a novel which has clear affinities of form with Kluge's concept of offensive realism through the medium of aggressive montage and at the same time, again like Kluge, emphasises the utopian element. On the most straightforward level of this complex novel *Die Verwilderung* concerns itself with Blumer, a journalist deeply involved in the events of 1968 and who has since drifted almost to the brink of despair. He is saved from suicide only by meeting Rob and Leni, a couple who are setting up a cooperative in the old 'Huppergrube' in an attempt to create a new and freer life style. The otherwise sceptical journalist, attracted to them and, in any case, without any real alternative, joins the enterprise. In time, others swell their ranks, until the point is reached where the group formally decide to constitute themselves into a democratic cooperative that will turn its back on exploitation, the competition ethos, bourgeois notions of jealousy and property. For the citizens of Jammers, however, the 'S' cooperative is an outright provocation which they destroy violently through the agency of the 'Freiwillige Aktion zur nationalen Sicherheit ASS', killing Rob and Leni in the process.

The story element of the novel is, however, only one strand amongst many. The narrative is constantly intercut with other

10. Quoted in Gisela Ullrich, 'Urs Jaeggi', *KLG*. p. 4.
11. Walter in conversation with W. Martin Lüdke, 'Es hat sich etwas verändert . . . ' in Lüdke (ed.), *Nach dem Protest. Literatur im Umbruch*, Frankfurt, 1979, pp. 103, 124. All quotations in the text from *Die Verwilderung*, Reinbek, 1977.

material, most importantly: biographical details about the main characters; 'Kalendergeschichten' (reports from the Zurich *Zeitdienst* of political and commercial news from Switzerland); 'Neues vom Tag' (fictional accounts of right-wing tendencies, especially the growth of the ASS); information about life in the blocks of flats near the 'Huppergrube'; 'Aus einer alten Geschichte' (extracts from Keller's novella *Romeo und Julia auf dem Dorfe*); 'Skizzenbuch' (Blumer's notes for an as yet uncertain book project, containing novelesque and autobiographical material, seen essentially as 'Schreibtherapie'; 'Balladen von der Herbeiführung erträglicher Lebensbedingungen für alle' (the evocation of a better, more humanitarian society in the near future); 'Für Liebhaber von Theoretischem' (extracts from theoretical works on various aspects of the novel, including the analysis of oligarchical systems). The emulsion of these various colloidal parts forms the totality of the novel.

As compiler of this material, the author is no neutral reporter. His sympathies clearly lie with the drop-outs, as the worthy citizens of Switzerland would term the central characters, and many of Blumer's positions coincide with the known views of Walter, who also feels that our 'Hochleistungssystem, auf liberale Demokratie kapitalistischer Machtordnung gegründet, . . . im Prinzip veränderbar [ist], durch Revolution oder Reform' (19). Of course, the question must be asked: 'Veränderung — wohin? Im Namen wovon bin ich auf der Seite der nicht Angepaßten?' (19). The answer given in the novel corresponds entirely to Walter's own stance: 'Das, wogegen sie [Rob and Leni, KB] sind, halte auch ich für nicht menschenwürdig'. This critical stance is complemented by a positive utopia — the attempt in the cooperative to create a different pattern of social existence that is the first step towards a 'auf demokratischem Weg herbeigeführte grundsätzliche Veränderung der Gesellschaft, mit dem Ziel . . . , die Produktionsmittel in die Selbstverwatung der Produzenten zu überführen'.[12] The 'Balladen von der Herbeiführung erträglicher Lebensbedingungen für alle' offer a prognosis of how such change can be brought about by the year 2000. But Otto F. Walter is realist enough to recognise that social reality will not be changed so easily and so this dimension of the book is counterbalanced by a negative utopia that avoids the vision of the future appearing as naïve wishful thinking; this 'besteht darin, daß das faschistoide Potential in der Schweizer Gesellschaft, auch in der Schweizer Gesellschaft, dargestellt wird, das dann tatsächlich in der Machtübernahme durch die Ordnungskräfte kulminiert'.[13] The forces operating against positive

12. *Nach dem Protest*, p. 123.
13. Ibid., p. 123.

change in society are revealed through the 'Kalendergeschichten', which tell of rising unemployment and political discrimination, the 'Blockberichte', which demonstrate the impact on ordinary people of highly conservative media treatment of anything remotely unconventional, and, above all, the growing strength of the ASS. Once a local branch of this organisation is formed, it poses a real threat to the cooperative, culminating in the murderous attack. In the short-term, at least, these negative forces are shown as the stronger, but the determination which is expressed in the final pages, in some way to continue the initiative, keeps alive the hope for change, without its being an unworldly dream ignoring social reality.

The various aspects of the novel revolve around two opposites: at one pole, the desire for, and work towards, a world with a greater content of human dignity; and at the other, a realistic assessment of the latent opposition in society at large to such possible change. Much as Walter identifies with the endeavours of his positive figures, he recognises the literary consequences of the nature of the world as it is: he avoids the dangers of oversimplification inherent in a linear narrative that merely follows through the author's personal position and operates, instead, with possible scenarios, trying to assess how, and according to what determining factors, people are likely to behave in certain situations. Like Wellershoff, Walter is in no way an omniscient narrator, but one who simulates hypothetical situations, with the structure and narrative pattern of the novel reflecting his own uncertainty as to how events would probably develop in the real world. The break with the conventions of the novel tradition, which such a stance involves, is a conscious one: Walter, through Blumer's notes in his sketch-book, asks whether the writer can reject the assumptions of the established novel 'ohne es auch formal zu versuchen?' The montage novel is his attempt 'den Rhythmus *dieser* Jahre hereinzuholen. Operative Montage als Prinzip, das hart geschnittene Blöcke verschiedenartiger Texte assoziativ zu einander in sich steigende, sich ergänzende, sich irritierende Beziehungen setzt' (170). These ideas suggest affinities with a number of other writers, from Döblin through to Heißenbüttel; the closest similarity is, however, with the early Arno Schmidt, in the way in which the component parts are not interwoven to create a kaleidoscopic picture of society, but are, in effect, sustained in parallel throughout, with the one pole thus constantly relativising the other. This is the formal equivalent of the consciously hypothetical nature of Walter's approach and, at the same time, of his determination not to adopt a firm, more or less traditional, authorial stance. Walter's expressed wish 'Co-Autoren ein[zu]beziehen' can be seen to some extent as a remnant of attempts made by writers close to the Student Movement to democratise literature, but his integration of such authors through montage, has nothing of the jokey quality of Chotjewitz's *Die Insel* or Faecke and Vostell's *Postversand-Roman*. The various textual components are designed to force the reader out of a purely contemplative attitude and to release his energies for 'kreatives Lesen':

> Indem ... Brüche, eine Diskontinuität der einzelnen Erzählstränge hergestellt werden, werden Freiräume geschaffen für den Leser. ... Das Erzählen wäre so zu demokratisieren, daß der Leser Vorschläge und Angebote bekommt, die einzelnen Elemente des Buches aufeinander zu beziehen, daß er sie mit eigenen Erfahrungen ergänzen kann, daß er zu einer größeren Bewegungsfreiheit kommt in dem Buch, als wenn er von einem festgelegten Konzept geführt wird (120).

The very formulations used here evoke the spirit of 1968, but this democratic element of the book has a much more important function: by incorporating a range of ideas from different authors, it allows for the widest possible response to a central thematic concern that cannot possibly be dealt with by a single individual and is thus an important part of the novel's realism.

One of Walter's 'co-authors' is, as we have said, Gottfried Keller. The carefully chosen extracts from *Romeo und Julia auf dem Dorfe* (alluded to in the title *Die Verwilderung*) add a historical dimension to the novel's portrayal of present-day personal relationships. While the suicide of Sali and Vrenchen is the ultimate and moving consequence of the obstacles to their love posed by their fathers' mutual loathing, it was portrayed in the newspapers of the day as an affront to established moral values: 'man nehme an, die jungen Leute haben das Schiff entwendet, um darauf ihre verzweifelte und gottverlassene Hochzeit zu halten, abermals ein Zeichen von der um sich greifenden Entsittlichung und Verwilderung der Leidenschaften' (241). By contrasting the deep morality of the young couple's love for each other with their fathers' bitter hatred and the coldness of the public moral code, Keller's novella represents an implicit plea for a change in existing ethical values. In the same way, the tenderness towards each other shown by all the members of 'S' — not just Rob and Leni — contrasts with the aggression shown as inherent in bourgeois society and brings out its lack of human warmth and tolerance. Through the focus on the relationships in the cooperative, Walter, indeed, attempts to go even further. One principle in the constitution of 'S' is that its members do not have the right, 'einen Menschen als seinen Besitz zu betrachten oder zu behandeln'

(164–5), which is applied to all aspects of their life, including the sexual. The triangular relationship between Rob, Leni and Blumer is meant to expose prevailing attitudes as being based on jealousy and narrow-minded concepts of partner as property and to call into question, through the co-existence of this new sort of relationship and that in the Keller novella, 'die bürgerliche Auffassung von der Einmaligkeit des Partners und der damaligen Konstellation, in der zwei Menschen einander treffen'.[14]

The various revolutionary social ideas contained in Blumer's notebook and in the story itself — the alternative ideas on corporate democracy, the family and sexual repression, expressed in the discussions and life style of the members of 'S' — are commented on and essentially supported by selections from theoretical works (Erich Fromm's *Autorität und Familie* and *Haben oder Sein*, Wilhelm Reich's *Der Einbruch der sexuellen Zwangsmoral* and his *Massenpsychologie des Faschismus*, Ernst Bornemann's *Das Patriachat*, Denis de Rougemont's *Liebe und das Abendland* and David Cooper's *Von der Notwendigkeit der Freiheit*). Even the sceptical reader takes such notions and their implicit or explicit criticism of society somewhat more seriously, despite the fact that — as Walter admits in a postscript to the novel — the theory behind them cannot yet to said to be 'wissenschaftlich gesichert'. Through their wider focus on social institutions, the professional witnesses, as they might be regarded, transform the reader's possible view of the cooperative as a dubious isolated phenomenon, so that it is seen much more as the working-out in miniature of long-established critical theories.

A final aspect of the consciously experimental thrust of the book has yet to be considered: the ending. Throughout the novel the author has been anxious to keep the course of events plausible and to maintain a realistic balance between the positive and negative utopian forces at work in it. Even some of the members fail to be convinced that the cooperative is the best way of fulfilling their personal needs and, from the beginning, Blumer, though alert to what he has gained from his younger companions, nevertheless views developments somewhat quizzically: 'War, was sie da ansteuerten, wirklich ein neuer Versuch? Das hatte er doch x-mal erlebt: dieser Elan junger Leute, damals, 68, 70, wie sie sich zu Kommunen zusammentaten' (152–3). His motto is: 'Bleib skeptisch, Blumer'. He does, in fact, leave the 'Huppergrube' for a while and return to his previous life in Zurich in order to evaluate his

14. Ibid., p. 103.

experience in the cooperative; his conclusion is that he has 'tatsächlich einen Zipfel vom Leben entdeckt. Ein ungeheuer gefährdetes Stück des sehr widersprüchlichen Anfangs von Neuem Leben. . . . Mit denen, die den Akt riskieren, will ich jetzt leben und arbeiten' (241). He therefore goes back, but others in their turn decide to leave, seeing 'S' as 'eine Insel für Priviligierte', existing in idyllic circumstances outside an exploitative society, without really challenging it. Their decision is 'Eintritt in eine revolutionäre, eine kommunistische Partei. Und gemeinsame Arbeit, Stadtteilarbeit, Aufklärungsarbeit' (235–6). This tension between positive and negative is maintained up to the end of the novel: the author does put forward an 'unlikely ending', which consists of a convivial party in the 'Huppergrube' with local residents, but this is more than offset by 'das wahrscheinliche Ende' — the far more convincing vicious attack in the name of decency and civil order by the ASS on the 'anarchistischen Vöglerclub', which culminates in arson and the murder of Rob and Leni. The cooperative, in which Blumer has invested so much optimism, is destroyed and the dominance of negative forces, in the form of militant conservatism, seems assured; a glimmer of hope is, however, kept alive by the determination of Blumer and an unknown sympathiser somehow to keep it going.

This sober evaluation by Walter of the aggressively antidemocratic forces hidden beneath the surface of Swiss society was widely received in West Germany as equally valid comment on that state.[15] The Seventies, far from having brought about the changes that might have been expected from a liberal coalition government, had seen the introduction (initially by the ruling SPD in Hamburg) of the 'Radikalenerlaß' and the creation of an atmosphere of political distrust. The witch hunt conducted by the Springer concern against the Left and the intensification of surveillance necessitated by the wave of terrorism induced at times widespread near-hysteria and a suspicion of institutionalised politics among the idealists of 1968: in many cases this paved the way to introspective withdrawal. In this situation it is not surprising that the optimism of the early Autoren-Edition novels seemed particularly misplaced and that the social novel soon came to be dominated by a series of works which, like *Die Verwilderung*, gave a gloomy prognosis of an embattled state that was now widely viewed with disaffection.

The best known example of these novels — Schlöndorff's film version served to complement the media furore caused by its initial appearance — is Böll's *Die verlorene Ehre der Katharina Blum* (1974).

15. Ibid., p. 103.

As in his contentious attack on the over-hasty condemnation of Ulrike Meinhof in the Springer Press, 'Will Ulrike Meinhof Gnade oder freies Geleit?' (*Der Spiegel*, 1972), Böll here endeavours, 'die Eskalation der terroristischen wie der polizeilichen Gewalt zu bremsen und einen gesellschaftlichen Denk- und Lernprozeß über die Frage einzuleiten, "wie Gewalt entstehen und wohin sie führen kann"'.[16] Although, as the narrator ('der Berichterstatter') tells us, the case of Katharina Blum is 'mehr oder weniger fiktiv', its authenticity — underlined by the quasi-documentary style — was immediately obvious to the public at the time; indeed, as Böll wrote somewhat ironically in the preface, 'Ähnlichkeiten mit den Praktiken der "Bild"-Zeitung sind weder beabsichtigt noch zufällig, sondern unvermeidlich'.[17]

Despite the clear polemical intent of this short novel, it once again provides a variation of Böll's archetypal image of woman as Madonna, typified by a mixture of innocence and, behind an apparently prudish façade, genuine sensuality. This familiar figure must then face the restriction of personal freedom through the power of social institutions, here the press and the police; the novel is thus another reworking, perhaps the most intense of all, of Böll's major theme. Böll once described the task of literature as 'die Suche nach einer bewohnbaren Sprache in einem bewohnbaren Land',[18] and *Die verlorene Ehre der Katharina Blum* documents, more than any previous work, how far short the language — and with it the country — falls short of his ideal of habitability: the newspaper reports, amounting to a witch hunt against Katharina, her family and friends, manipulate statements, exaggerate, insinuate and lie, while the language of Police Commissioner Beizmenne constitutes a less public, but semi-official assault on her decency. The appalling treatment of Katharina constitutes the negative utopia of degradation of the individual by authority that is at the heart of this author's work, right up to *Frauen vor Flußlandschaft* (1985), while the central character herself, like so many of Böll's Madonnas, represents the positive utopia in her embodiment of important human attributes threatened by the existing social order.

Central issues in *Die verlorene Ehre der Katharina Blum* are again taken up and varied in Böll's penultimate novel, *Fürsorgliche Belagerung* (1979). The literary treatment of the tension between the indivi-

---

16. Jochen Vogt, 'Heinrich Böll', *KLG*, p. 15.

17. *Die verlorene Ehre der Katharina Blum* (1974), Munich 1976 (dtv), p. 5. All quotations from this edition.

18. Heinrich Böll, *Frankfurter Vorlesungen* (1964), Munich, 1968 (dtv), p. 45.

dual and social institutions in this much criticised novel[19] proceeds from the terrorist threat to Fritz Tolm, the president of the newspaper publisher's association, and to his family. The novel is far more concerned, however, to examine how almost all areas of the family's life are affected by the constant surveillance under which they are forced to live, and to show the introspection induced by this extreme situation and the consequent social isolation — which in some cases results in quite extreme personal revaluation. The actual terrorist threat comes to nothing, but the book reveals the drastic effect on individuals of the necessary countermeasures. All members of the family, even the most conformist (such as Fritz and his daughter Sabine) are changed by the experience into 'Gegner des Systems'.

Although, as critics have put it, Böll yet again 'sich fortschreibt', a striking difference between this novel and its forerunners (even *Die verlorene Ehre der Katharina Blum*) is the total absence of the irony and other forms of humour that generally mark his work. The only plausible interpretation is that this is a response to a sensed deterioration in the political and social climate of the Federal Republic (the external context of the novel is determined by a security situation that corresponds to the time of the 'deutsche Herbst', when Hanns-Martin Schleyer and Jürgen Ponto were kidnapped and murdered). The surveillance of the Tolm family is so strict that Fritz wonders whether 'diese Sicherheit, die keine war, nicht doch zu teuer erkauft [war]' (170–1); the Tolms too have become prisoners and just have to accept 'daß wir in der Sicherheit, vielleicht an der Sicherheit zugrunde gehen' (163). The security net is so tight that normal contact with others is impossible; everything has to be carefully planned, spontaneity is excluded from all aspects of life. Even the lives of people not directly affected are dramatically changed. But even worse than the actual state of siege is the effect of the threat on the mentality of those who, once alerted to the existence of internal and external enemies of the status quo, whip up an atmosphere of hostility to anyone suspected of dissidence. Rolf, Tolm's second son, a former political activist who has forsworn all forms of violence and lives a quiet life in a rural commune, is categorised as a security risk; his brother-in-law Fischer, a thoroughly corrupt person, refuses to have anything to do with him, since Rolf had 'nach November 1974

---

19. Cf. in this connection: Rudolf Augstein, 'Gepolter im Beichtstuhl', *Der Spiegel*, 30.7. 1979, p. 139; Marcel Reich-Ranicki, 'Nette Kapitalisten und nette Terroristen', *Frankfurter Allgemeine Zeitung*, 4.8.1979; Wolfram Schütte, 'Lauter nette Menschen', *Frankfurter Rundschau*, 4.8.1979. All quotations from *Fürsorgliche Belagerung* from the first edition, Cologne, 1979.

noch ein Kind Holger genannt' (46; the reference is to the terrorist Holger Meins). Fischer is prepared to subject critics of society like Rolf 'dem Geschwätz unserer Mitbürger . . . , durch Spitzel, Schnüffler, Berufsverbote' (306). The intensity of public hatred generated against such innocent people is seen in the changed attitude of the rural community to Rolf and his wife Veronika. It becomes known that they had received prison sentences for having set fire to cars during the time of student unrest and they are now so harassed that they are afraid of the villagers setting their house on fire. Even worse and far less explicable is the attack on Veronika's father, who has practised as a doctor for thirty years in a neighbouring village: 'hab nie meine Hilfe verweigert, dreißig Jahre lang und auch nicht in den schlimmen Nachkriegsjahren, als es gefährlich war, nachts auf die Straße zu gehen — und dann schmeißen die dir plötzlich die Scheiben ein, knallen dir dein Arztschild kaputt, beschmieren dir das Haus' (236). Heinrich Schmergen, a friend of Rolf, tells how he was reading a book called *Castros Weg* on the bus on the day when the newspapers were full of the death of the terrorist Bewerloh, when he noticed 'daß alles stumm und feindselig auf ihn, auf das Buch gestarrt hätten, . . . "als würden sie mich jeden Augenblick erwürgen"'. The threat to Tolm has intensified and brought out into the open the constant surveillance normally used, not only against terrorists, but against the activities of a generation critical of society. Rolf complains to Holzpuke, the official in charge of the guard on the Tolms: 'wir kennen unsere Zahl nicht, Sie müßten sie kennen, schauen Sie sich diese Armee, diese Geisterarmee an — mustern Sie sie — lassen sie diese Hunderttausende junge Frauen und Männer und deren Kinder aufmarschieren, wenn auch nur vor Ihrem geistigen Auge, und fragen Sie sich, ob deren Ausbildung, deren mögliche Intelligenz, deren Kraft und Herrlichkeit nur dazu da sein soll, überwacht zu werden' (310). Schmergen's experience on the bus suggests the press's part in implanting a general suspicion of any form of apparent dissidence. This, the central theme of *Katharina Blum*, is an important subplot in *Fürsorgliche Belagerung*. Tolm is shown to be a liberal, decent newspaper proprietor, whereas his rival Zummerling publishes a yellow-press rag dealing in scandal about prominent people. More importantly in this context, Zummerling collaborates with the police in suppressing a letter of vital public interest and in nourishing the hysteria about the supposed threat from the Left.

The other side of the 'Sicherheitsgetue', the siege mentality of social organisations and, it would appear, even normal citizens, is represented in the novel by the motif of 'ringsum Chaos, Auflösung'

— the concern of Fritz, Hubert and Sabine Tolm that, beneath the surface of a society that seems intolerant of fundamental criticism, developments are taking place which represent an even more basic threat to civilised values. The most obvious sign of this tendency is the public aggression shown to Rolf and others, but some aspects are more subtle. One of the various subplots concerns the environmental threat posed by, amongst other things, the lignite industry and the spread of power stations. A more or less 'Green' campaign against such threats is led by Hubert Tolm and apparently financed to some extent by Fritz Tolm's wife Käthe; but it is opposed by an alliance of industry, the unions and the Church that takes scant regard of the interests of workers. We should remember at this point that Böll, in conversation with Heinz Ludwig Arnold, some years earlier described the 'Mechanisierung der Welt' as 'eine Erscheinungsform des Faschismus',[20] and Fritz Tolm, continuing this thinking, becomes increasingly fearful of a drift towards an authoritarian state, in which a combination of tight security and close cooperation between powerful interest groups would put the individual at the mercy of the system, as well as ignoring vital environmental questions.

The other aspect of the 'Chaos, Auflösung' motif is the suggestion of societal decay, particularly in the decadent figures of Bleibl and Fischer. Bleibl, now a successful businessman, is a former SA officer, whose post-war rise is based on money obtained through bank-robbery and murder; he has moreover — this is of great significance in Böll's moral code — been married five times. Fischer's fortune (as owner of a successful chain of boutiques) derives from his exploitation of cheap labour in Eastern Europe and the Far East. His decadence, like that on Bleibl, is further reflected in his private life. During his frequent and lengthy business trips he indulges in a series of sexual adventures, and his marital relations with Sabine are devoid of love or tenderness; sex is degraded to the level of a quick, superficial thrill, indeed, his language to her is that of the driver of fast cars.

As in so many other of Böll's works, such corruption is countered by a system of authentic human values embodied by figures who are essentially outsiders. The central character of the novel, Fritz Tolm, seems to be anything but a nonconformist: although from a modest background, he was put in charge of the 'Blättchen' by the Allied occupiers after the war and his success has recently been crowned by his appointment as chairman of the 'Zeitungsverband'; he lives in

---

20. Heinrich Böll, *Interviews I, 1961–78*, Cologne, 1979, pp. 170–1.

regal style in Schloß Tolmshoven. Despite this, he has always felt a certain schizophrenic attitude ('meine Zweibahnigkeit') towards his business activities: external success means nothing to him and, prior to his recent appointment, he had been so bored with his work as to consider resigning. He has failed in his self-appointed task of using the newspaper to counter the 'Nihilisierung durch den Nazismus'. After the suicide of his friend Kortschede, Tolm admits that his sons 'recht haben': 'mir ist es nicht gelungen, das System zu täuschen, das System hat mich getäuscht' (349). His sympathies lie increasingly with the opposition of the young and, generally, there is considerable affinity between the positive portrayal of the younger generation in the novel and those put forward by Böll himself in a number of interviews during the latter Seventies. For example, Tolm's sons and their friends reject 'Hasch und Stärkeres, Porno und Schlimmeres, auch Besaufen und Ähnliches' (176), just as Böll, in conversation with René Wintzen shortly before the publication of *Fürsorgliche Belagerung*, spoke of the development of ascetic life styles as a necessary part of social reform. The younger generation is seen as embodying high idealism and real human potential while, in contrast, in upper Catholic circles (it is hardly surprising that the Church is here seen as part of the rotten Establishment) 'eine Art Porno-Katholizismus oder Katho-Pornismus' is practised (176).

The youthful opposition, while not without its faults, is shown as offering real potential for social regeneration, unlike the terrorist scene, which represents idealism run amok. The young Tolms have learned from their earlier mistakes — Rolf now rejects every kind of violence, even against property, and Hubert concentrates his energies on lawful campaigning for the environmental lobby — but their former friend Heinrich Bewerloh, once a protégé of Fritz Tolm and a close friend of Sabine, is unwilling to compromise and opts for the most extreme expression of opposition: terrorism. German terrorism is portrayed as a madly aberrant form of specifically middle-class protest — emphasised both by the close relationship between the Bewerloh group and the Tolms and by the 'Nettigkeit' of the two sides — yet it proceeds from concepts that are 'abstrakt und absurd' (as Böll put it in an interview). Nevertheless, the novel implicitly shows a certain fundamental agreement with some of Bewerloh's criticisms. Had he continued a financial career he would have 'mehr Geld verdienen können, als er je würde gebrauchen können'; capitalism is, he declares, a 'wuchernde, wachsende Unermeßlichkeit, die niemand gebrauchen konnte, zu niemandes Nutzen war, sich nur selbst heckte und deckte und beheckte in obszöner Inzucht' (230). To help bring about the victory of their notion of socialism, the terrorists are prepared not only to kill other people ruthlessly, but, if necessary, to sacrifice their own lives. While originating in the same circles as the Tolms, they develop in such a way that they have more in common with present opponents than with former friends: 'they share . . . their cold calculating rationality, which enables them on the one side to accumulate wealth and power or devize total security precautions, on the other to construct booby-traps and ways of penetrating these security precautions'.[21] Here Böll once more expresses his belief that 'nicht Dogmen oder Prinzipien retten die Menschheit vor Verzweiflung — und dem Selbstmord —, sondern Spiel', by which he means the living out of true human qualities.[22] One cluster of such qualities, here set against the coldness of the system and its terrorist opponents, is constituted by the true intimacy of the close private relationship, which he calls the 'Theologie der Zärtlichkeit'.[23] As in so many of Böll's novel and short stories, though, the real strength of his realist portrayal of contemporary society lies in his demonstration of its faults — here the cold rationality of established society (and its enemies), its moral decadence and intolerant rejection of any nonconformist behaviour, such as the rural commune. His countervailing positive utopia, however, is more problematical. A knowledge of the moral indicators seen in Böll's earlier work can certainly be applied here to identify what is to be seen as positive in the relationship of Fritz and Käthe Tolm, and this emerges much more clearly when contrasted with Bleibl's private life. The love-affair between Sabine and her police guard Hendler is, however, very difficult to comprehend. Admittedly her sexual contact with him is very different from the abhorrent coupling with her husband Fischer, but Hendler's marriage has clearly been a good one and the abandonment of his wife seems to trample on the positive values which Böll is advocating. The greatest difficulty lies, however, in Tolm's remarks at Bewerloh's funeral, which have provoked much discussion — 'Daß ein Sozialismus kommen muß, siegen muß . . .' (414). It is undoubtedly significant that he speaks of 'a' socialism (which should presumably be understood as the realisation of a world embodying Böll's set of values), and this contrasts with the far more dogmatic formulation left behind as a suicide message by the distraught Verena Kortschede ('*Der* Sozialismus wird doch siegen'). Even allowing for this distinction, however, Tolm's remark lacks any sort of motivation. In any event, as Böll

21. J.H. Reid, 'Back to the billiards table? — Heinrich Böll's *Fürsorgliche Belagerung*', *Forum for Modern Language Studies*, 1983, p. 130.
22. Böll, *Interviews I*, p. 323.
23. Heinrich Böll and Christian Lindner, 'Drei Tage in März', in *Interviews I*, p. 323.

himself had already noted, problems are inherent in the very use of the word: 'Es ist schwer mit dem Wort Sozialismus in der Bundesrepublik. . . . Ich glaube überhaupt, daß man Worte wie Sozialismus oder Kommunismus ganz neu definieren muß, vielleicht neue Worte dafür finden'.[24] The problems raised by Tolm's words, together with the general reaction to them, confirm this conclusion.

In terms of the narrative technique adopted, *Fürsorgliche Belagerung* marks a departure from its immediate predecessors. Instead of using the first person or a single narrator, Böll reverts here to the polyperspectival approach of his earlier *Wo warst du, Adam?*, *Und sagte kein einziges Wort*, *Haus ohne Hüter* and *Billard um halbzehn*. Narration from twelve points of view (other commentators have come to a slightly different figure) enables Böll to build up a series of layers that add up to a more or less panoramic view of a particular segment of society. He has been reproached for not using 'Rollenprosa'; quite apart from the consideration that this would have been a risky undertaking in the context, such criticism ignores the fact that, in the very lack of linguistic differentiation between the characters, Böll is here underlining one of his major points: the close similarity between people ostensibly representing very different positions. By a mixture of inner monologue, free indirect and direct speech, the author builds up a series of subjective viewpoints, from which we observe external reality. As in real life, its component details only slowly and apparently haphazardly form a recognisable (but by no means complete) jigsaw puzzle. As in other Böll novels, the author makes no attempt to give psychological insight into the behaviour of the various characters, who — quite realistically, since they are by no means intellectuals — tend to react intuitively and to show a certain vagueness in their thinking. Böll has been strongly attacked for the use made by a number of figures of the word 'nett', but a close reading of the novel shows the term to be perfectly understandable and normal: moreover, it is one of several leitmotifs in the work which are anything but a tired use of 'Stereotyp-Kennzeichnungen' to bolster failing narrative powers, as Rudolf Augstein asserted.[25] As always, Böll's realism does not exclude the integration of such leitmotifs and other symbolic elements, spinning with their help and that of '"realistischen" Vokabeln, Haltungen und Reizworten eine Kunstwirklichkeit aus'.[26]

One point of interest in the critical reception of *Fürsorgliche Belage-*

24. Ibid. p. 589.
25. Rudolf Augstein, *Der Spiegel*, 30.7.1979, p. 139.
26. Joachim Kaiser, 'Heinrich Bölls heikle Innen- und Außenwelt', *Süddeutsche Zeitung*, 25–26.8.1979.

rung is the way in which, with almost indecent haste, Böll was accused of disappointing the reader, who was apparently entitled to expect 'das intensivste, umfassendste, "realistischste" Roman-Bild oder Panorama dieser Zeit'.[27] He was, in other words, blamed for failing to achieve exactly what literary criticism, quite correctly, had said was no longer possible in the novel: a more or less total re-creation of reality in the style of the nineteenth century. His realism lies precisely in the way in which this novel evokes a social world that he 'immer nur komplex und widersprüchlich, gleichsam unsauber, dafür allgemein faßlich aus der diffusen Unüberschaubarkeit herausgehoben hat'.[28] Even the polyperspectival presentation of this reality is, as we have said, by no means complete: not only do some characters speak only once, other important figures — Amplanger, Fischer, Breuer, Bewerloh and Kortschede — are given no chance to open their mouths and we have to rely on other characters' reports for information about them. Very important details of the various story lines are not explained; we do not know the extent of Käthe Tolm's involvement in the ecological cause, the contents of the suppressed suicide letter from Kortschede or the reasons behind the conversion of former middle-class terrorists. The book's open-endedness is an appropriate reflection of our necessarily incomplete view of any complex issue (the implicit conclusion of such documentary works as *Missing* and *The Killing of Karen Silkwood*, which aimed precisely to find out 'the truth'). Yet, despite its realistic incompleteness, *Fürsorgliche Belagerung* reveals a great deal about key aspects of an uncomfortable phase of the Federal Republic's history — matters which the average citizen refused to recognise or which were obscured by the wave of public hysteria. By this means, the author demonstrates that 'seine Sache war und ist, unübersichtliche Zustände und das Leben des Menschen in ihnen erzählend deutlicher, wahrnehmbarer zu machen, als sie es von sich aus gewöhnlich sind'.[29]

At a very early stage, Böll had recognised the consequences of public anxiety about terrorism, particularly as whipped up and turned against innocent individuals by unscrupulous sections of the press: later he had personally experienced the results and he was, moreover, the first to write about them. By 1977/8 there was widespread fear amongst the German Left, difficult perhaps to comprehend today, but vividly documented in Luise Rinser's account of what happened to many innocent people during the

27. Schütte, 'Lauter nette Menschen'.
28. Heinrich Vormweg, 'Entlarvende Belagerung', *Merkur*, 34, 1980, pp. 85–6.
29. Ibid., p. 87

hounding of those labelled 'Sympathisanten'.[30] There is, in addition to such testimony, an extensive cultural legacy of the 'deutsche Herbst' — the films *Deutschland im Herbst* and Margaretha von Trotta's *Die bleierne Zeit*, songs like Ina Deter's 'Viele Gräber auf meinem Weg' and Degenhardt's 'Bumser Pacco', and a range of literary responses to the mood of the time. Peter O. Chotjewitz's 'Romanfragment' *Die Herren des Morgengrauens* was the most spectacular victim of the intense suspicion of the Left amongst establishment circles. This work had already been accepted by the editors of the Autoren-Edition but was rejected by Bertelsmann for very dubious reasons without consulting the editors; the Autoren-Edition's protests led to cancellation of its contract with Bertelsmann and Chotjewitz's novel had to apppear in the Rotbuch imprint.

Die Herren des Morgengrauens (1978)[31] is concerned with the emotional effects of proceedings instituted, on apparently questionable legal grounds, against Fritz Buchonia, defence counsel for a leading terrorist. Worse still, an unofficial statement released by the *Bundeskriminalamt* to the media labels him as a terrorist sympathiser. Because of this, he suffers a feeling of intense isolation and is virtually ostracised by the inhabitants of the village where he lives. The office of the State Prosecutor is by no means unsympathetic in all this, but can do nothing against faceless officialdom. Adverse judgements, 'die in einem anderen Land undenkbar waren' (137), as he says, make Buchonia think of escaping to the simple life in Sicily, or even of emigrating to the GDR. At the same time, the novel represents his endeavours to find the appropriate literary expression for his experiences and records his ideas on Kafka's *Der Prozeß*, with which *Die Herren des Morgengrauens* has a number of similarities.

The fragmentary novel is based on Chotjewitz's own experiences: as the publicly funded defence counsel chosen by Andreas Baader he had circulated a letter to his colleagues in the Writer's Union, attempting to draw attention to the living conditions of the terrorists in Stammheim during their hunger strike; an appended statement from the prisoners led to proceedings being instituted against him 'wegen öffentlicher Aufforderung zur Begehung von Straftaten' that were not laid aside until two years later. Despite this background and the closeness of scenes in the novel to actual events, it is in no way a documentary work. The essentially autobiographical material forms the basis of a complicated fictional text narrated in the third

30. Cf. Louise Rinser, *Kriegsspielzeug. Tagebuch 1972–78*, Frankfurt, 1978, pp. 167–72.
31. Berlin, 1978. All quotations from this edition.

person 'mit dem oft verwirrenden In- und Durcheinander von Wirklichkeit und Alptraum' that was, according to Christian Retsch, forced on Chotjewitz 'von der Wirklichkeit und seiner Angst'.[32] This is certainly true as far as the mixture of dream and reality is concerned, but it ignores the Kafka dimension and the reflections on problems of writing, both of which add to the complexity of the work.

Besides the narrator's interpretation of parts of *Der Prozeß*, unambiguous allusions and a large number of direct quotations, two whole chapters are taken almost directly from Kafka's novel. This extensive instrumentalisation is meant to serve Buchonia/ Chotjewitz in highlighting the concrete social forces that have caused his problems. The narrator wonders whether the explanation for Kafka's novel (also) remaining unfinished is that he 'den Widerspruch zwischen den realen Verhältnissen und der metaphysischen Deutung, die er ihnen durch seine literarischen Erfindungen gab, nicht mehr ausgehalten hatte?' As a result he had described 'einen zwar bedrohlichen, aber realen Vorgang' as a 'metaphysisches Ereignis' (133). The logic of this is that, confronted with the path Kafka had taken, Buchonia should be able to see which literary solution is best able to reveal the real causes of his neuroses (and thus finish the novel!), but, in the event, through the form of *Die Herren des Morgengrauens*, the 'Justizapparat [wird] zum Gericht hin dämonisiert und damit die Realität verrätselt'.[33] At times the novel reads like an updated version of the Kafka, complete with the metaphysical presentation of the court, at others the literary game Chotjewitz plays with Kafka (Spot the Reference!) serves further to obscure our view of reality, which ultimately can only be unravelled with the aid of external information. In the event, a relatively conventional story might well have been more realistic, and this would certainly have been so with a quasi-documentary novel like Chotjewitz's earlier *Der dreißigjährige Friede* (1977) or a Wallraff-type reportage — and, interestingly enough, Buchonia himself says in this connection that he tries 'Literatur zu produzieren, wo Klartext erforderlich wäre'. Perhaps the most suitable form of all would have been a montage novel, in which Chotjewitz could have so arranged documentary material and sections from, or comments on, *Der Prozeß*, that he could indeed have hoped to bring out something of the nature of the 'realen sozialen Kräften' that lay behind the confused and confusing events.

32. Review in *Tages-Anzeiger*, Zurich 6.12.1978.
33. W.M. Fues, 'Die Wirklichkeit der Unwirklichkeit. Über Peter O. Chotjewitz' Romanfragment *Die Herren des Morgengrauens*', *Basis 10*, 1980, p. 99.

The advantages of such a novel, putting into practice important parts of the theoretical work of 'Sprachrealismus', are shown in a further novel on terrorism and the surveillance-state, F.C. Delius's *Ein Held der inneren Sicherheit* (1981). A late response to this thematic area, clearly inspired by the kidnapping and murder of Hanns-Martin Schleyer, this book deals ostensibly with the response by the staff of the 'Verband der Menschenführer' to the abduction of their president, Alfred Büttinger, but this outline plot is used by Delius to focus from various perspectives on power and its administrative apparatus. Far from creating a political thriller that concentrates on the central character and his fate, Delius — whose Büttinger is 'eine Modellfigur und kein literarischer Abklatsch' of Schleyer[34] — hypothesises about the possible consequences for such an organisation if one of its leading personalities is kidnapped. It is not the effects of power on innocent but critical figures like Fritz Buchonia that we see, but the way in which it 'sich als ein Magnetfeld aufbaut, dessen Stärke sich an den magnetgeladenen Wörtern ablesen läßt'.[35] The means Delius adopts to analyse the apparatus of power is, therefore, not a more or less convincing reconstruction of events, but an examination of the language of power and of those who wield it.

The novel is narrated primarily from the point of view of Roland Diehl, Büttinger's ghost-writer, in a mixture of the third person, with or without narratorial empathy, perspectivisation and free indirect speech, the latter style particularly highlighting the language of his own thought-processes. A much wider focus is, however, attained by integrating into the total montage the life-histories of his girlfriend Tina and Büttinger, together with the latter's 'full and frank' disclosure of his relationship to National Socialism, 'Nachrichten und Kommentare' on the abduction, further newspaper reports and 'Notizen zu einer Rede'. Whereas Chotjewitz's evocation of the language of power rapidly turned into caricature, with Delius — and this is hardly surprising, in the light of his earlier works, linguistically closely observed, *Wir Unternehmer* (1966) and *Unsere Siemenswelt* (1972) — we find a highly skilled reconstruction of these various language areas, based on his use of texts available to the public.

Apart from the personal response of Diehl to the crisis, a major theme of the novel is the role of former Nazis in the upper echelons of West German public life. Like Schleyer, whose Nazi past had first been the centre of literary attention in Engelmann's *Großes Bundesver-*

34. 'Wie Macht wirkt', *Die Zeit*. 24.4.1981. All quotations from *Ein Held der inneren Sicherheit*, Reinbek, 1981.

35. 'Wie Macht wirkt'.

dienstkreuz, Büttinger had occupied a position of importance in the Third Reich. While he is portrayed in a tribute from the 'Verband der Menschenführer' as 'ein Mann der Freiheit . . . und des Rechts', he is described by a 'Linksaußenblatt' as the embodiment of 'einer Kontinuität, die nicht sein dürfte, wenn der Faschismus als das Verbrechen bewußt wäre, das er war' (142). Büttinger has been clever enough to conceal his career in the SS and when he is exposed is able, undoubtedly with the help of the skilful Diehl, to excuse his past and to relativise the real nature of National Socialism. He now emphasises the 'sozialen Komponente' of the movement, which in the later phases of the Third Reich were, he says, so far forgotten that Nazism turned out to be 'trügerisch'. After the abduction an even thicker veil is drawn over the past; Büttinger, a high official in the Organisation Todt, is now presented by Diehl as having been 'schon damals ein Sozialpolitiker', a 'Diener fürs Gemeinwohl, soweit die Verhältnisse es zuließen' (123). Behind the distortion of historical reality effected by this clever use of language we can detect, if not a continuous system of power unchecked by changes on the political stage, then, at the very least, a self-perpetuating cadre exercising power from the wings.

Whilst astutely formulated public statements serve to protect the image of the kidnap victim and thus of the VM from 'Mißverständnissen', the members of the organisation and, above all, its leading officers recognise that this incident has given them the opportunity 'wie nie zuvor, unsere Position auszubauen' (142), so that the rescue of Büttinger would be a disaster for them. He has to be 'geopfert', come what may, and his death exploited to bolster the sense of need for public order — and thus to consolidate the manipulation of power. Only Diehl, who viewed Büttinger as his 'Beschützer', fails to see this and still hopes for his release. As a social climber who has not long been with the organisation, he has to learn that even the most prominent figure, no matter how important he and the image of him promoted for public consumption may be, is ultimately dispensable if the interests of the whole, the cadre, demand it. If he really wishes 'zu den Siegern zu gehören', he has to come to terms with the fact that his former boss, to whom he feels he owes so much, is now a dead man: 'Es war ihm, als begriffe er etwas. In der Sache Büttinger ist nichts so fehl am Platz wie Mitleidsgefühle, nichts so gefährlich wie ein persönliches Interesse an Büttinger. . . . Und er, der Chefdenker Roland Diehl, hatte das vier fünf Wochen lang nicht kapieren wollen, was sonst alle offenbar wußten' (211). Büttinger's death actually gives him the chance of career advancement, of starting to take decisions himself, instead of merely assisting others to decide. Delius's depressing but by no means implausible thesis is, therefore, that power is not an anonymous, metaphysical force, nor is it exercised by groups of conspiratorial politicians; it is controlled, in reality, by individuals in their capacity as members of an indefinable body of interest groups, for which politics are only the means to their end — ruthless self-interest.

The persuasiveness of *Ein Held der inneren Sicherheit* lies in the precise linguistic analysis of the manifestation of power and in the sober investigation of its nature. The ending offers nothing like the easy solutions of Engelmann's *Großes Bundesverdienstkreuz* — which, though focusing on very much the same subject area, naïvely suggests that the misuse of power can be brought to an end by exposing the opportunism of a few individuals. As in Walter's *Die Verwilderung* and Böll's *Fürsorgliche Belagerung*, the didactic emphasis of Delius's novel is on arousing in the reader a sensitive and critical awareness of how far a social problem may extend, not on the supposedly representative nature of one person's behaviour. (It is worth noting in this context that Delius's later novel, *Adenauerplatz*, 1984, which does concentrate solely on the experiences of a single individual, is far less convincing than its predecessor.) The openness of the literary form would seem to correspond to the position of these writers as politically engaged, but free-floating (in the sense of party politics) intellectuals; conversely, we find that a more clearly defined political position can still lead to the retention of the Socialist-Realist 'Entwicklungsroman', in which the belief in change following from personal conversion is added to the claim to representativeness.

Franz-Josef Degenhardt's *Brandstellen* (1975)[36] is perhaps the clearest example of such a novel. It traces the development of Bruno Kappel, a Hamburg lawyer, a man of the Sixties (whose contemporaries have either made their careers in the State Prosecutor's office or become terrorists) from a dissatisfied, but successful, careerist into an activist in the local politics of his home town where, more or less by accident, he has become involved in a protest campaign. It must be said that the dense intertwining of this main theme with a number of subsidiary plots demonstrates Degenhardt's clear ability to tell a story, and above all, to evoke a locality through local gossip, command of dialect, sketch-like scenes and thumbnail portraits of local characters: these are the skills already known from his songs. In addition, the descriptions of the local campaign to prevent local common land being taken over for Bundeswehr exercises, especially

36. Munich, 1975. All quotations from this edition.

the linguistic precision of the fictional police records, are well done. But the garrulous story-teller cannot resist the temptation to drift away from this potential core into other subplots of questionable relevance, dealing with motor repairs, sexual encounters, an international football match, pub-crawls and Kappel's meeting with a terrorist, a former lover. Even here, the skill in sketching a scene is beyond question, but such episodes add little or nothing to our understanding of the reasons for Kappel's change. The renewed appeal of his home town seems to rest on the sexual appeal of his new lover and on a romantic, completely illusory dream of the simple life: 'Die menschliche Bleibe weit und breit ist ein Tisch unter einer Kastanie auf einem Hof, in dem Kinder spielen und Hühner gackern' (148). The regeneration of his political commitment is even less well motivated. Kappel had admittedly taken part in demonstrations against Springer and against the CRS (in Paris) in 1968, but this activist phase is seen merely as the working out of a childhood dream, and does not, in any case, seem to have lasted for very long. Suddenly, however, this resigned man begins once again to respond spontaneously and romantically. The disturbing actions of the police and border police in breaking up the protest movement, coupled with the local activists' determination, in spite of that, to carry on with their work, bring about his 're-conversion': '"Drüben stehen die Faschisten, drohend am Horizont. Kämpft Genossen". Das war kein Traditional mehr, kein Lied aus vergangener Zeit. Das Lied war wieder aktuell, jetzt nach der ersten Hälfte des Jahres' (314). As an emotional response to the excesses of the state forces that are portrayed this is perhaps understandable, but — bearing in mind the short-lived nature of his earlier activism and his apparently unstable character — hardly a pointer to a long-term politicisation; it is as questionable an ending as that of Timm's *Heißer Sommer*.

Degenhardt's third novel, *Die Mißhandlung* (1979) adapts the form of the 'Entwicklungsroman' in a way that, while not eradicating all the problems, leads to a far more convincing novel.[37] Whilst we witness the transformation of Kappel, but — as in so many such novels — not his subsequent life, *Die Mißhandlung* retrospectively depicts the process leading to the change in Hans Dörner and at the same time presents us with an idea of his life afterwards. Moreover, while the conventional third-person narration in *Brandstellen* underlines the suggestion that Kappel is to be understood as an example, the first-person account by Hans Dörner of his development from a

---

37. Munich, 1979. All quotations from this edition.

conformist opportunist into a critic of society is clearly a personal one, and all the more realistic for that.

Dörner is a social climber. He comes from a modest background and has to take his *Abitur* at night-school, but goes on to study law, to become a judge and to marry the daughter of a respected upper-class, highly conservative senior colleague. He is very skilled 'im geschmeidigen Anpassen', as he puts it, and so makes rapid professional progress. His whole life centres round his career and his — seemingly intact — family life. His pleasant existence is suddenly disturbed by a case involving the ill-treatment of a child. As the case is politically delicate, in the light of a current campaign against forced adoptions in the GDR, Dörner is urged to rule on the matter quickly and without drawing attention to it. For reasons that he himself cannot identify clearly — although the arguments of politically active (left-wing) colleagues and the memory of the cruel incarceration of a Russian youth by his father during the war have played their part — he drags his feet. His indecision is such that a colleague feels he has started to question whether his own interests are the same as those of his father-in-law and his class: such agonising is 'heute ziemlich verbreitet bei der Zwischenschicht-Intelligenz' (129), a colleague tells him. Indeed, Dörner, who would earlier have considered it 'unangemessen, verdächtig, wenn ein Richter da Zusammenhänge herstellen wollte' (6) and also dismissed 'Vereinfacher', comes to envy others a coherent view of the world. His peace of mind is disturbed and his growing conviction that the German legal system is class-biased and by no means free of political influence leads to increasingly unpredictable behaviour, expressed first and foremost in anger, through which — as he can now recognise — he tries to protect himself 'gegen Änderungen, die mir drohten' (247). But whilst his father-in-law sees the eventual change in Dörner as determined by his working-class background, the character himself ascribes it to a much vaguer, humanitarian concern: 'Der Radke-Fall bewegte mich, und diese Bewegung hält an' (5).

Nevertheless, a number of other factors which have apparently influenced Dörner's personal development argue against either interpretation of his conversion into a dedicated activist for human rights who, through his refusal to compromise in the Radke case, ruins his chances of further promotion. His father's imprisonment of the young Russian has, as already mentioned, clearly left behind strong guilt feelings; Dörner's unpredictable angry behaviour can be traced back into childhood; above all, there is the collapse of his family life: all these seem to play important parts in his change.

Indeed, the discovery of his wife's unfaithfulness appears to free him from the constraints of previously sacrosanct obligations and facilitates the release of hitherto suppressed feelings. The achievement of the novel lies in this open-minded exploration of Dörner's radicalisation. Compared with *Brandstellen* this is a far more plausible presentation of the utopia of progressive personal change — here in an apparently highly conformist individual — and if we take note·for a moment of Degenhardt's own didactic aims, it is much more likely to lead to thoughtful reflection by the reader.

In the evaluation of realist novels with an avowedly political intent, such as those of Degenhardt, the category of their usefulness has to be included. If a novel aims at direct political effect, full assessment of it should also consider that intention and, moreover, how the work has been received. In this context, it is interesting to note the vastly differing responses to Degenhardt's novels, ranging from uncritical near-adulation through critical, but positive appreciation, and on to almost instinctive dismissal, with the critical evaluation being directly related to the political position of the reviewer, particularly as reflected in aesthetic matters. Thus, while some — continuing the anti-realist tradition — view any social novel as inherently trivial, others welcome the more popular style and content of his work, precisely because they believe that here is a political author with the same chance as the thriller-writer of reaching a mass audience. The delicacy of balance between the various component parts, when a novel is consciously written with this aim in mind, is shown, we would argue, by the 'Tatsachenromane' of Engelmann and the later novels of Max von der Grün, *Flächenbrand* (1978) and *Die Lawine* (1986), in which the inadequacies in plot, characterisation and language seriously undermine any possible political impact. Degenhardt's novels successfully avoid the worst pitfalls and benefit greatly from the linguistic precision used in the portrayal of particular milieus — the working class in *Zündschnüre* and *Brandstellen*, the legal world in *Die Mißhandlung*. Both the novels examined here succeed in drawing attention to worrying aspects of the law in practice, but *Die Mißhandlung* is ultimately a more convincing work because of the deeper psychological dimension in the characterisation of Dörner and the tighter, generally more satisfactory form. Undoubtedly, though, some would argue that, compared to its successor, precisely the broader canvas of *Brandstellen*, its tenser plot, the love interest and the local colour, are all more likely to appeal to a popular market and, in the process, to spread its political point of view to more readers. Such a counter-position serves, in turn, to make it clear that the evaluation of the reception and possible 'usefulness' of a literary work is a thorny problem and one which certainly goes beyond the scope of our enquiry.

The demand for literature with direct political effect is also central to discussions in the Seventies that aimed at producing a new working-class literature. The authors of Gruppe 61 in no way wrote 'als Arbeiter für Arbeiter', but, as Fritz Hüser put it, wanted 'einen Beitrag leisten zur literarischen Gestaltung unserer von Technik und "Wohlstand" beherrschten Gegenwart'; such works were, it was emphasised, to be assessed strictly according to aesthetic criteria. The new Werkkreis Literatur der Arbeitswelt, however, defined the purpose of literary activity 'nicht von den Erfordernissen der Literatur her, sondern aus den Erfordernissen der Arbeiterbewegung'.[38] The products of the Werkkreis 'wenden sich vor allem an die Werktätigen',[39] in an effort to help, 'die gesellschaftlichen Verhältnisse im Interesse der Arbeitenden zu verändern';[40] literature is understood very much as a means to a political end. It is impossible to assess adequately the 'effectiveness' of the range of publications by the Werkkreis, but, even within the context of the so-called 'Literaturbetrieb', the success of the Fischer-Bücherei series is impressive: by 1977, Helmut Creutz's 'Betriebstagebuch' *Gehen oder kaputtgehen* (1973) had reached sales of 35,000, Josef Ipper's *Der Kanthaken* (1974) 15,000, Margot Schroeder's *Ich stehe meine Frau* (1975) 23,500 and Hermann Spix's *Elephteria oder die Reise ins Paradies* (1975) 13,000. The sales figures of these novels, which compare most favourably with those of 'bourgeois' novels, show that the Werkkreis, for all its programmatic statements, has become part of the wider literary scene; debates within the organisation have, indeed, had their influence outside it and this is particularly true in the case of the vigorous discussions about realism in the early Seventies.

The major stimulus to the foundation of the Werkkreis was the irresoluble tension in Gruppe 61 between the activists, who saw 'Arbeiterliteratur' as one of several possible means of political influence, and those who maintained that literary criteria alone should be the determining factor. The general politicisation of literary discussion in the late Sixties and the concomitant criticism of established literary forms as bourgeois and, therefore, incapable of contributing to social change also played their part here. As a result, the initial debates within the Werkkreis were, dominated by

38. Erasmus Schöfer, 'Rede zur Eröffnung des Werkkreises 1972' in *Realistisch schreiben*, Erkenswick, 1972, p. 26.

39. 'Programm des Werkkreises'.

40. Ulla Hahn and Uwe Naumann, 'Romane mit Gebrauchswert', *Basis 8*, 1978, pp. 155–6.

those who saw documentary literature, exemplified in Günter Wall-raff's reportages, as representing the only possible literary path in keeping with the organisation's political aims. Very soon, though, leading theoreticians of the Werkkreis, like Erasmus Schöfer, were forced to complain of a 'Trend zur Literarisierung' in the first publications, which were dominated by short stories, satirical texts and poems. In the opinion of younger members who had joined the Werkkreis after the collapse of the Student Movement, such agitatory texts as were produced did not, in any case, have their intended effect, but simply preached to the converted. These members, familiar with the 'Rote-Eine-Mark' series of the 'Bund proletarisch-revolutionärer Schriftsteller' and with the 'Expressionismusdebatte' of the Thirties, at this point advocated the virtues of the novel with mass appeal. At the Werkkreis conference of 1972, dealing with the topic 'Realistisch schreiben', it became clear that there was the very real danger of a split between a Brechtian and a Lukácsian position within the organisation, with one group stressing the need to accord 'dem realistischen Schreiben Weite und Vielfalt' and the other claiming that realist literature should aim to reproduce 'gesellschaftliche Wirklichkeit nachvollziehbar, d.h. verbindlich'.[41] In the event the threat of polarisation was not fulfilled, and the novels subsequently produced from within the Werkkreis tend to demonstrate a fruitful synthesis between the two positions: the re-creation of external reality frequently breaks new ground and is, as such, highly informative, but writers also have considerable success in avoiding the simplifications of the Socialist-Realist 'Entwicklungsroman' and show instead considerable formal flexibility. A good example of this blend is given by *Ich stehe meine Frau*.[42]

Margot Schroeder's novel is a first-person account of a phase in the life of Charlie Bieber, who is housewife, mother of two children, cashier in a supermarket and union representative, although far from active in union affairs. The external framework of the novel is provided by her reaction to a letter from the owner of her block of flats to all the residents, complaining that children have spoiled the lawn; because of this, she determines to get a decent play-area constructed. She enlists the help of neighbours and, when the owner refuses to cooperate, mounts a public campaign. As Charlie herself comes to realise, however, the letter was merely 'der letzte Anstoß' to her rebellion against a number of irritants in her life — the cramped flat, the frustrations at work, the double burden of being an

---

41. *Realistisch schreiben*, pp. 62, 88–9.
42. Frankfurt, 1975. All quotations from this edition.

'Auch-Mutter' and the constrictions of marriage, particularly the role of domestic servant and sex object that it imposes on her; this has led, understandably enough, to the book being received as an important feminist text. The novel is, in effect, Charlie's recollections of a period in the life of a woman wanting to be 'was wert sein', in which she attempts for the first time to be 'wie ich sein möchte, nicht wie ich bin' (27). The process of self-assessment on which she embarks is reflected in the composition of the novel, which is made up of stream-of-consciousness passages, monologues and remembered discussions between Charlie and others; through these elements we gain a vivid impression of a lively, articulate woman of real character who is concerned about the quality of her life. The problems that beset her are, however, by no means peculiar to Charlie: the conversations with her neighbours that the campaign helps to bring about demonstrate that her situation has much in common with the lot of other women. This, the new growth of awareness that what had seemed purely personal problems are part of a collective burden, is an important dimension of the novel. There is, however, no development of a committed collective leader here; instead, in a way reminiscent of *Berlin Alexanderplatz*, the need for interaction between the individual and the collective is counterbalanced by a tension inherent in that relationship which prevents any easy solution. Charlie certainly sees the advantages of corporate activity, but in practice it arouses great emotional problems in her — for example, she feels envious if others take on positions of responsibility. She is also honest enough to see that her energetic involvement in the campaign is more the result of existential need than any sense of political conviction. If she is not the pivotal figure of activity she becomes restless; as she herself can see, her emotional make-up requires the constant onrush of a 'Dauerinitiative'. These problems lead to excessive drinking and a situation of, as she puts it, near emotional bankruptcy; she is, however, able to pull herself together and determines to cut down on alcohol. The ending of the novel tells us nothing about the course of the public campaign for a children's playground, offers no immediate solutions to Charlie's personal problems or any indication as to the path her future life might take, but she is left with a much clearer sense of her identity and emotional needs than before.

Margot Schroeder has been criticised for her use in this novel of first-person narration, which, it is said, gives only a shadowy impression of other characters. While it is inevitable, given the narratorial perspective, that these do not acquire the depth of focus that marks the portrayal of the central figure, this criticism ignores the fact that the astute Charlie gives us very vivid thumbnail sketches of her neighbours Frau Ludwig and Frau Conrad, particularly in the way that she captures the quality of their speech in a few sentences, and that the relatively vague image of Werner, her husband, is an accurate reflection of the lack of communication and alienation that mark their relationship. More serious is the charge that Margot Schroeder shows 'wie bestimmte gesamtgesellschaftliche Zusammenhänge, vermittelt über soziale Verhältnisse der Hauptfigur, sich auf die psychische Situation und das Verhalten des Individuums auswirken', with social reality being used as 'bloßer Anreger seelischer Erlebnisse' (Brecht, KB).[43] Such criticism, based as it is on an inflexible reading of Brechtian theory, nevertheless ignores the fact that the concentration on Charlie and the highly personal narrative perspective lead to a penetrating analysis of the interaction between the individual psyche and external reality: moreover, this style enables us to follow closely the realistic portrayal of the gradual emergence of Charlie's ability to view herself and society with critical insight. The plausibility of the novel stems from the fact that the experience and insights gained never go beyond those of a woman like Charlie, who can only react to what she and others around her actually undergo; no more than any other modern individual, she cannot provide an account of her life which will demonstrate the 'gesamten sozialen Komplex', which Brecht once described as the task of realism. The weakness of novels such as *Heißer Sommer* and *Brandstellen* lies in their implicit claim to meet this impossible demand; the persuasiveness of *Ich stehe meine Frau*, on the other hand, lies in its modest concentration on an educational process set in motion by personal experience, individual suffering and contact with others and which, in turn, confronts the reader with human problems in a particular social context.

While *Ich stehe meine Frau* is the successful transformation of what is essentially autobiographical material, the other important novel from the Werkkreis represents another key aspect of writing within the organisation: Hermann Spix's *Elephteria oder die Reise ins Paradies*[44] was the first novel to fulfil the programmatic demand that works should be planned and written within the local literary workshop. It was, moreover, written in collaboration with union colleagues and some of those involved in the real events on which the novel is based, and thus exemplifies the determination within the Werkkreis to collectivise literary production. It also shows the folly of the argu-

43. Hahn and Naumann, 'Romane mit Gebrauchswert', pp. 166–8.
44. Frankfurt, 1975. All quotations from this edition.

ments as to whether documentary or fictional writing was the most appropriate choice for Werkkreis authors: the strike in Pierburg led to three different literary treatments of it — a full documentation, essentially for internal use, a reportage (which was published in the volume *Dieser Betrieb wird bestreikt*, 1974) aimed at a wider public, and *Elephteria*. The documentation was intended to give 'ein weitaus zusammenfassenderes Bild der komplexen Zusammenhänge' than the other two, according to Werkkreis theoretician Peter Fischbach,[45] but its length and complexity were clearly such as to deny it broad interest. The reportage is the compromise between the documentation and the novel, but also appealed mainly to the politically committed. However, the novel, which also has a large documentary dimension, but which concentrates its attention on the portrayal of human problems stemming from the working conditions in the plant, quickly aroused wide public attention.

While *Ich stehe meine Frau* demonstrates the hesitant beginning of awareness as to the wider social context of apparently merely individual problems, *Elephteria* is an outright operative text deliberately using a particular case study to induce further collective political action. The major criticism levelled at Spix — that the psychological portrayal of his heroine is far from adequate — fails to recognise the function of the novel. Elephteria, as the central character, is a sort of literary litmus paper, whose reactions are more or less representative of her fellow-workers. It should be conceded that, in the first part of the novel, Spix does not seem to have realised fully the persuasive force she can exert, and the focus is blurred somewhat by the completely irrelevant sex scenes between Elephteria and her husband. Later, however, details of their private life are reduced to the anecdotal, with the result that her representative public existence is shown in greater detail. It was perhaps to some extent inevitable that the choice of a non-German female worker as the central figure should bring the danger of wandering off the main point into other, though in themselves important, issues: on the other hand, it is the very focus on a person like Elephteria that enables Spix so neatly to avoid the risk of clichéd character development. Just as the figure of Étienne Lantier in *Germinal* enabled Zola to portray life and working conditions in Montsou, as well as the strike, with the vividness born of the outsider's sensitivity to the new, so here the persuasiveness of the novel lies to a considerable extent in Spix's ability, through the character of Elephteria, to

45. Peter Fischbach and Maria Meyer-Puschner, 'Für eine Literatur der Arbeiterklasse' in Manfred Brauneck (ed.), *Der deutsche Roman im zwanzigsten Jahrhundert*, vol. 2, Bamberg, 1976, p. 319.

provide the detailed information (so necessary for the uninformed reader) in a way arising naturally from the text. The sensitivity of the central figure enables him to expand on various themes — such as the housing shortage, the exploitation of foreign workers, particularly women, the prejudice against foreigners, even in the union, the role of shop stewards and trades union, language problems and the impact of work on leisure time — without these intruding on, or digressing from, the main story.

The vividness of the more or less conventionally narrated parts of the novel derives from the blend of direct, indirect and free indirect speech and the almost filmic series of individual episodes making up the narrative. These elements are then interwoven with the documentary material — including factory regulations, wage agreements, flysheets put out by the strikers, announcements by management and union representatives and evidence of the distorted or tendentious reports by press and police (the real names of firms, newspapers etc. being given throughout), which gives the narrative a considerable degree of authenticity. The use of the montage technique serves at every moment to place individual experience in the context of empirical research of the situation, to blend the subjective with the objective and, at the same time, to allow the reader *post hoc* to assess the advisability of individual and corporate action at the time. In this sense *Elephteria* has, apparently, been found to be most useful in trade union courses and therefore was republished in 1984.

The strength of the Werkkreis novels is that, instead of attempting to portray social totality, they proceed from the assumption that the contemporary individual subject can no longer hope to come to awareness of the full nature of external reality through personal experience or contact with others. In their writing practice, therefore, these novelists have implicitly rejected Lukács's stance in the 'Expressionismusdebatte', which seemed to have considerable support in the initial discussions within the Werkkreis. In the Thirties, the disputants on both sides had an understandably simple view of the world as one threatened by National Socialism and their aesthetic ideas were exclusively addressed to the need to triumph over the arch-enemy. In the late Sixties the political situation seemed to many naïve enthusiasts to be equally straightforward, so that they turned uncritically to the rediscovered debate on Expressionism as providing the magic key to contemporary realist writing. The attempts to emulate BPRS novels or to put Lukács's theory into practice (e.g. in the early novels of the Autoren-Edition) failed to take account of the inherent strength of an increasingly multinational capitalist system. Much more, these writers ignored those features of present-day capitalism directly affecting political realism: the increasing isolation of the individual within a political reality that essentially exists in a realm outside his awareness; the influence of the mass media in determining what he might consider as his knowledge of the political sphere; and, immediately linked with that, the role of public language in obfuscating reality. Moreover, the post-war political world is far removed from that of the Thirties and the era of fascism, while the factors determining the reception of literary works have also changed greatly. The bulk of the ideas generated within the 'Expressionismusdebatte' were a response to an exceptional historical situation and, as such, are by and large irrelevant today; instead the realist writer has to take note of Brecht's cautionary words: 'Es verändert sich die Wirklichkeit; um sie darzustellen, muß die Darstellungsart sich ändern'.[46] This view has, unfortunately, rather been lost sight of by those who rather uncritically advance Brechtian ideas on realism. The flexibility inherent in his position allows for a modern reinterpretation of many of his thoughts, but a number of his major points are highly questionable today. In particular, his demand that realist writing must concern itself with the exposure of the 'gesamtgesellschaftlichen Kausalkomplexes', with the aim of advancing the possibility 'einer Lösung aller gesellschaftlichen Probleme' is realisable in neither East nor West. The political aim of the Werkkreis is undoubtedly, like Brecht's, the transformation of society 'im Interesse aller Werktätigen' (i.e. some form of humanitarian socialism), and its consciously anti-capitalist literature does seek to expose social injustice and to demonstrate the need for change in society, but at all times it reflects an awareness of the problems concerning modern realism. No naïve hope of immediate and radical change is put forward, attention is instead concentrated on negative utopias, in the sense of demonstrating just how far aspects of contemporary society fall short of a humanitarian ideal. The limited perspective of the Werkkreis novels, with their focus on individual experience of specific social problems — such as inadequate working conditions, redundancy threats, housing shortages and prejudice against minorities — enables them to produce highly readable works that can inform both members of the same social group and sympathetic outsiders and thus help, to the extent that any literature can, in creating wider critical awareness.

The didactic novel, meant to draw attention through literature to working-class problems, is by no means peculiar to the Werkkreis in

46. Bertolt Brecht, *Über Realismus (1937–39)*, Leipzig, 1968, p. 124.

the Seventies. The increased literary exploration of the world of labour — previously neglected in West German literature — particularly through the reworking of personal experiences or researched material by such novelists as Chotjewitz, Ingeborg Drewitz, Gerd Fuchs, Karin Struck, Michael Scharang and others, certainly seems to owe something to the influence of the 'Sprachrealisten'. However, it also demonstrates the wider impact of Werkkreis ideas. The fourth novel of Max von der Grün, co-founder of Gruppe 61, seems to have benefitted considerably from this influence. *Stellenweise Glatteis* (1973), based on the author's careful research, lacks the clichéd metaphorical portrayal of working conditions that marred his earlier work (*Männer in zweifacher Nacht*, 1959, *Irrlicht und Feuer*, 1963 and *Zwei Briefe an Pospischiel*, 1968). The discovery of listening devices in a firm's vehicles leads to tension and, finally, strike action; but another result is to reveal the compromised position of the union, which is ready to extend its holdings by taking over the firm and is, therefore merely irritated by its members' acts. Events are unwittingly set in motion by Karl Maiwald, through whose eyes the reader views events, and whose personal development runs parallel, to some extent, to the increasing tension in the firm. Previously he wanted nothing more than '[sich] um nichts kümmern . . . und in Ruhe gelassen werden', but is now alerted to workplace practices affecting him directly. He soon realises that he can achieve nothing as a loner and that success is more likely through collective action, yet, at the end of the novel, he is still far from a political activist, remaining uncertain and confused as to how to act. The realism of the novel consists as much in the depiction of his inability to draw appropriate conclusions from the situation presented by the narrator, as in the slow building up of a body of information that, true to real life, remains an unfinished jigsaw.

The demonstration, as in *Stellenweise Glatteis*, of the process — even though incomplete — of an individual's growing awareness as to the objective nature of his position, with the intention of persuading the reader along a parallel path of enlightenment and, thus, to political engagement, is one of the basic structuring principles of political realist writing. Yet, if such an example is to be realistic, it must take due account of the obstacles already mentioned to growth in political insight; and there is no doubt that, for the working class, language limitations particularly bedevil self-orientation. Michael Scharang, whose earliest literary work (*Verfahren eines Verfahrens*, 1969) is part of that complex known as 'Sprachrealismus', has made this problem the central theme of his work. The eponymous central figure of Scharang's novel *Charly Traktor* (1973)[47] is as politically naïve as von der Grün's Maiwald, but is considerably more disadvantaged in his efforts to maintain some degree of human dignity at his place of work by his inability to express himself adequately. He instinctively resents the authority of his employer, but, since he cannot put his frustrations into words, this frequently comes out in the form of angry outbursts. Those parts of the novel narrated by Charly himself, so very reminiscent of Scharang's 'O-Ton' radio plays, through their sharp contrast with the more dispassionate and articulate sections narrated by an authorial voice, testify to these difficulties. On one level the novel is yet another story of the growth of individual political awareness, but this is seen at all points as being hampered by Charly's linguistic and conceptual problems. He slowly comes to realise that the working conditions in his factory are no worse than those elsewhere, but his first, scarcely voluntary, attempt to represent grievances to the management on behalf of the workers is a disaster: he cannot cope with questions put to him, is humiliated, and angrily vents his frustration on the time-clock and the rack of clocking-in cards. His former girlfriend considers Charly, the 'Tölpel vom Land' to be too stupid, 'mit den politischen Möglichkeiten, die sich geboten haben, etwas an[zu]fangen' (120), but the sympathetic narrator, always anxious to put Charly's point of view, sees his real problem as lying in his isolation from any political organisation that might help him. Charly eventually comes into contact with a friendly shop-steward, who starts on his political education. He is no longer on his own: 'Wenn der Kollege es nicht weiß, wird er jemand wissen, an den ich mich wenden kann' (139). There is no dramatic improvement in working conditions, Charly has not become a dedicated activist, but he feels he has made a start at understanding something of his position and of acquiring the language necessary to this understanding.

Scharang's message — of the need to educate the working class to a point where they can begin to understand their social situation and the need for group action, if this is to be improved — is also that of August Kühn's family chronicle, *Zeit zum Aufstehn* (1975), intended, at the same time, as a sort of history book for workers.[48] It provides a vivid survey of political and social history in Germany over the last hundred years through the annals of the Kühn-Zwing family from their move to Munich in the latter part of the nineteenth century up to the present. The more or less chronological family history, based

47. Michael Scharang, *Charly Traktor*, Darmstadt & Neuwied, 1973. All quotations from this edition.
48. Frankfurt, 1976 (Büchergilde Gutenberg). All quotations from this edition.

on oral traditions and a whole range of documentary material from local Munich archives, is intercut with episodes from the life of the present family in the Seventies, which serve to bring out the way in which, even in such a relatively short time, the wheel of history has kept on turning. The everyday problems of today's Zwing family are shown as continuing those of their forebears, while they expose as myth the notion that modern society is marked by constant social improvement for all; the life of the family, as far as living standards, unemployment and housing are concerned, constitutes an eternal recurrence of the same social disadvantages. But the authorial voice is also anxious to stress 'daß jede Generation dieser Arbeiterfamilien ihre eigenen, schmerzlichen Erfahrungen machen mußte', that little helpful information is passed on from one generation to the next, 'weil die Väter und Mütter abends zu müde sind, um mit den Kindern über das zu sprechen, was die Lehrer in der Schule nicht wissen können' (11). He asserts that the official history of Germany draws a veil over the social history of the working class and is thus instrumental in bringing about its disastrous lack of collective consciousness. The novel is conceived, then, as a graphic alternative chronicle of the last hundred years, intended to help create a critical awareness, hitherto lacking, among a working-class readership; it is, yet again, impossible to assess whether it had any such success, but the large imprint of the novel in the Büchergilde Gutenberg could well be seen as pointing in this direction.

From the structure adopted in *Zeit zum Aufstehn*, it is clear that Kühn is concerned to counter any nostalgic tendency in his readers to distort the view of the past through selective memory, triggered off by his account. In the Seventies it was widely held that this understandable human inclination had been intensified by the high level of general prosperity for the West German workforce since the Fifties, leading to amnesia, as far as a historical awareness of the working-class movement was concerned, and 'false consciousness'. The experiences described in Peter Schneider's *Lenz* — the shattering of his hero's naïve belief in an uncomplicated sense of solidarity between himself and the workers — are typical of many such in the late Sixties and were seen as clear evidence of the lack of political consciousness amongst the West German working class. The conclusions drawn by the activists of the Seventies were that the precondition for any attempt to involve the mass of workers in the democratisation and general improvement of working and living conditions was an education in the social history of modern industrial society. By this means, members of the working class would be enabled to take a critical view of their own experiences and their

145

family's before them, to be concerned with their own objective interests and thus to become politically aware.

This didactic purpose lies, ultimately, behind all the working-class novels examined; in the case of Kühn's *Zeit zum Aufstehn* and Hans Dieter Baroth's first novel, *Aber es waren schöne Zeiten* (1978), it stands centre-stage.[49] In this highly autobiographical work, the narrator — like Baroth, a working-class child who becomes a professional writer — confronts himself with his own past, in order to show those he left behind how life really was and is in such an environment — anything but 'schöne Zeiten'. He feels that he has now learned 'seinen Standpunkt [zu] verteidigen und Ansprüche [zu] begründen' (297) and uses his advantages to write about 'seine Klasse und eine Zeit' (the post-war period), in order to counter what he sees as a tendentious historical picture put over by the educational system. In school 'wurden diejenigen ausgebildet und vorprogrammiert, die später einige Schritte weiter auf der Zeche ihr Brot verdienen mußten' (65), rather than their being educated as such. Their choice of work was 'Ausweglosigkeit'. Economically and unsentimentally, Baroth evokes a graphic picture of the harsh life in a mining community — the shortage of food, the poor housing conditions, the constant threat of accidents to loved ones, the gradual wearing down of people and their general degradation. He does not forget the joys of childhood and other pleasurable moments in such a life, but the overall impression that emerges is of how the strain imposed by the working and living conditions takes its toll on the quality of human relationships, which are bitter, even brutal. In many respects, the picture has changed little since *Germinal*, but the anecdotal form of the novel, with its lack of pathos or dramatic highlights is reminiscent of Turek's *Ein Prolet erzählt*, and Baroth, like Turek, is here consciously attempting to write an un- or anti-bourgeois novel. While the conventional form concentrates its attention on the 'besonderen Menschen', 'damit jeder unten glauben kann, als einzelner Mensch könne er es schaffen, auch oben zu sein' (298), *Aber es waren schöne Zeiten* describes the everyday life of ordinary people for the 'Mann am Straßenrand'.

Baroth's second novel, *Streuselkuchen in Ickern* (1980) is to some extent a continuation of this story, with the focus moving on to the relative prosperity of the Fifties and Sixties. The misery of the immediate post-war period has given way to a life of dissatisfaction, with the dream of making money and the craving for new possessions having so enslaved people that they now seem incapable of

---

49. *Aber es waren schöne Zeiten*, Cologne, 1978. All quotations from this edition.

enjoying anything. Socialisation through the school, the family and the community has produced spiritual cripples, incapable of even the modest happiness that the improvement in their material standard of living would seem to guarantee. Even family life, which once offered a degree of consolation for life's troubles, is now portrayed as a depressing cohabitation devoid of sense and human warmth: the petrification of personal relationships seen in his first book has here intensified considerably. Work offers no satisfaction at all and, although increasing leisure time offers the possibility of people spending more time together, there is no sign of this leading to group reflection on their collective position, still less political activity; conversation, once so lively despite miserable conditions, is now reduced to empty chatter. The need for a programme of political education, in which literature can play its part, as well as the necessity of training workers to make productive use of increased leisure, emerge clearly from this chilling picture of the dark side of modern industrial society.

In the context of this analysis of the overtly didactic novels of recent West German political realism there remains the question of the relevance here of Peter Weiss's *Die Ästhetik des Widerstands*, often seen as the epitome of the modern political realist novel. We, however, view this monumental work as essentially unrealistic, and Peter Weiss himself stressed the need he felt in writing the novel 'die Phantasie auf dem Boden der Wirklichkeit zu errichten, der Erfindung jede nur irgendmögliche Realität zu geben . . .'.[50] Despite the realist framework and the realist nature of whole sections of the book, this statement makes it clear that the central 'Wunschautobiographie', as it has been called, of the first-person narrator is essentially a device that enables Weiss to explore his real theme. The portrayal of the narrator himself is, in any case, anything but realistic: 'Wenn es eine Lebensgeschichte gäbe wie die des Ich-Erzählers . . . wäre sie ein existenziell konkretisierender permanenter Dialog mit dem Weltgeist in diesem Jahrhundert gewesen, eine individuelle Verwirklichung der geistig-politischen Hauptfragen der Epoche'.[51] The novel is, ultimately, not concerned with the development of an individual (interesting though that is in the context of Weiss's recurrent treatment of problems of identity), but represents a massive attempt to work out 'eine kämpferische Ästhetik' (Weiss). His aim is certainly similar to that of a number of the authors examined in this chapter, but his methodological

50. Peter Weiss. *Notizbücher 1971–80*, 2 vols., Frankfurt, 1981, p. 701.
51. Heinrich Vormweg, 'Peter Weiss', *KLG*, p. 2. Cf. further in this connection Vormweg's *Peter Weiss*, Munich, 1981 (Autorenbücher).

premises are quite different and his essentially pessimistic conclusion (in the third volume) as to the possible influence of culture on the course of politics is in marked contrast to the inherent optimism of these didactic novels. *Die Ästhetik des Widerstands* is a major literary achievement and, at the same time, the culmination of Weiss's literary oeuvre, but is irrelevant for this analysis, in that it is, as Heinrich Vormweg has put it, 'ein Roman von provozierender Irrealität'.

In examining the novels of the Werkkreis Literatur der Arbeitswelt and of Franz Josef Degenhardt we were several times confronted with the question of their 'usefulness'. To some extent, any political realist work, since it is written with the intention of influencing the reader and changing his political consciousness, raises questions about its reception and possible impact. The novels examined in the latter part of this chapter, as well as the early Autoren-Edition books, may well have had an informative or solidarising function amongst left-wing readers and even liberal sympathisers — a limited but perfectly legitimate role for political realism. It is, however, most unlikely that they had any wider impact. Those novels by Böll, Walter and Delius which we have evaluated particularly positively — and to which we should perhaps add the markedly similar documentary novels of Kluge and Franke and Uwe Timm's historical novel, *Morenga* (cf. Chapter 7) — are anything but popular ('volkstümlich' would be Brecht's term) in concept. Moreover, their complex form, so close to that of 'Sprachrealismus', would render any broadly based impact impossible. Given this, and bearing in mind the operative intent of political realism, Brecht's stress on the need to develop forms of writing which retained the utopian element of the desire for social and political change, but which were 'den breiten Massen verständlich', had a certain logic. Nevertheless, it is doubtful whether, even if those authors (Timm, Engelmann and Degenhardt, in particular) influenced by Brechtian thinking had been able to avoid the major weaknesses of their avowedly 'popular' novels, any literary work can achieve the wide political impact needed here. The sad conclusion of the final volume of Weiss's *Die Ästhetik des Widerstands* would seem to be that high culture, being ultimately concerned with the visionary and the utopian, can have no direct influence on political events,[52] and this is all the more likely to be the case in the modern era of advanced information technology and media industries. It is clear that no literary work today can attain the mass impact of *Holocaust* or *Heimat*, from which

---

52. Cf. *Die Ästhetik des Widerstands*, 3. Bd. II. Teil, Frankfurt, 1981, p. 187.

we should perhaps conclude that modern popular political realism could only be achieved in a television series. If this is so, we then have to ask what possible role is left for the political realist novel of quality. If the writer does want to intervene directly in political events of the day — to comment on the Flick affair or on the dangers of the arms race — then he is certainly able to use his status as respected writer and intellectual to gain special attention for his views; he has, indeed — as Walter Jens put it over twenty years ago — 'keine andere Wahl, als sich, auf moralische Integrität und artistische Meisterschaft pochend, *unmittelbar*, mit Hilfe von Manifesten und Pamphleten, Gehör zu verschaffen'.[53] In his literary work, on the other hand, he can only hope, through his analytical treatment of social concerns, to draw attention to what he sees as the need for change in the existing social order and thus contribute to a more broadly based process of general political education that will, at best, be long drawn out.

53. Walter Jens, *Literatur und Politik*, Pfullingen, 1963, p. 17.

7

The Beginnings of a New Historical Novel

The politicisation of the Sixties led to a new critical awareness that questioned not only established literary forms and traditional literary history, but — since they were bourgeois and, as such, highly tendentious — all historical disciplines. The young generation of literary and social historians began to turn its attention to the exploration of hitherto neglected subject areas: one particular concern was to supplement existing historical analyses in an attempt to understand more fully, through examination of the failure of democratic movements, the origins of the German state and, hence, the reasons for the lack of a strong German tradition of democracy. From the end of the Sixties onwards, a large number of dissertations and monographs were published on aspects of the revolutions of 1848–9 and of 1918–19; other common new themes were the industrialisation and urbanisation of the German state, with particular attention being paid to the development of a modern capitalist economy and of colonialism (and we may note here the continuation of interest in the Third World). Another major focal point of analysis was the rise and triumph of National Socialism in Germany and of fascism in general. A survey of publications in the first half of the Seventies, in particular, clearly indicates how widespread was this redefinition of the historical base over a range of disciplines. Some indication of the drastic shift in the understanding of *Germanistik* about that time, is given by the change in the title of Ullrich Krause's dissertation (in Timm's *Heißer Sommer*): he abandons his work on Hölderlin's odes and chooses as his new theme 'Die Arbeiterliteratur der zwanziger Jahre im Spiegel der Kritik'.

Krause's change of title indicates how a new awareness of earlier socialist literature had emerged within the area of literary scholarship. Whole bodies of theoretical debate, forgotten texts from the nineteenth century and, above all, writings from the Twenties were republished, and this renaissance certainly played its part in bringing about the large amount of political realism in the early Seventies. The new sense of the inadequacy of established historical perspectives also led to writers, in fiction and non-fiction, turning increasingly to historical topics. One indication of this is offered by Bernt Engelmann's polemical quasi-documentary novels *Großes Bundesverdienstkreuz* and *Die Laufmasche* and his series of studies on the social history of National Socialism: the work of Alexander Kluge and Manfred Franke's *Mordverläufe* exemplify another, more complicated response to historical material. Both these writers attempt to analyse recent historical phenomena but, at the same time, the difficulty of actually reconstructing any history is part of their theme. Their work is testimony to the fact that it is impossible for one person to arrive, even through the most careful research, at an unambiguous understanding of a complex body of historical material; this being so, the writer who works in such areas can only hope to present something of the complex in its entirety by refraining from imposing his own interpretation on it. He as non-historian has the relative freedom that allows him to present a subject in a way that precisely exposes the contradictions and the problems, rather than arriving at a neat but distorting thesis. All this is relevant to the new historical novel that emerges during the Seventies. The work of Kluge and Franke differs, however, in that they are concerned primarily with the implications for literary form of this view of history, rather than with the work of fiction's interpretation of its matter as constituting the pre-history of the present, correctly identified by Georg Lukács as an essential feature of the historical novel. But the mere drawing of parallels between the historical subject-matter and the present does not suffice to constitute a historical novel, as is shown by Elisabeth Plessen's *Kohlhaas* (1979).[1] Plessen's material seems ideally suited to an historical novel, with Kohlhaas clearly lending himself to portrayal as a fighter for individual freedom against the constraints of state power, whose struggles prefigure those, for example, of contemporary activists in various pressure groups. She does base much of her novel on a reading of old documents and chronicles (such as Peter Haffnitz's *Märkische Chronik*) and has come to the conclusion that they do not provide her with 'die reine Wahrheit, die ich dann für immer in mein Notizbuch eintragen könnte' (135); she also sees in the torture of Kohlhaas's supporters '[w]ie sich die Tradition gemütvoller Schlachter durch deutsche Geschichte zieht'. At times she tries to establish further links with the present by using modern expressions: she compares Kohlhaas with Astrid Proll and, at other points, presents him to us as a Red Indian with a tomahawk, as a Western hero and as walking through Manhattan with

---

1. *Kohlhaas*, Zurich & Cologne, 1979. All quotations from this edition.

'Mrs. Cölln'. She has stressed that her novel is 'nur scheinbar der Vergangenheit zugewandt', but, despite the unhappy attempts to link Kohlhaas to the modern age, it is essentially nothing more than a reinterpretation of the historical figure. The dominant impression is of an emotional need to rescue Kohlhaas from, as she has called it, 'Kleistsche Staatsfrömmelei', rather than any real concern to explore through him aspects of the relationship between the individual and the State that are still relevant today.[2]

Unlike the costume drama, which early established itself in the cinema and has also long had an equivalent in popular novels (and Plessen's *Kohlhaas* represents but a modish development of this), the true historical novel always makes a real connection to the present. Its classic form, an essential component of the bourgeois novel, always tended to reflect the dominant attitudes and values of the educated reading public with regard to the historical identity of the state. In the case of Germany, the hypersensitive concern with national history, produced by late unification, led to a series of historical novels heroising the German past and, in effect, legitimising the 'kleindeutsche Lösung' — the most obvious examples being Freytag's *Die Ahnen* and Dahn's *Ein Kampf um Rom*. The radical social changes throughout Western Europe in the late nineteenth century induced in most novelists of quality a far more problematical, often highly critical, authorial relationship to society: Fontane's *Schach von Wutenow*, which, in its critical treatment of the Prussian ethical code, prefigures *Irrungen, Wirrungen* and *Effi Briest* (thereby demonstrating the close link of the historical with the mainstream novel), is a clear indication of the nature of the historical novel at that time. Through its graphic presentation, in a historical context, of inhuman patterns of social behaviour still pertaining in his day, Fontane established a historical link that underlined their outmodedness and implicitly made the case for the necessity of future social reform.

Today's historical novel, like the bulk of contemporary realist writing, we would argue, has clear parallels, in terms of authorial point of view, with its predecessors of the late nineteenth century. This can, perhaps, be seen most clearly from the example of Uwe Timm's second novel, *Morenga* (1978), which, at the same time, demonstrates a full awareness of how problematical is the act of narration for the modern author.[3] In *Morenga*, which amounts to an

---

2. Elisabeth Plessen, 'Über die Schwierigkeit, einen historischen Roman zu schreiben' in P.M. Lützeler and E. Schwarz (eds.), *Deutsche Literatur in der Bundesrepublik seit 1965*, pp. 195–201.
3. Munich, 1978. All quotations in the text from the editions given here.

alternative account of the colonial era to that provided by the 'Kolonialroman', the personal interpretation of history of the authorial voice is supported, as in many a documentary work, by quotation from authentic source material. The author, essentially operating as a compiler of information, concentrates our attention on the experiences of Gottschalk, an army veterinary surgeon in German South-West Africa (modern Namibia) by extensive and, to some degree, fictionalised extracts from his diaries. Gottschalk's otherwise unremarkable story is, however, then placed in a wider political and social context by use of the montage technique: thus the individual experience, through its fusion with transindividual information of an historical kind, is drawn upon to facilitate a critical examination, from both sides, of the colonial system and its nature.

The Gottschalk presented at the outset of the novel is a minor European colonialist, by no means untypical, full of ambition, but from a modest background, seeing his best chance of 'getting somewhere' as lying in the overseas territories: 'Wonach Gottschalk Ausschau hielt, war Farmland, auf dem er, in einigen Jahren, mit seinem ersparten Geld Rinder und Pferde züchten wollte . . . für Angehörige der Schutztruppe gäbe es zinsgünstige Kredite, wenn sie im Südwest Land erwerben wollten' (19). Once in the colony, however, the critical remarks of his colleague soon alert him to the systematic starvation and extermination of a high proportion of the natives in order to acquire land for settlers. He starts to look searchingly at all that is going on around him, becoming aware of the large profits that the colony makes for the business community and the German tax-payer. While the occupying forces view themselves as 'Träger der Kultur und Zivilisation', and are presented as such in their homeland, for the decent Gottschalk they quickly emerge as just the opposite: 'Wie will man ein Land kolonialisieren, wenn man sich nicht einmal die Mühe macht, die Eingeborenen zu verstehen, hatte Gottschalk einmal in Keetmannshoop gefragt. Mit Hilfe eines Dolmetschers und einer Nilpferdpeitsche, hatte Leutnant von Schwanenbach geantwortet, einer internationalen Sprache' (99).

Gottschalk continues his enlightenment by reading Kropotkin's *Mutual aid: a factor in evolution* and Westrup's notes and marginalia on its contents. The reader follows the course of his 'Verkafferung', as his colleagues term his change of attitudes, which emerges particularly clearly from the increasingly critical diary entries: 'Der südöstliche Teil des Landbesitzes der Topnaars war gegen 210£, 60 Flaschen Branntwein (deutsches Fabrikat), 20 Flaschen besten Kubarums (weiß!), 15 Kg. Tabak, 25 Kg. Kaffee sowie ein perlmutternes Opernglas an die Landgesellschaft gegangen' (289).

Understandably enough, Gottschalk is increasingly alienated from his colleagues and slowly slumps into gloomy resignation; he abandons his dream of becoming a farmer and returns to Germany. The last few entries in the diary tell us nothing of his state of mind in the final months.

Unlike its predecessor *Heißer Sommer*, however, *Morenga* is not a simple 'Entwicklungsroman'. Not only is Gottschalk a far from active hero, whose future remains unknown to us, his story — as the title indicates — is by no means the only strand of the novel. His diary is supplemented and qualified, as far as concerns its descriptions of the prevailing attitudes in the Second Reich towards the colony, by the insertion of minutes taken at meetings of both the German High Command in South-West Africa and the government in Berlin. Reichskanzler von Bülow, for example, apparently opposes 'die vollständige und planmäßige Ausrottung der Herero', since they are 'sowohl für den Ackerbau und die Viehzucht als auch für den Bergbau unentbehrlich', but General von Trotta takes the view 'daß die Nation als solche vernichtet werden muß' and Generaloberst Graf Schlieffen agrees that the 'entbrannte Kampf ist nur durch die Vernichtung einer Partei abzuschließen' (29–30). In addition to the military records, the intercut documentary material includes reports on the opening up of the region by German missionaries, who initiate the process of subjugating the Hereros ('Landeskunde I') and details of business dealings by German firms exploiting the primitive tribespeople by exchanging expensive ostrich feathers for cheap brandy ('Landeskunde II'; as in North America, alcohol seems to have been used extensively as a means of stupefying the natives). In the light of all this, it is no surprise that the long-suffering Hereros eventually rebel. The insurrection and the countermeasures taken by German troops, which provide another crucial strand of material, are presented antithetically; on the one hand, through the long-lost diary of Morenga, the Herero leader, and, on the other, by documents from German war archives. Although the 16,000 German troops are opposed by a mere handful of rebels (ca. 260, we are told), a certain Oberst von Deimling soon has to record that 'der Krieg . . . im herkömmlichen Sinn gar nicht mehr gewonnen werden konnte' and that, as a result, '[d]rakonische Strafen gegen gefangene Rebellen und Sympathisanten' have to be developed (362). After the declaration that the state of emergency is at an end, the 'Grundbesitz und das Vieh aller aufständischen Stämme der Hereros und Hottentotten' is seized by the German authorities; in addition, laws are passed, 'die es den Eingeborenen verboten, Grundstücke zu erwerben, ebenso Großviehzucht zu betreiben und

Reittiere zu haben. . . . Mehr als zehn Eingeborenenfamilien durften nicht zusammen auf einem Grundstück wohnen' (365). In the
account of the final phase of the rebellion — the desperate fight to
the end by Morenga and his closest aides — it becomes perfectly
clear that Uwe Timm's critical exposure of conditions in South-
West Africa is not to be understood as an attack on German
colonialism in particular, since Morenga's band can only be defeated (with the leader himself being killed) as a result of a pact
made with the British.

Our analysis thus far would seem to suggest that Timm's novel
amounts to nothing more than a carefully researched reinterpretation of an historical phenomenon, but this is by no means the case.
Gottschalk's individual confrontation with colonialism, since it is so
different from that of most settlers and, indeed, his own expectations, forces the reader to re-examine existing attitudes towards the
colonial experience in general and the role of the colonists in
particular. The suppression of the uprising brings out vividly the
cultural and political role of the European nations as a collective
force in Southern Africa: indeed, the collaboration of the British
with the Germans in finally crushing Morenga is particularly significant, making it clear to the native — as von den Hagen, a member of
the German General Staff, puts it — 'daß er nicht mehr gegen den
Deutschen oder Engländer oder Holländer usw. kämpft, sondern
daß jetzt die weiße Rasse geschlossen gegen die schwarze steht'
(393). Colonialism is shown, therefore, as the collective suppression
and exploitation of backward people by Europeans, rather than as
an expression of the ambition of an individual nation. The location
of the novel then makes the point that this is by no means peculiar to
an earlier era, since Namibia, effectively a part of South Africa, offers
daily eloquent testimony to the continuing suppression of Blacks by
Whites. The contemporary relevance of Timm's theme was highlighted particularly strikingly on the evening in 1985 when the final
part of the television film of the novel was transmitted, the preceding
news bulletin having shown scenes of extreme police brutality
against Blacks during a funeral in a Johannesburg township:
Timm's point was made. Nor are the links between the novel and
the present confined to the parallels between colonialism and current racial oppression. Morenga himself has great importance as the
first rebel to use a new means of warfare (which would today be
called guerrilla tactics). In Morenga, the 'Napoleon der Schwar-
zen', Uwe Timm rediscovered a historical figure who can be considered in many ways as the prefiguration of the great freedom fighters
in the developing countries and the Third World. Largely as a result

of this novel, which was soon afterwards published in English in Southern Africa, Morenga was quickly taken over by SWAPO as a key symbolic figure of their continued struggle for freedom in Namibia. Timm thus confronts the modern reality of Southern Africa with its past through a figure who, in his day, fought for the kind of human dignity still not respected there and, through his example, still inspires a modern generation involved in the same struggle.

Morenga is a skilfully crafted work which demonstrates the vast potential of the modern historical novel. The fusion of the critical, clearly subjective, positions of Gottschalk and the narrator with the body of documentary material, which supports and develops their points of view, simultaneously illuminates a suppressed chapter of European history and a dark aspect of modern political life. It marks the potential beginning of a significant chapter in the German historical novel, but gets no further, in that no other historical novel of similar quality has been published in West Germany in recent years. Nevertheless, enough novels — varying in quality — delineating the immediate relationship between aspects of the past and the present, have been produced since the mid-Seventies as to indicate the existence of a widespread new historical awareness among younger German writers that has made its mark on the contemporary novel. An interesting example in this connection is August Kühn's *Zeit zum Aufstehn* (see Chapter 6), which recreates a hundred years of German social and political history through the experiences of a working-class family in Munich and, through continuous intercutting to the life of the present-day family, brings out its relevance to the present-day. The novel is at times crudely didactic and the amount of information given exceeds what the story demands — reflecting Kühn's avowed intent to write an alternative social history —, but, within its modest limits, it succeeds in producing a readable and vivid account of working-class life in the context of Social Democratic politics in the past century. Walter Kempowski's series of novels, constituting a 'Deutsche Chronik', is intended to contribute, through the account of the family's history over the last few generations, to the better understanding by the present-day generation of recent German history, of 'das deutsche Problem', as he has put it; the sad reality is that the novels constitute a rather nostalgic reconstruction of German social history, and seem to have been received as such. Peter Härtling's 'Geschichten gegen die Geschichte' are clearly written with a similar intent, but, again, the relationship to the present is far from clear. In *Eine Frau* this vagueness is completely in keeping with the memory process of an elderly woman, but his latest novel, *Felix Guttmann* (1985), confirms a growing impression that the only connection between the historical material and the present is the author's own interest in the past: in this case memories of conversations with the lawyer AB, the model for Felix. Letters, diaries, books from the lawyer's library, the tape of a radio interview with him in 1974 and books on the Third Reich are used to create a most interesting and highly competent account of the life of a Jewish lawyer in the Twenties and Thirties, but without establishing any immediate relevance to the Federal Republic of today. A last example in this context is Peter Weiss's *Die Ästhetik des Widerstands* (see Chapter 6) which re-creates the history of the broad spread of anti-fascist resistance in the Thirties and the Second World War and thereby commenting, to some extent, on what socialist activists and artists are doing today. Despite the portrayal of individual fates in this unique work, it is essentially a protracted dialogue by the author with himself about aesthetic questions which, though undoubtedly still relevant are, in the main, dealt with abstractly. This applies particularly in the discussions about the significance of the Pergamon altar, the realism debates during the Spanish Civil War, the analysis of Géricault's 'The Raft of Medusa' and the lengthy discussions with Brecht in Sweden.

There is little doubt that, in its latest phase, the treatment of the importance for present-day Germany of the Nazi past has up to now constituted the most fruitful area of work for the renascent West German historical novel, even if none of the works involved have reached the standards set by *Morenga*. It should be said at the outset that the experiences of the previous generation and, to some extent, of writers themselves by no means constitute obvious material for an historical novel. Indeed, it could be argued that such matter conflicts with the nature of the literary form. The real question here is as to how the term 'historical' is to be understood. Of particular relevance here is the factor of rapid social and technological change during the past hundred years, which has accelerated unbelievably since the Fifties, so that the narrator Plauth in Peter O. Chotjewitz's *Saumlos* notes, on returning to the village where he had spent part of his childhood: 'Das Dorf hatte sich in den letzten dreißig Jahren verändert, mehr als in den dreihundert Jahren davor' (18).[4] Colour television seems to drive even recollected experiences — in black and white, i.e. from a technologically inferior age — from childhood into an indefinite past. To this general tendency of the recent past

4. Königstein, 1979, p. 11. All subsequent quotations from this edition.

retreating ever more quickly into history must, in the case of West Germany, be added a number of other special factors: while the end of the war was in no way a socio-economic 'Stunde Null', in that much property was restored to the large industrialists after the currency reform, it nevertheless marked an important psychological caesura for the population. The Nazi seizure of power in 1933 had already meant radical change, marking, in effect, the end of an era that began with the establishment of the Second Reich, but the defeat of 1945 and its consequences on the stage of world politics confirmed and intensified the sense of a break with a state which, in any case, had but a brief history. The loss of the Eastern Territories to the USSR and Poland, the subsequent difficulties of access during the cold war to cities and regions that had played important parts in Germany's cultural history and, above all, the division of Germany into two states signified the final dissolution of Germany as a familiar political and cultural entity. For those born during and after the Second World War the cultural history of Germany before 1933 is that of a lost country, one that they never knew. In the Forties and Fifties the full and radical significance of 1945 was not recognised by the adult generation, not only because many still clung to the idea that the post-war division of Germany was merely provisional, but because they had experienced the old country at first hand; it had not died, since they still carried it in their hearts. The generation politicised in the Sixties, however, clearly viewed things differently; amongst other things the sovereignty of both German states was self-evident to them, and their relationship to National Socialism, too, differed from that of their fathers. Since they had in no way been involved in the Third Reich, they could — and here the Frankfurt Auschwitz Trials of the early Sixties and Peter Weiss's *Die Ermittlung* clearly played their parts — view Nazism more critically and were anxious to evaluate fully its relationship to the Germany of the (then) present. One consequence of this, coupled with the politicisation of the time, was that the political and economic elite of the Federal Republic was, in effect, put on public trial. In the Seventies this process continued and, in addition, the post-Thirties generation extended its focus of critical examination to take in everyday life in the Third Reich and the relevance of this shaping experience for themselves. Here, the most harrowing aspect was a scrutiny of the parental involvement. A number of literary essays and a sequence of so-called 'Väterromane' testify to the attempt by younger writers to exhume what had hitherto been a suppressed part of their parents' earlier life and to assess its relevance to their own upbringing and family relationships. (The best known of these works are Bernward

Vesper's *Die Reise*, 1971/7, Ruth Rehmann's *Der Mann auf der Kanzel*, 1976, Günter Seuren's *Abschied von einem Mörder* 1980, Peter Härtling's *Nachgetragene Liebe*, 1980 and Christoph Meckel's *Suchbild*, 1980.) For others this interest in wider aspects of National Socialism took the form of unearthing from the prehistory of the Federal Republic important chapters which, it was felt, had been wrongly neglected.[5]

An early example of this sort of historical novel was Franz Josef Degenhardt's first novel, *Zündschnüre* (1973). In terms of location, language and, in part, story material, this novel is closely related to his early 'Schmuddelkinder' cycle of songs, but here the focus is moved back to the last phase of the war. The main concern of the novel is the activities of a group of young Communist resistance fighters, somewhat akin to the 'Edelweißpiraten' (who, in 1973, were also virtually unknown). They hide people on the run from the Nazis — an English officer, a Polish girl, a deserter from the Hitler Youth, a Jewish woman and a Frenchman — and, in addition, generally do whatever they can to foul the works of the Nazi war machine, even attacking fanatical members of the SS who try to prevent the townspeople capitulating to the advancing Allies. Their parental generation are, for the most part, those local Communists who have avoided being sent to concentration camps. They are shown as a highly self-aware proletariat, strongly anti-fascist, but also having great vitality and a lively cultural life (particularly in terms of 'Arbeiterlieder'). It was clearly Degenhardt's intention not only to counter the carefully nurtured — as many would argue — popular impression, which existed into the Seventies, that the Kreisauer Kreis was the only organised opposition to the Nazis, but also to draw attention to the consistent, brave and unambiguous opposition of certain groups on the Left. At the same time, with this positive picture of KPD activism, he was, it would seem, intent on 'correcting' what had become the official account of the last phase of the war. He saw that version as falsely legitimising a state which had not only banned a party that had played such a part in opposing National Socialism but was also less than tolerant of its successor — Degenhardt's own party. By his amendment of the accepted story, the author drew attention to what he saw as ignored or betrayed opportunities for the development of post-war Germany.

5. Cf. in this connection Norbert Elias, 'Gedanken über die Bundesrepublik', *Merkur*, 39, 1985, pp. 733–55. This essay, written in 1977 but only recently published, gives a fascinating reading of the mood of Germany at the time and, in particular, of the new sense of the importance of the legacy of the Nazi past for a younger generation.

The same theme of opportunities missed by West Germany in the cauldron that was the end of the war, but without the element of party propaganda, is taken up in Gerd Fuchs's *Stunde Null* (1981).[6] As the title indicates, the novel depicts the period immediately after the war has ended, particularly as experienced by the Haupts, a middle-class family in a small town in the Hunsrück. Like any decent family, of course, they had nothing but contempt for the Nazis, but had nevertheless — according to the provisional mayor appointed after the capitulation — 'so getan . . . , als wäre nichts geschehen' (12). War has, however, taught the older Haupt son much about National Socialism and he is appalled at the behaviour of most people in the town after the cease-fire: 'Sie machen einfach weiter . . . , gehen zur Tagesordnung über. Ich werde das nie begreifen' (12). The younger son Georg is even more forthright in his criticism of how the same people went along with the Nazis until the very end, but then put everything behind them: 'Vom Endsieg habt ihr gefaselt und von Wunderwaffen und vom Durchhalten, und dann seid ihr in den Garten gegangen und habt eure Parteiuniformen vergraben' (20). While the Haupts are deeply concerned about such problems, most of the townspeople are quite willing simply to come to terms with the new situation in which, for the first time, the SPD is responsible for administration (the past difficulties of the party are brought out by the story of the radical parson Veit). The new civic fathers order 'die Entfernung von Nationalsozialisten, Militaristen und Personen, die den Alliierten feindlich gegenüberstehn, aus Ämtern und verantwortlichen Stellungen, einschließlich privater Unternehmungen', but then, even the CDU has ruled that 'die Vorherrschaft des Großkapitals, der privaten Monopole und Konzerne werde beseitigt' (124; the reference here is to the 1947 Ahlener Programm). The local furniture factory is requisitioned and its business continued by the council. Zander, the owner of the factory and the richest man in the district, is portrayed as a typical opportunistic capitalist: his family has always managed to surmount local difficulties and to exploit shifts in the political situation to its advantage, even backing the Nazis to ensure the continued prosperity of the firm (without their assistance 'wäre die NSDAP längst bankrott gegangen', he freely admits to Haupt, 307). Despite the factory requisition, he continues to live opulently even in the desperate days of the post-war period, calmly biding his time. He rightly guesses that the political climate will change to his advantage: in the first free elections the CDU sweeps the board, with not a single

6. Munich, 1981. All quotations in the text from the editions given here.

member of the SPD elected, and Zander immediately gets his factory back, while the de-Nazification procedures are stopped. Things quickly change; even Olaf, Zander's son, who had previously told his father that 'das deutsche Unternehmertum ist nicht unschuldig an dieser Katastrophe' (146), soon accepts the new situation. He tells Georg: 'Ich verabscheue die Nazis genauso wie Sie. Aber irgendwann muß ein Schlußstrich gezogen werden' (323). In the Currency Reform, the position of people like the Zanders is cemented at the expense of ordinary citizens, and the foundation of the Federal Republic is portrayed as confirming and intensifying this tendency.

Stunde Null is a novel with a double historical perspective, in that the post-war period is not only an important part of the prehistory of the Federal Republic, but itself the continuation of an established historical pattern. In his conversations with others, Haupt hears for the first time something of the history of the region and discovers that what is now happening is nothing new: all attempts at reform aimed at a more equitable distribution of wealth and power are blocked by the few who enjoy these privileges. The story of Schinderhannes, the Robin Hood of the Palatinate, presents him as the embodiment of all the various efforts at democratisation in the region; he represents an 'irrsinnige, wilde Hoffnung auf eine Herrschaft, die nicht in Frack und steifem Hut ging, sondern im Kittel kam und fröhlich war und lachte und arglos war bis zum Schluß' (335). The restoration of the status quo after the Second World War is but the latest in a line of such defeated hopes of significant change. What is presented as the missed opportunity of a reformist break with the past in the years 1945–9 has, then, both a past and a future — the contemporary State in which the German reader lives and which is thereby shown in a critical light.

A similar pattern — the analysis of the recent past acting as a springboard for criticism of the Federal Republic of today — is to be found in Peter O. Chotjewitz's *Saumlos* (1979). Like Manfred Franke's *Mordverläufe*, this novel is concerned with the persecution of the Jews in the Third Reich, and especially the excesses of the Reichskristallnacht, but Chotjewitz in no way restricts himself to an attempt at reconstructing the events of November 1938. The journalist Eric Plauth, looking for a house after returning to West Germany from a lengthy stay in Rome, decides to pay a passing visit to the village of Saumlos where he spent part of his childhood. Mechanical trouble necessitates a somewhat lengthier stay, a man is found dead — the signs point to suicide, but murder cannot be excluded — and Plauth gets to know an expert in local history, who excites his interest in

161

unravelling the mystery of the fate of the local Jewish population thirty years before. He had, in any case, in thinking back to his childhood, remembered the old village synagogue and begun 'darüber nachzudenken, daß es früher in Saumlos Juden gegeben haben mußte, die schon vor seiner ersten Ankunft spurlos verschwunden waren' (52). Through material given him by the local historian, reading the old school chronicle, conversations with the few people in the village who are prepared to discuss the topic, and later through official records, he slowly builds up a picture of the past. There had previously been more Jews than Christians in the village, but they were poor folk — grain merchants and craftsmen — and completely assimilated: they were conservative, nationalist and loyal to the Kaiser. By and large Jews and Christians lived peacefully together, but, despite this, there was always a certain local anti-Semitism and, during the 1848 Revolution, there were attacks on local Jews. In 1933 the Jewish community did everything possible to adjust to the new way of things, with Jewish teachers distributing the appropriate coloured pencils at the time of the Presidental election, in order to avoid the suspicion of casting their votes against Hitler. Nevertheless, pressure on the Jewish community increased: in 1933 there were 172 Jewish villagers, but only 87 by October 1938. During the Kristallnacht Jewish businesses and houses were laid waste, the synagogue was set on fire, the livestock dealer Katz robbed and killed; afterwards, all Jewish males were shipped off to Buchenwald. Official reports stated that Katz 'habe vor Erregung einen Herzschlag erlitten', when neighbours broke down the door of his house, 'um ihn ins Feuerwehrgerätehaus zu bringen' (108). Plauth discovers that most of the assaults on the Jews were carried out by village youths, who had, in reality, been incited by the village teacher and the parson. Between 1938 and 1939 there had been compulsory purchases of Jewish property and a number of villagers had made their fortunes from the departure of the Jewish community.

It is not easy for Plauth to establish the facts: most villagers refuse to discuss this chapter of their history and an elderly woman, who clearly would like to tell him something, is silenced by her family. Even old Herr Holzhacker, who talks in general terms of what had happened, stresses: 'Ich will nichts gesagt haben. . . . Aber von mir erfährt keiner was. Ich will keinen Unfrieden stiften' (108–9). Many aspects of the matter are ignored in Plauth's initially crucial source of information, the school chronicle; moreover five 'missing' pages would have covered the period from October 1938 to September 1939 and, thus, the events of the Kristallnacht. When the mayor discovers why Plauth is consulting the school records, a demand is made for the return of this 'amtliche Urkunde': no one is prepared to talk openly of the expulsion of the Jewish community.

The section of the school chronicle for the period since 1945 shows that a similar attitude has been maintained throughout the post-war period. In the first free mayoral election, says the old schoolteacher, the villagers had set out to find a man 'der keinen Unfrieden stiftete im Dorf und nicht immer in diesen Sachen herumrührte, die vorgefallen waren bei den Nazis, das mußte ja aufhören. Man kann in einem Dorf nicht zusammenleben, wenn man dauernd Angst haben muß, angezeigt zu werden' (110). A 1946 report made by an officer of the American occupying forces describes how the only villager prepared to testify against those suspected of setting fire to the synagogue was publicly hounded as a traitor and suffered considerable professional damage. In 1947, according to a newspaper item, the village school's parents association successfully requested the transfer of a teacher, 'weil er Unfrieden im Dorf gestiftet habe, indem er Mitbürger vor die Spruchkammer gebracht habe' (102). The official history of the village after 1945 does not mention the former Jewish community and Plauth is granted access to civic records only on condition that he 'die Persönlichkeitsrechte der erwähnten Personen nicht verletzen [darf]' (147). No one, not even old Holzhacker, who admits to being saddened by the fate of the Jews, will admit that any inhabitant of Saumlos took part in their ill-treatment, indeed, the 'Gerede von den nationalsozialistischen Judenverfolgungen, das sei doch überwiegend kommunistische Propaganda' or an attempt by those in the East (i.e. the DDR), 'anständige Bürger zu beschuldigen' (144).

Chotjewitz is not, however, interested merely in unravelling the suppressed past: he sees his topic as having contemporary relevance in the continuation of old prejudices. Thus, even the basically decent former village teacher, Leimert, who obtains the school chronicle for Plauth, continues to put forward a notion which in the context of the history of Saumlos is totally false: the supposed 'Zinsknechtschaft' imposed by the Jews on their fellow-villagers in the nineteenth century. He claims to have nothing against the Jews, who are to him 'so lieb wie jeder andere Mensch', but 'Juden und Christen in einem Dorf, das geht nicht zusammen'; even attempted assimilation through baptism fails to eradicate 'seine artfremden Eigenschaften, und auch bei den sogenannten Mischehen rasseechter Juden mit Ariern behält nachweislich das jüdische Blut immer die Überhand' (91–2). In conversation with another villager, a workman, Plauth is further confronted with similar ideas, also couched in the language of the Thirties. Despite the horrors of the Kristallnacht and the continuing anti-Semitism after the war, the narrator suggests that the attitude of villagers to the Jews has to be looked at in a wider context: the villagers have always tended to be apolitical, with the ability to get on with neighbours being more important than party allegiance. The village has a strong sense of corporate identity, expressed, it would appear, particularly forcefully in suspicion and even intolerance of any sort of outsider figure. Plauth remembers how a homosexual was driven out of the village in the Fifties and is horrified to find his former school friends talking today about opponents of atomic power, 'Radikalen', 'messerstechenden Türken' and homosexuals in language similar to that used by the Nazis about the Jews. There are even those who long for 'einem starken Mann, wie Hitler einer war, der würde schon aufräumen. Todesstrafe' (143). This intolerance seems sometimes to appear as a sort of lynch law: it transpires that the case of suicide (the official verdict) was really the murder of a local recluse while he was drunk by two of his neighbours, themselves relatives of people responsible for the excesses of the Kristallnacht. The only witness to the murder is another outsider — a half-Italian girl from 'Klein Chicago', the poorest part of the village, who is despised and sexually exploited by the male villagers. She has learned the rules of village life well enough to know that her best course is 'nichts zu sagen: Man würde ihr sowieso nicht glauben, und es ersparte ihr viel Ärger' (47). The murderers, like the men who killed the livestock dealer Katz, go unpunished.

Like Fuchs's *Stunde Null*, Chotjewitz's novel is a critical exposé of a suppressed chapter of recent German history, based on research material and, to some extent, personal experience, which is then shown to have relevance for the present-day Federal Republic. Further evidence was provided, incidentally, by the publication of a companion volume, *Wer mit Tränen sät* (1979) comprising interviews in Israel with members of the former Jewish community of Saumlos. In order to authenticate his controversial charges, within the novel he makes the formal distinction between documentary and fictional material by dividing the text up into blocks, in the manner of the early Arno Schmidt. To make the novel more 'readable', however, he fuses the documentary with the form of a thriller (at one point the unmistakable figure of Chotjewitz appears, in the style of Alfred Hitchcock), made up of the investigation into the alleged suicide and the search for material on the Saumlos Jews. The mixed form is not always successful, however: several coincidences defy belief, the sexual relationship with the comely local historian is superfluous, and the bringing together of the evidence (far more complex than that in any Agatha Christie novel) is achieved unbelievably quickly. In addition, the links to the present are somewhat sketchy, but, despite these weaknesses, *Saumlos* does generally succeed in its aim of providing a vivid account of such important material.

While *Schach von Wutenow* represents the transition from the affirmation of the classic historical novel to a humanitarian critique of society, the analyses of *Morenga*, *Zündschnüre* and *Stunde Null* serve to show how the contemporary historical novel tends to go further than Fontane and offer an ideological interpretation of the past that is, in turn, a criticism of the political present; their proximity to political realism is clear. *Saumlos*, on the other hand, takes up a much more general critical position, and this is also true of Alfred Andersch's last novel, *Winterspelt* (1974).[7] To some extent this fine work takes up Andersch's old theme — the free will of the individual — but lacks the crude symbolism of *Sansibar oder Der letzte Grund* and the theme is here dealt with in a far less abstract manner. The central character, Major Joseph Dincklage, has much in common with earlier Andersch figures, having become an officer '[um] den Nationalsozialismus auf halbwegs saubere Art zu überwintern' (39). At the end of 1944 he finds himself commanding a battalion in the Ardennes and confronted with a rapidly worsening military position. In this situation Andersch then creates a literary 'Sandkastenspiel', as he calls it, in which he 'spielt eine Möglichkeit durch', rather than providing a strictly historical account of events.

The novel is based on an extensive body of documentary material and the model for the village of Winterspelt was 'ein im östlichen Teil des Landkreises Prüm gelegenes Dorf' (129). The book is, moreover, dedicated to a person 'die von 1941 bis 1945 in der Westeifel gelebt hat' and who claimed, 'des öfteren Gespräche deutscher Offiziere mitangehört zu haben, in denen Pläne erörtert wurden, die denen des Majors Dincklage entsprachen' (22), and Andersch lists the names of other informants, written sources, and the various Anglo-American histories and biographies consulted. He was clearly anxious to get the most accurate picture possible of the situation from both sides and the three main characters — Dincklage, the resistance fighter Käthe Lenk and Captain John Kimbrough of the American Army — would seem to be based on real persons. Nevertheless, it is not Andersch's intent to produce the best possible authentic recreation of events, but to use the documentary sources to

---

7. Zurich, 1974. All references to this edition.

heighten the plausibility of his scenario. The narrator, indeed, continually stresses the fictionalisation of the material used and that he himself neither knows the person on whom Dincklage is modelled nor has any information enabling him to achieve a psychologically realistic portrayal. He is not concerned, 'sich mit den Beweggründen zu beschäftigen, die den Major Dincklage zu seinem Anschlag gegen den Krieg veranlaßt haben', since there is enough literature 'zum Thema der Aufstandsversuche deutscher Offiziere gegen Hitler, welche die Überlegungen, weltanschauliche Motive, Argumente und Gefühle dieser tragischen Gestalten . . . auf das minuziöseste katalogisiert. Ihr kann nach Belieben entnommen werden, was am Bild der Ursachen von Dincklages Projekt fehlen mag' (64). Dincklage's 'project' is the offer to surrender his force to the Americans; 'in erster Linie faßte er seinen Entschluß aus fachmännischen Gründen. Bekanntlich teilten im Herbst 1944 die meisten deutschen Offiziere Dincklages Ansicht, daß der Krieg militärisch verloren und deshalb auf der Stelle zu beenden sei' (64–5). The plan fails to come to fruition, since his troops are transferred to another command and statistical details of German losses during the Ardennes Offensive of 1945 (594–5) show that it would have had no military relevance, even if it had been successful. The narrator is not, however, interested 'ob und wie es dem Major Dincklage gelingt oder mißlingt, ein nahezu kriegsstarkes deutsches Bataillon den Amerikanern zu übergeben' (63), but is concerned with the interplay between the German officer and the Americans, brought about by Käthe, whom Dincklage has told of his plan, passing the information on to Captain Kimbrough. She has recognised that Dincklage's idea was a totally abstract one — as it must have been for many others at the time — until she forces his hand. But the response of the Americans, who, like their German counterpart, belong to the 'Internationale der Offiziere' is highly sceptical and, in addition, they want 'mit einem Verräter nichts zu tun haben': the actions and thought-patterns on both sides are governed by an unwritten code of officers' behaviour. Dincklage, although he is fully aware that his proposal is only sensible and humanitarian, nevertheless keeps hesitating, seems incapable of reconciling the planned act of treason with his officer mentality, and the Americans, in their turn, cannot rid themselves of their misgivings, until it is too late. While the other participants in the sand-pit game are seemingly free to decide on their actions, the military players are paralysed. It is implied that the Americans, because of their suspicion, do not give Dincklage sufficient room to move or come to a final decision and there is criticism — supported by a quotation from the war historian Liddell Hart — of the Allies' 'unkluge und kurzsichtige Forderung nach bedingungsloser Kapitulation', which restricted the scope for action of senior army staff opposed to Hitler (588). The narrator's lack of interest in the possible consequences of Dincklage's actually surrendering his unit, together with the structure of the novel and the narratorial style adopted, make it clear that no attempt is made here to reinterpret a critical phase of the war, nor to criticise the attitude of the Allies as such, but that it is intended to highlight the officers' lack of freedom, the constraints imposed by normative behaviour. It is no coincidence that this novel was written during the Vietnam War, which, amongst other things, slowly exposed the one-sided, simplistic morality of the victors in 1945 for what it was, particularly since individual officers were posed the same moral questions as in the Second World War and were then restricted in their response by the codified thought-patterns that are at the heart of any military organisation. *Winterspelt*, in taking up the same moral dilemmas that were being discussed in the West in response to American actions in Vietnam and in making its strong plea for all individuals to be able to take decisions of their own free will, establishes the strong connection of its theme to present-day concerns.

All the novels so far examined in this chapter have a considerable documentary quality, which is necessary for the author to authenticate his material and place an otherwise apparently random series of events in a wider context; the relevance of the historical to the present is then, in turn, all the more likely to appear as something other than coincidence. The Seventies and Eighties also see the emergence of an historical novel based on autobiographical material, in the sense that the individual life story is not portrayed as an interesting and essentially unique whole, but as having a considerable degree of historical typicality and, as such, able to contribute to an understanding of an earlier phase of social existence and its after-effects on present-day society. To some degree, this sort of novel has similarities with the documentary life stories published by Erika Runge and Martin Walser in the late Sixties, but it lacks the interpretative intervention of a third person. The authors of these newer works are mature people who have, in the course of their life, undergone a process of growth in consciousness: this has, amongst other things, brought home to them the historical significance of their earlier experiences and development as part of a complex of social phenomena still relevant today.

Hannsferdinand Döblers *Kein Alibi, Ein deutscher Roman 1915–45* (1980) concerns itself with the writer's childhood in a conservative ('deutsch-national') family, his youth in the Third Reich and his war service.[8] The writing of the novel would seem to have been precipitated by the question he felt forced to ask when, in 1966, he was reporting on a war crimes trial, namely: 'bin ich ein besserer Mensch? Oder nur ohne eigenes Verdienst ohne Schuld?' (229). He engages on a process of research amongst family records and comes to the realisation that his is more than an individual story, that it epitomises the demise of a lost epoch, that the fate of the family reflects in miniature 'die Zerrüttung der alten Bourgeoisie'. To bring out this wider significance of his story, Döbler avoids the conventional autobiographical approach adopted by a number of writers who, coincidentally, also published descriptions of their youthful war experiences in 1980 (Dieter Borkowski, *Wer weiß, ob wir uns wiedersehen*, Eugen Oker, . . . *und ich der Fahnenträger*, Elisabeth Heinisch, *Der Hirseberg* and Jochen Ziem, *Der Junge*), and opts for the autobiographical novel form.

As the son of an academically trained 'deutsch-national' father, Döbler is confronted very early with ultra-conservative ideas at home. The range of prejudices against so-called inferior races, particularly the Jews, is an integral part of his socialisation, as is his involvement in the Youth Movement (the 'bündische Jugend'). This education is complemented by the obligatory reading of conservative texts, and he even comes into contact with 'national-revolutionär' literature, such as Franz Schonauer's *Aufbruch der Jugend*. His father is one of those conservatives who underestimated National Socialism and naïvely imagined that the 'nationale Bewegung' would be able to realise its aims through the NSDAP, with Hitler as an obedient puppet, while the son, like many of the 'bündische Jugend', has an ambivalent attitude to the Nazis, born of a dislike for the plebeian nature of the Hitler Youth. His view of the Third Reich is ultimately influenced by conscription into the *Reichsarbeitsdienst* and rapid advancement to officer rank. The oath of allegiance he takes in the army (and which the author still knows by heart today) is seen as sacrosanct and as determining his behaviour during the war. Total loyalty to the army enables him to accept and even to justify such terrible things as the mass deportation of Jews from Holland (in which he was not involved): 'hätte man ihn gefragt, was er denn so davon hielt, so hätte er geantwortet: Dieser Anblick [of the railway trucks used, KB] ist zwar unangenehm, aber Härte ist notwendig, und das wird schon alles seine Ordnung haben. Er jedenfalls sei Frontoffizier und nicht dazu da, sich mit dem Schicksal der Juden zu befassen' (235). When, in 1944, he hears that officers, and not

8. Frankfurt & Berlin, 1980. All references to this edition.

foreign slave workers, had carried out the attempt on Hitler's life, his reaction is one of shame at such conduct: 'Offiziere hatten die Hand gegen Hitler erhoben — also mußten Offiziere diese Schmach mit ihrem Blut tilgen. . . . Mehr denn je handele es sich darum, als Offizier seine Pflicht zu tun *Deutschland muß leben und wenn wir sterben müssen* [italicised in original, KB]' (276). This fanatical allegiance to his oath as an officer comes out, however, most decisively in his behaviour during the last weeks of the war: 'Wir beschlossen, Rachetrupps im Stil einer Freiheitsbewegung zu bilden, die getrennt operieren sollten. Ihre Aufgabe sollte sein, besonders grausame Besatzer, besonders wüste Gesellen unter den Angehörigen der feindlichen Armee, umzubringen — notfalls unter Opferung des eigenen Lebens' (303–4). Only when he has to give orders for a whole village to be burnt to the ground does he start to question actions that, for once, cannot be dismissed on the grounds that 'Befehl ist schließlich Befehl'.

This critical examination of the officer corps' behaviour-patterns, as determined by a military code of honour, is in parts very similar to Andersch's *Winterspelt*; Döbler's approach to his topic, however, concentrates especially on the particular role of language in shaping and mediating these values. To highlight this aspect of the problem, Döbler as narrator, looking back from the late Seventies on his past, tells the body of the story and comments on particular features of it in the preterite, but the language the younger Döbler would have used is given in the present tense, and, where he can remember the exact words used at the time, these are printed in italics. Where Döbler wishes particularly to emphasise the distance between his present and his former self, the third person is employed. These stylistic devices are designed to heighten our sensitivity to the way in which the younger Döbler in 'Klischees aufgeh[t]' and responds to 'die leeren Worte' of the earlier time. He has so absorbed the language of his ideological environment that he uses the sloganised language of the Nazis even in private; in 1938, for example, he records in his diary: 'Die Einwohner sind alle P.G.! Neu-Bentschen ist judenrein!' (50). When, during the war, a non-commissioned officer protests against an order to shoot prisoners, Döbler rejects his 'Humanitätsduselei', and his thoughts on the matter are especially revealing.

Weshalb müssen sie denn nur die Gefangenen erschießen, sagt er, das sind doch auch Menschen wir wir. Außerdem ist es verboten.
Ich sehe ihn erstaunt an, ich habe mir darüber noch nie den Kopf zerbrochen: diese kahlköpfigen stinkenden Russen mit ihrem stumpfen

Blick, die wie Untermenschen wirken? Was heißt das schon: Menschen wie wir, das ist eben eine andere Rasse (191).

In this language, which really is from the 'Wörterbuch des Unmenschen', the inhumanity of the regime and Döbler's internalisation of its values emerge vividly. Yet this question of personal moral guilt, sparked off by the trial in 1966, was not, in the end, the most important point that Döbler wanted to make in the novel: in his preoccupation with that area of history he had come increasingly to feel that all forms of official documentation of the period, including even films, gave a spectral, unreal impression of the Nazi past. The book is ultimately conceived less as a literary *mea culpa*, than as the reworking of a period of Döbler's life, which — as the subtitle indicates — is still of significance today. In confessing and doing penance for his own past, he draws attention, in the first instance, to the unscrupulous opportunism of the bourgeoisie, the middle class from which he comes: 'Heute sehe ich: der Enkel des Bilderbuchkapitalisten aus Berlin-Charlottenburg, der Sohn des glücklosen Architekten und der sozialen Absteigerin hatte sich seinen Platz in der Gesellschaft gesichert wie aus bürgerlichem Instinkt: nicht den eines Rebellen . . . , sondern den im Glanz der faschistischen Macht' (257). Alongside the criticism of what is portrayed as a middle-class predisposition to act short-sightedly and only with an eye to its own social and economic interests there is implied a strong criticism of military behaviour-patterns. The Second World War, in which 'man von taktischen Atomwaffen, mit Napalm erzeugten Flächenbränden, fall out und den Wüsteneien des modernen Kriegs noch nichts wüßte' (143), seems to belong to a past age in which it still seemed possible to satisfy the 'äußerste Bedürfnis' of the officer, 'sich auszuzeichnen, mit einer einzigen kühnen Tat alle Augen auf sich zu ziehen' (154) — to become a hero. The implication is that this notion was illusory, in that it ignored moral consequences of the horrors of the actual war, which in the most recent theatres of war have become even more fearful, but which are still accompanied by the inculcated need of the officer to distinguish himself: the emphasis on war as glorious action, rather than moral bankruptcy. Döbler suggests a clear parallel between the position of the officer corps in his day and the war as fought in Vietnam, but it can clearly be drawn more widely than that: Döbler's theme is anything but *past* history.

The new historical awareness of modern authors not only seems to assign the Third Reich to a time long gone, but also gives that past a relevance for the present by bringing out the pattern of historical continuity, including the continued existence of phenomena in conflict with basic human values. Even much of the life of the Federal Republic (which, after all, has now lasted over twice as long as the Weimar Republic) is viewed by younger writers as a piece of history, rather than the near-present, as older people tend to see it. Proof of the younger generation's attitude is provided outside the sphere of literature by, for example, Fassbinder's films *Die Ehe der Maria Braun* and *Lola*. These portray earlier phases of the Federal Republic as period pieces that are, however, important for the understanding of the present (as emphasised by the series of stills at the end of *Maria Braun*), in the manner of the new historical novels just examined. In their treatment of the war, the post-war period and the Fifties, the time of the 'Wirtschaftswunder', the novels of Hans Dieter Baroth offer an alternative account of times that have, in the main, passed into legend. They also offer insights into the historical origins of existing social and educational problems and the false values of the present-day working class. One novel, however, Peter O. Chotjewitz's *Der dreißigjährige Friede* (1977) lays specific claim to providing an alternative version of West German history, showing the impact of its earlier aspects on life in the present.

This novel, based on an actual human drama and drawing on reports and conversations with almost all the major participants, describes the life of a lower middle-class family over the period suggested by the title: the end of the war up to the middle of the Seventies.[9] Adolf Schütrumpf's experiences in the immediate post-war period are typical of many: he is a prisoner of war until 1947 and on his release can only survive by black-market dealing. However, the currency reform of 1948 enables him to set up as an independent craftsman, which to him seems a real social advancement. His subsequent career is shown as reflecting the fact that he is still tied to the values of his class. He rejects, with fateful consequences, the opportunity to expand his business because he does not want to incur debts, and the conformism to petty bourgeois values decisively prevents his eldest son Jürgen from attending the *Gymnasium*; his teachers say the boy has the ability and recommend that he should go, but Schütrumpf is anxious that his son should not 'auffallen', and Jürgen is educated at the *Realschule*. The real focal point of the narrator's attention is the character of Jürgen within the constraints imposed on the development of his personality by his home environment. He makes sporadic attempts, 'die unlösbaren Konflikte seiner Persönlichkeit auszudrücken' (46), for example through his music, but, by and large, his own authentic needs are so suppressed that by

9. Düsseldorf, 1977. All references to this edition.

the age of twenty his 'Anpassung an die elterlichen Lebensver-hältnisse' is complete (76). Then, through a stay in Italy and social contacts with students, he comes into contact with a style of life that he sees 'als dauernde Kritik an der eigenen Lebensweise' (106). The effect of these experiences outside the confines of his normal exist-ence leads to his being different from his contemporaries in a number of ways — he has no interest, for example, in cars or sport, unlike his brother Herbert. For a while Jürgen in effect leads a split existence, but, as a result of this vicarious involvement in something more in keeping with his needs, feels all the more sharply that there is ultimately 'keine Flucht aus dem vorgezeichneten Leben in N.' One of his difficulties, the narrator tells us, is that the young man, like 'fast alle Jugendlichen der Nachkriegsgeneration . . . so gut wie keine politische Erziehung erhalten [hat]' (163). Jürgen himself, on coming into contact with political activists in the factory, realises just how little he knows of politics and is anxious to make good the deficit. Yet the dramatic consequences of his apparent politicisation — his setting fire to the factory, which drew great public attention to the original case — demonstrate more clearly than anything else just how much his behaviour is determined by the petty bourgeois role expectations he has internalised. The apparently political action is really caused by his fear of losing his girlfriend Giovanna because of her doubt that he can act decisively — possession of a woman being perceived as one of the most important male roles in Jürgen's social world. Through this figure and his action, criticism is directed at the political immaturity of the petty bourgeoisie; at the failure of the SPD and the trade union to act in the case; at the activities of a capitalist industry — both in the Third Reich and in the Federal Republic — portrayed as ruthlessly and exclusively concerned with its own interests; at the press; and at the intolerance of a supposedly democratic state. This criticism is, however, undermined by the heavy-handedness of the narrator, who over-schematises Jürgen's experiences and interprets them rather glibly in generalising sociological-psychological jargon; in this respect *Der dreißigjährige Friede* most readily recalls the editorial interventions by those re-sponsible for the taped life stories of the 'non-authors' at the end of the Sixties, also designed to draw attention to the social disadvan-tages of the lower middle classes. These writings, however, lacked the historical aspect, which is the strongest feature of this novel. For all the glibness of occasional narratorial guidance, Jürgen is shown as the product of a particular milieu, including his family life, at a particular time. The simultaneous focus on Jürgen's childhood and youth, on the one hand, and on his parents' existence, on the other, produces a lively picture of the early years on the Federal Republic, in terms of the human consequences of the actions of the stage of high politics, examining from this perspective the values on which the state was built. Adolf, the decent little man who goes along with all that the new age stands for, during his last illness expresses the keen sense of disappointment with his life that he has come to feel: all his endeavours have come to nothing, he has been deceived by the grand lie 'daß wir in einer glücklichen Zeit leben und froh sein mußten'. His life has been a continual grind — he has only 'geschafft und noch mal geschafft' — and he has been let down in his belief that 'im Leben sollte eigentlich doch mehr herauskommen als ein paar glückliche Stunden und daß Du über die Runden gekommen bist. Daß Du satt zu essen gehabt hast und Dich fortgepflanzt hast' (277). The presentation of the lives of Adolf and Jürgen, his successor, throws the Fifties and Sixties into critical relief in a way designed to call into question the established self-awareness of West Germans today. This is where the strength of the book lies and what makes it part of the new historical novel.

The discussion in the Women's Movement about the historical novel also falls within the context of this chapter. An important and integral part of the process of self-realisation amongst women in recent years has been the discovery of, and concern with, historical representations of the social role of women, as a means of better understanding the historical process that has generated their present-day social conditions. Earlier imaginative literature by women has been included in the rediscovered material and has clearly served to adduce vivid testimony to the historical lot of women. It has also brought strongly to the fore questions about the nature of women's writing *per se*. Since the inception of the contemporary feminist movement in the Federal Republic the autobiographical statement has played an important role in highlighting aspects of the modern woman's identity problem — obvious examples in this connection are Karin Struck's *Klassenliebe* (1973), Verena Stefan's *Häutungen* (1975) and Angelika Mechtel's *Wir sind reich, wir sind arm* (1977). These autobiographical works, whatever influence they may have had in stimulating discussion within women's groups or in inducing others to reflect on the question of their own identity, are written by younger women and, as such, lack the historical perspective of Ingeborg Drewitz's novel *Gestern war heute* (1978), which presents personal experiences within the framework of a historical development starting in the last century and going on into the generation after her own.

Gestern war heute, in the words of its subtitle, tells of 'Hundert Jahre

Gegenwart'[10]: the narrator retraces not only her own life, but delves back before the turn of the century by using the reminiscences of older family members. The historical background to her own life-story is provided by a range of documentary information, inserted collages of newspaper items and news reports, the everyday life of the family being reconstructed as precisely as possible from her own memories and those of her parents. Despite this broad social and historical canvas as background, the foreground of the novel is always concerned with the identity problems of the narrator, Gabriele M., seemingly modelled largely on the figure of Ingeborg Drewitz herself. The first sense of a crisis in self-awareness for Gabriele comes at school: her parents' initial, intuitive response was to reject the Nazis with contempt and so, since she is not 'organisiert' and still lacks the 'Kraft zum Alleinsein', she becomes most upset that she 'in der Schule gehänselt wurde, weil sie keiner Jugendorganisation angehörte, keine Uniform besaß, kein Abzeichen trug' (87). She is, therefore, delighted that she can become involved in the gymnastic display for the Berlin Olympics of 1936, in which she can at last 'WIR sein', if only for a while. She is torn between her desire 'dazu zu gehören' and her dislike of a mass movement, secretly joins the BDM for a while, but has the courage to leave it after the Reichskristallnacht. The isolation into which she is thrown is relieved during the war by 'die graue Lehrerin', who puts her in contact with an underground organisation helping refugees. To some extent she is taught by her former teacher 'der Anpassung zu widerstehen', but the reader is always aware of her need to be with others. When the war is over Gabriele initially plunges into work with a group of young people publishing a (short-lived) periodical: she feels that this activity enables her to catch up on experiences she has missed during the war and to define her own existence in terms other than those of mere survival. With the energy and enthusiasm so typical of many of her generation in this situation she starts studying, but feels confidence in herself only when involved with others. This insecurity leads quickly to marriage and the birth of her first child, Renate. Despite the hope that marriage and motherhood will mean a fresh start — symbolised in the name chosen for her child — she finds that the domestic role impedes any possibility of self-fulfilment: 'Ich lerne, daß ich nicht BIN, um zu sein, sondern um zu sorgen. . . . Ich gebe mich preis' (210). After some years, though, she is able to resume and complete her studies and begin a career as a radio journalist; now she feels

---

10. Düsseldorf, 1978. All references to this edition.

that she is at last offering 'Widerstand gegen die Zerfaserung des einzelnen, des ICH', rebelling against 'das Schema Mannfraukind' as she calls it (186), though later she has to admit that she is gradually losing sight of 'das ICH als Ziel' in her life.

In one sense Gabriele is a woman living between two eras. By leaving home for a while, writing her doctoral thesis and establishing a successful career, she probably gains more independence than most women of her generation (she was born, like Drewitz, in 1923). When she is alone she lives, as a former colleague puts it, 'aus der Fülle', but, when she returns to family life after the death of her second daughter, her life is marked by 'die zunehmende Unschärfe des ICH'. Her husband has no understanding at all of her real needs, thinking that their measure of happiness has been achieved in prosperity. She cannot forget what she calls her 'Wachträume', her dreams of true fulfilment, but in her relationship with him she feels that 'die Rolle ist stärker als der Mensch' and, lacking the courage to challenge what is expected of her, she relapses straightaway into a traditional pattern of wifely behaviour. During the time of the Student Movement, which she supports in an abstract sort of way in her capacity as journalist, she reacts as a mother very emotionally, suffering great distress when Renate leaves home and is not heard from for a long time. She is concerned about the nature of the freedom which the students 'sich genommen haben und die sie mit der Freiheit verwechseln, die sie suchen' (353), failing to recognise, it is implied, that Renate is at the same stage of her life as Gabriele herself was after the war; the daughter, however, is far more determined not to compromise in her striving for self-realisation.

In the attention that is drawn here to Gabriele's initially somewhat blinkered view of her eldest daughter's development and in other ways too Ingeborg Drewitz avoids a simplistic and falsely reassuring picture of the gradual emergence of female self-possessedness. While Renate is more consistent in her position than her mother, Gabriele's other surviving daughter Claudia seems totally ensnared by the traditional role of woman, believing that true fulfilment is to be found in the roles of wife and mother. In the light of her own experience, Gabriele cannot share her daughter's faith in the redemptive power of marriage, indeed, the idea had filled her as a young woman with 'Angst vor der Immer-Wiederkehr: Mann und Frau und Mann und Frau. Angst vor dem Leben, das Mutter gelebt hat und Großmutter und Urgroßmutter: Draußen die Welt und hinter den vier Wänden — nein, keine Geborgenheit' (196). She nevertheless went ahead with her marriage, behaving, as she now sees, just as short-sightedly as Claudia today: 'als gäbe es nur das.

Anfangen, sich lieben, ein Kind haben, keine Fragen, keine Zweifel keine Erinnerung an das alte, immer neue Elend der Vielen. Als gäbe es diese Angst nicht, die Renate umtreibt' (381). She has come to recognise that her discontent with her lot as woman and the compromise represented by her marriage has a historical context. Nevertheless, although Renate seems to embody some hope for more drastic change in the future, her mother's inconsistency and the development of Claudia indicate that the most recent phase in the social history of women is still marked by their difficulty in committing themselves fully to the cause of self-fulfilment. The delivery of Claudia's baby at the end of the novel links back, moreover, to Gabriele's own birth at the very beginning, the suggestion seeming to be that over Gabriele's lifetime little has changed. The central concern of the novel is located in the wider context of a general historical struggle for social emancipation by the leitmotif of Gabriele's uncle's involvement in 1905 in a mass demonstration at St Petersburg 'für Gerechtigkeit und Schutz'. While her husband, like — we are told — many other citizens of the Federal Republic, lives complacently in an ahistorical, affluent present, Gabriele feels that she cannot live without the varied forms of historical awareness that she has acquired and which inform and enrich her view of present-day social problems. The novel is testimony to such sentiments and at the same time, like the other historical novels examined in this chapter, represents a plea for the wider recognition of the need for such a perspective in any would-be dynamic society.

8

Realism and 'Neue Subjektivität'

In an earlier chapter we examined the frequently propounded view that the Seventies in West German literature represented a turning away from the politicisation of the Sixties and a subsequent flight into inwardness and subjectivity. Not only is it far from true that the Seventies were unpolitical (cf. Chapter 6), but the notion that 'Neue Subjektivität' (as a special tendency within the general pattern of more subjective literature) stemmed from a 'Rückzug ins Innere' caused by a reaction against the experiences of the Student Movement is, certainly in relation to the novel, not without its problems. In lyric poetry after 1970, and as far as poets like Delius, Krüger, Theobaldy, Born and Ritter are concerned, Peter Rühmkorf may well be right in his claim that 'die Geburtsstunde des neuen Ich-Gefühls mit Zerfall der Studentenbewegung [datiert], Erst mit der Zerlösung des sozialen Integrals, so lesen wir, konstatieren wir, wurde ein Selbstbewußtsein virulent, seltsam gemischt aus Isolationsschaudern und der trotzigen Lust, das eigne Oberstübchen neu zu vermessen'.[1] As to the prose of the period, Marcel Reich-Ranicki identifies 'das Individuum, der leidende Mensch' in his 'Selbstbeobachtung, Selbstforschung, Selbstdarstellung' as the — far vaguer — dominant tendency here, with the autobiographical writing of the Seventies being particularly significant within this. David Roberts identifies 'die persönliche Krise' as the 'vorherrschende Thema der Literatur der neuen Subjektivität', stemming in part from the increased awareness of the 'existenzielle Entfremdung in der modernen Industriegesellschaft' that the Student Movement brought with it; this crisis is also, he states, 'von einer Todesangst geprägt, die zur "authentischsten" Erfahrung der Isolation und Entfremdung der siebziger Jahre wird'.[2]

If we accept Roberts's understanding of 'Neue Subjektivität', it can hardly be considered new, in the sense of marking a departure from existing major thematic concerns of contemporary literature.

1. Peter Rühmkorf, 'Kein Apolloprogramm für Lyrik', in *Walter von der Vogelweide, Klopstock und ich*, Reinbek, 1975, p. 188.
2. 'Tendenzwenden. Die sechziger und siebziger Jahre in literarhistorischer Perspektive', *Deutsche Vierteljahresschrift*, 56, 1982, p. 302.

While Dieter Wellershoff's first novel, *Ein schöner Tag* (1966), fuses together the thought-processes of three figures, the focus in *Die Schattengrenze* (1969) is sharpened, with the neurotic state of the single protagonist portrayed from the individual's subjective point of view, in a way that anticipates the introversion in many novels of so-called 'Neue Subjektivität'. As early as 1972 — i.e. before the 'Tendenzwende' that allegedly induced widespread inwardness — Kurt Batt drew attention to the treatment of the middle-class intellectual's isolation in novels such as Walser's *Die Gallistl'sche Krankheit*, Gabriele Wohmann's *Ernste Absicht* (1970) and Ingeborg Bachmann's *Malina* (1971), as well as the exploration of the 'Abbruch der Beziehungen zur Mitwelt' in Thomas Bernhard's *Frost* (1966) and *Das Kalkwerk* (1970). In all these novels, Batt states, '[wird] das, was nicht im unmittelbaren Bezug zur eigenen Innerlichkeit steht, mit Unmut registriert oder als Störung empfunden'.[3] The stereotyped picture of the so-called 'new' in the literature of 'Neue Subjektivität' has to be further qualified by reference to the full nature of the politicisation of literature in the late Sixties, which consisted only partly in the call to subordinate literary activity to political goals. The Student Movement was seen as an integral part of a broadly based struggle for change in both the subjective and objective realms and, as such — although this frequently seemed at variance with individual political engagement — it involved an intention to stimulate and demonstrate new modes of behaviour freed from the constraints of traditional normative categories, representing a new, expanded and radical subjectivity. Herbert Marcuse, for example, argued the need for a 'neue Sensibilität', in the sense of a 'humane Sinnlichkeit', that would break 'das Diktat der repressiven Vernunft', and Rolf Dieter Brinkmann stressed in his afterword to the anthology *ACID* that this 'neue Sensibilität' had nothing to do 'mit politischem Inhalt', as 'dieses Thema nicht die Relevanz besitzt, wie es das Klischee wahrhaben möchte'. The emphasis on the dynamic and revolutionary force of the individual's 'innere Bedürfnisse', based on a heady cocktail of the ideas of Ernst Bloch and Marcuse, the early writings of Marx and Leslie Fiedler, and represented at its most extreme by the publications of the März Verlag, seemed to find a resonance in student and intellectual circles: this was, indeed, such that Martin Walser, who at the time took the view that literature needed to play its part in political activity, considered it necessary to issue a public warning (in *Kursbuch 20*) against this 'Neueste Stimmung im Westen'. Looking back

3. Kurt Batt, *Die Exekution des Erzählers*, Frankfurt, 1972, p. 11.

on the Student Movement, Rolf Hosfeld went so far as to call it a revolt intent on a 'Politisierung des Interieurs', its 'wesentlichste literarische Ausbeute' being 'der Rückzug auf die Existenz' (*Kursbuch 48*).

The stress on emotional life, subjective needs and personal relationships is, therefore, far from new in the context of the literature of the time: it represents, rather, a continuation of existing literary themes and a more intensive concern with integral aspects of that complex which is the Student Movement. It must nevertheless be conceded that, in certain circles of politically committed students, it was realised after the event that, as Uwe Timm has put it, 'im Denken über soziale Veränderung persönliche Bedürfnisse zu kurz gekommen sind'. There are numerous literary examples of the way in which, after the elections of 1969 and the demise of the APO, the sense of the neglect of emotional needs comes out. In Karin Struck's *Klassenliebe* (1973) — the novel which, together with Peter Schneider's *Lenz*, is frequently cited as heralding the reflection in literature of the 'Tendenzwende' — the narrator is dissatisfied in her relationship with H., because he 'ist immer noch infiziert vom Abscheu vor der Subjektivität. Unter Ausschaltung aller Subjektivität solle man aufopferungsvoll für die Revolution arbeiten' (146). In Hermann Kinder's *Der Schleiftrog* (1977) the narrative voice describes the great day of his 'Rückkehr zu mir, zu dem, wo ich bei mir war und für mich selbst, die Rückkehr zu meinen Gefühlen, meinen Sorgen, meiner Wirklichkeit, der große Sieg meiner Subjektivität, die Befreiung von Gertruds Vernunft und dem Gehorchen: die Freiheit von den politischen Sollvorstellungen, vom Zwang und Müssen'.[4] Much the same is true of *Lenz*. The eponymous central character embodies 'die Irritation des bürgerlichen Intellektuellen angesichts seiner schlechten Vermassung und Entindividualisierung in den doktrinären politischen Gruppen und Parteizirkeln der niedergehenden Studentenbewegung'.[5] He develops a 'Haß auf die fertigen Sätze' and the 'hohle Gerede' in his study group, whereas Italy 'löst seine Wahrnehmung aus dem Korsett der Begriffe' (320) and his new start promises to achieve a balance between inner and outer existence. *Lenz* can, indeed, also be read as a literary reaction against the propagation by some in the Student Movement of Socialist Realism, which tends to neglect precisely the inner life of the protagonist.

Although Lenz's development stems, in one sense, from his

4. Zurich, 1977, p. 205.
5. Michael Schneider, 'Von der Alten Radikalität zur Neuen Sensibilität' in *Die lange Wut zum langen Marsch*, Reinbek, 1975, p. 329.

reaction against the neglect of individual emotional needs in student political discussions, his involvement in the *Studentenbewegung* and his integration into the community in Trento are indicative of the — possibly illusory — sense shared by many, that the burdens of individuation could be suspended by participation in the collective. This re-emerges as a literary theme in Walter's *Die Verwilderung* and Karlheinz Frank's *Willi kalt und heiß* (1978). The emergence from communal existence often meant a renewed and more intense exposure to the isolation of the individual in the modern, increasingly atomised, society that has resulted from the dissolution of traditional social ties: *Lenz* and *Der Schleiftrog* are testimony to the difficulties experienced outside the collective, and a number of so-called 'Neue Subjektivität' novels portray the existential crises of the re-alienated individual and the consequent attempt to escape fear of death, heartache, loneliness or a sense of aimlessness, by withdrawing into the inner world of the self.

Nicholas Born's *Die erdabgewandte Seite der Geschichte* (1976) has, with good reason, been widely viewed as the prime example of this sort of novel.[6] It depicts — through what later turn out to be diary entries — 'ein langsamer Boykott aller Tätigkeiten des Überlebens' on the part of a radio journalist. He does occasionally fear that life is passing him by, but he is far more afraid 'alle Fäden wiederaufzunehmen, die ich ja ohnehin nicht halten konnte' (12). He occasionally enjoys the 'angenehme Gefühl einer Zugehörigkeit, einer gesunden Übereinkunft mit einer ruhig vorangehenden Gesellschaft' (20; this is, bizarrely, provoked by going to post a letter!), but on the whole he seems to enjoy his retreat into what is a 'wohltätige Einsamkeit'. Although the collapse of his marriage, very vaguely described as a 'falsches Leben', could well have been one cause of his later emotional paralysis, the structure of the novel and his later relationship with Maria make it clear that both his problems in an emotional relationship and also his general sense of alienation from the environment ultimately stem from the existential need to cut himself off from others: he can only find peace when he '[sich] ganz leer fühlte'. The first-person narrator blames society for the disintegration of his personality: 'die Gesellschaft erschöpft einen so, die Gemeinschaft der vielen Menschen, auf die du deine Aufmerksamkeit verteilen mußt, die Teams und Gruppen höhlen dich aus, verdünnen dich. . . . Das Kollektivgespenst gegen das Individualgespenst. Die Erde wird letzten Endes der Vernunft geopfert' (150–1). He rejects the organisations founded on the basis of a

6. Reinbek, 1976. All quotations from this edition.

consensus to work for human progress through discussion and action, while the political activity of that progressive, middle-class reference group to which he himself once belonged, is, more than anything else, now viewed as a stumbling-block to individual self-fulfilment: a concept like 'Solidarität', for example, 'käme mir wie ein angstvolles Beschwörungswort vor, mit dem die ruhlosen Wünsche der einzelnen gebannt, die unberechenbaren Energien gebunden werden' (195). He can now only take part in discussion with former friends by role-playing, but, despite all inability to continue as a full member of the group, he envies 'die Wirklichkeit aller anderen, die schon das eigentliche Leben führten, während bei mir alles immer noch nur Vorbereitung und Provisorium war' (22). He can no longer accept the norms of his own social circle and yet, somewhat perversely, finds the family life of his hospital room-mate attractive and, for a while, the 'Einschränkungen und die damit verbundenen Beschränkungen wurden langsam zu Maßstäben für ein normales Leben' (137). It is clear, however, that he is incapable of leading such a life; in a way reminiscent of the early Benn, he really longs for a brainless corporeal existence, a vacuous state that he can apparently attain briefly though sex. Intercourse with Maria or her sister provides him with the 'Schutz einer vollkommenen Sättigung' that makes conversation redundant and frees him for a while from the confines of a relationship in which every 'freies Gefühl, das in mir aufkommen mochte, wurde erstickt von Marias übergreifenden Forderungen' (93). His dream of comfort is to be an 'empfindungsloser Körper, der wie ein Eiswürfel wegrutschte, sobald man ihn anfassen wollte' (104).

The narrator accuses the State of offering him nothing but 'die Regie . . . der äußeren Auflösung', yet he longs for his own internal dissolution. He waits for bad news after Maria's accident, so that he can 'endgültig zusammenbrechen', and hopes for serious illness, promising himself 'eine stille Einfältigkeit' if he abandons himself 'hemmungslos der Medizin'. His self-indulgent immersion in medical treatment is indeed successful for a time and he notes how 'das Gefühl allgemeiner Paralyse war zu einer lieben Krankheit geworden, mit der man auch alt werden konnte und die aus sich selbst heraus immer neue, immer detailliertere Auflösungsgefühle absonderte' (145). As he can only conceive of life as a living death, it is no surprise that his thoughts, as Maria observes, revolve 'unaufhörlich um den Tod', and that he toys with the idea of suicide.

Nicholas Born claimed in his Preface to *Literaturmagazin 3* that the collapse of utopian thinking stemmed from the total efficiency of industrial society, and the narrator of this novel, as already observed, continues this thinking by blaming the State for his mental condition. The novel itself, however, would seem to show that the personality which claims to have to flee from the contraints of society is neither shaped by social forces, nor autonomous, but totally predetermined, according to the narrator's view of the world, by the universality of death. His alienation, as he presents it, is not socially induced, but derives from man's eternal and unchangeable fate. He attains the certainty 'daß es so bliebe, zeitlebens ohne Leben, bis zum Tode immer nur Anwartschaft auf Leben, ein hoffnungsloses Herumprobieren, als ob es darum ginge, die richtige Lage zu finden, wie beim Einschlafen. . . . Und dabei erschien es mir selbstverständlich, daß man diese Lage nur suchte für die lange Zeit des Totseins' (215). This insight leads to the narrator's determination to separate permanently from Maria and to cut himself off from the world: he at once feels 'stumpf und zufrieden' and all about him is at peace. The withdrawal into the self is complete.

The neurotic self-involvement of the narrator is perfectly reflected in the form of the novel: from the isolation of his writing-desk and from the perspective of the already completed withdrawal he describes the various earlier phases of the process. Anything which is not relevant to the self's view of its own development is excluded from the narrowly focused account of its retreat even from Maria: 'Nicht vor dem Hintergrund einer ruchlosen weltgeschichtlichen Spirale, deren Bewegungen immer enger und unentrinnbar wurden, spielte sich unsere Geschichte ab, vielmehr vollzog sich das gesellschaftliche Leben, dieser atemlose Stillstand in der Bewegung, vor dem Hintergrund unserer Geschichte' (203). The outer world as we know it has no direct relevance to the story, but exists only in so far as it reflects the inner mood and in any case, as he deduces from the objects in Maria's room, is unfriendly to him. The life to which he draws ever closer is far from the rich solipsistic existence of the later Arno Schmidt, but rather a self-indulgent concern with the self, the ultimate form of which, paradoxically, is seen as consisting in its own dissolution, as with some would-be suicides. The novel is, in a sense, the means whereby this process of self-erosion can be accelerated, since, the narrator himself tells us, he tries in his writing 'der Person ähnlich zu werden, als die ich mich beschrieb' (146), i.e. one who ruthlessly works at freeing himself from all ties, as being irrelevant to his concept of life — a waiting for death.

Nicholas Born continued this theme in his second — and last — novel *Die Fälschung* (1979).[7] The central character, Laschen, is again

---

7. Reinbek, 1979. All quotations from this edition.

a journalist and, like the narrator of *Die erdabgewandte Seite der Geschichte* he is 'ein ansteckender Fatalist', 'von der Vergeblichkeit durchdrungen' (132). He seems to have been like this for a long time, as he had 'ein halbes Jahr nach dem Abitur ... sich die Pulsadern aufgeschnitten' (63), but for a time he was able to distract himself from his inherently pessimistic view of life through his marriage to Greta, which, however, has now started to break down. The novel gives the initial impression that it is intended to portray how Laschen, during an assignment in the Lebanon where he is confronted with senseless sectarian killing, slowly comes to see the pointlessness of his profession. This is certainly the interpretation that Michael Krüger, amongst others, put on it: 'Mitten im Zentrum der Vernichtung spürt Laschen einen rapiden Lebensverlust, eine sich beschleunigende Ichauflösung angesichts der unverständlicher werdenden Realität'.[8] Undoubtedly, too, this was the central motif in Volker Schlöndorff's film of the novel and, indeed, the book several times draws attention to Laschen's dawning awareness in Beirut that he has been so desensitised to horror of any kind that he no longer knows 'Schmerz ..., an dessen Stelle vielleicht eine betäubte und deshalb unbegrenzte Fähigkeit getreten war, *Erlebnisse* aufzunehmen, zu speichern, wiederzugeben' (65). The fact that the murders he witnesses have little effect on him is attributed by the narratorial voice in part to the professional distance demanded of a journalist, while Laschen himself feels — with a sense of relief — that he 'krank geworden war an der Unbeteiligkeit und der Verantwortungslosigkeit des Berichterstattens' (168). But the truth of the matter is that Laschen, thrown in upon himself in the murderous world of Beirut, is constantly preoccupied with the problems of his false life and the absence of feeling between Greta and himself. Often withdrawing into his room, in three letters to Greta he tries to redefine his life, ignoring — as he is forced to admit — what is going on around him, since a 'Brief an Greta ist wichtiger' than the horrors outside. The plethora of details about the never-ending war and the extended episode with Ariane, who attracts him for a while, provide an exotic background to his introspection, but it is one of which he himself becomes increasingly unaware. 'Mitten in Ereignissen', his demeanour is characterised by 'Weltferne'; instead of becoming involved in what is happening around him and about which he is apparently still writing with great competence, to judge by the reaction of his editorial staff, his head is 'ein Leerraum des Nichthandelns ..., ein gelähmter Kern, eine Ferne von allen Ereignissen'

8. 'Krieg in Libanon — deutsche Eiszeit', *Die Zeit*, 12.10.1979.

(121). He is, in his own words, a 'Krüppel, ein tief gedemütigtes, in Auflösung übergegangenes Wesen' (216), but, although he 'lebt wie einer, der mit dem Leben abgerechnet hat' (290), it is his constant dream, 'ein neues Leben zu entwerfen'. After his return to Hamburg he resigns his position, but, far from being changed by the expected 'seelischen Zusammenbruch', his problem becomes 'nicht lösbar, sondern furchtbar erträglich' (317). At the end of the novel he slots back into his old 'false' life, climbing without thinking into bed alongside Greta. Despite the intensive activity of his inner life concerning fundamental questions of existence, his external life consists at the end, as the beginning, in his 'alte, sprichwörtliche Lethargie'.

The desire for radical change, for liberation from a false existence through a redefinition of the self is one of the basic themes of 'Neue Subjektivität', but in Born's case the exploration of what he termed the 'inneren Kontinente' of the soul ultimately seems of greater interest to his protagonists than a changed relationship to external reality. As in the early novels of Bernhard, in Gabriele Wohmann's *Ernste Absicht* and Ingeborg Bachmann's *Malina*, we find in Born's novels the portrayal of figures so self-obsessed that the outside world is relatively unimportant. The professional work of his journalists, just like those of the protagonists in the novels by Wohmann and Bachmann, is outside 'der immer ungeschriebenen Realität der Ereignisse' (DF, 239) and represents a 'raffiniertes System von Assoziationen, von Erinnerungen an *Das Leben*' (309) that has been lost to normal life. Born's figures prefer, however, the cosy world of their reduced existence and lack the drive to alter it or work for a positive change in the outside world that might restore to it those lost dimensions of which they are aware.

An actual break with an inadequate existence is the crucial event in Peter Handke's *Die Stunde der wahren Empfindung* (1975), a controversial novel proclaimed by some critics as an exemplary work of the 'Tendenzwende', and attacked by young critics and writers for its alleged 'abgestandenen Subjektivismus', based on a 'Konzeption der Innerlichkeit als eines nahezu autonomen Innenraums der reflektierten Empfindung und der empfindsamen Reflexion, der manischen Selbstbeschäftigung'.[9] The main character, Gregor Keuschnig, press attaché to the Austrian Embassy in Paris, is radically transformed by a dream in which he commits murder, and becomes so sensitive to the inadequacies of the life he has been

---

9. Roman Ritter, 'Die "Neue Innerlichkeit" — von innen und außen betrachtet', U. Timm and G. Fuchs (eds.), *Kontext 1*, Munich 1976, p. 249. All quotations from *Die Stunde der wahren Empfindung* from the first edition, Frankfurt, 1975.

leading that he is quite alienated from the world around him. Since everything seems to be carrying on 'elendig normal', at first he feels forced to lead a sort of double life, as he calls it, to survive. His press work now seems to consist of boring and meaningless routine and his personal relationships are repulsive — he loathes the sight of his wife and his regular lunchtime visit to his mistress Beatrice seems to be no more than an empty ritual: 'Das-die-Hose-über-den-Stuhl-Legen; das-sich-nebeneinander-ins-Bett-Legen; das das-Glied-in-die-Scheide-Aufnehmen' (29). He experiences hitherto unknown aggressive feelings and a heightened awareness of objects: as a result he comes to envy the 'ungebrochene Äußerlichkeit' of others. Soon, however, he recognises that for some time he has sensed a dissatisfaction with the dull routines of his private and professional lives and comes to see the positive potential of his 'komplizierten Seelenzusammenbruch'. Nevertheless, he finds it difficult to cope with the accompanying feelings of uncertainty and deep disgust with things around him; he is driven to the point of contemplating suicide. Suddenly, though, his eyes are opened and he can unravel 'das Geheimnis der Welt' and face the future with keen anticipation: the novel ends with his buoyant entry into a new life.

It is not at all clear how we are to understand the new and fuller life that lies before Keuschnig. Manfred Jurgensen maintains that the aesthetics of a 'Stunde der wahren Empfindung' lead directly to a preparedness for political action, although this is difficult to see, and Handke himself stated soon after the novel appeared that it was important 'künstliche Solidarität . . . aufzugeben und sich selber ohne Erbarmen zu erforschen'. Only by following the inward path could literature hope to be able to address itself again to the outside world ('Ohne Ausreden innerlich geworden, wird seine [the writer's, KB] Poesie ganz herzhaft ganz äußerlich werden können[10]). Not only is it difficult to know how Handke conceives of this happening, we would tend, in this connection, to go along with Hans Christoph Buch's view (which he applies to the tendency of 'Neue Subjektivität' as a whole) that an 'Innenleben, das sich nicht ständig an den Irritationen der Außenwelt bricht und korrigiert, ist keins'.[11] Keuschnig's metamorphosis — and the allusion to Kafka is consciously made by the author — is a completely unmotivated break with his former life; the change comes about as a result of a dream. He now looks at his wife and suddenly 'wünschte er nie mehr etwas von ihr zu hören oder zu sehen. . . . Sie hieß Stephanie und gestern

10. 'Die Tyrannei der Systeme' (a correspondence between Dieter E. Zimmer and Peter Handke), *Die Zeit*, 2.1.1976.
11. 'Vorbericht', *Literaturmagazin 4*, Reinbek, 1975, p. 15.

185

noch hatte sie ihn zumindest manchmal gerührt' (8). His wife, his mistress and his work now fill him with disgust — which the reader can only understand as the physical manifestation of some sort of spiritual break with his existing life, induced by the dream. But the novel does not offer a psychological interpretation of his change of consciousness, nor does it portray events within a consistent metaphorical framework, as is the case with Kafka. From the narrator, who suddenly pops up like Hitchcock in the figure of the 'dicke Schriftsteller', we are given to understand that Keuschnig feels at one 'nur mit Leuten, die in ihren Tätigkeiten keinen rechten Sinn sehen' (93), but at no point are we are told why the various segments of his former life were unsatisfactory. Keuschnig's metamorphosis provides no clue as to this or to the nature of his new existence, other than that it consists completely in a radical intensification of inner life, leading to a situation in which 'das Sehen und Beobachten und der Zustand, in dem dies geschieht, wichtiger werden als das Beobachtete und Gesehene'.[12] Keuschnig's heightened sensitivity leads to detailed descriptions of everyday objects, which would be completely justified if the novel were concerned to show, like Kipphardt's *März*, the mind of the psychologically abnormal, but this is merely a narcissistic process of observation, with the external world — as in Born's *Die erdabgewandte Seite der Geschichte* — existing only as a projection of Keuschnig's state of mind, the linguistic reflection of his alienation from the world as he has known it. We are completely uninformed as to the real reasons for Keuschnig's break with the past and, just as mysteriously, his state of alienation and disgust is overcome, enabling him to start a new life:

> Indem ihm die Welt geheimnisvoll wurde, öffnete sie sich und konnte zurückerobert werden. . . . Weit auseinander liegende Einzelheiten, ein von Eidotter gelber Löffel auf der Straße, die Schwalben hoch oben, vibrierten in einer Zusammengehörigkeit, für die er jetzt keine Erinnerung und keinen Traum mehr brauchte: ein Gefühl, daß man von jedem Punkt aus zu Fuß nach Hause gehen konnte (152).

He now realises, with the help of a crumpled letter he finds in the gutter, that he has been indifferent about everything in his life, but this 'schaurigste Zeit' is now behind him and the world round about

12. Stephan Reinhardt, '"Nach innen führt der geheimnissvolle Weg, aber er führt auch wieder heraus". Unvollständige Anmerkungen zum neuen Irrationalismus in der Literatur' in W. Martin Lüdke (ed.), *Nach dem Protest. Literatur im Umbruch*, Frankfurt, 1979, p. 179. Reinhardt's statement was directed specifically at Steffen's *Die Annäherung an das Glück*, but he himself makes the link to Handke which justifies its use here.

186

him is transformed. Just what this recapture of the world and the new correlativity of things consist in, and what sort of new work he finds, 'deren Ergebnis verbindlich und unverrückbar wäre' (161), we do not discover. We only know that, wearing a blue suit, white socks and yellow shoes, he 'an einem lauen Sommerabend über-querte die Place de l'Opéra in Paris. Er hatte beide Hände seitlich in die Hosentaschen seines sichtlich noch neuen Anzugs gesteckt und ging zielbewußt auf das Café de la Paix zu . . .' (167).

It would clearly be wrong for a reading of this novel to ignore the possible element of play in it and not to ask, therefore, whether the analysis thus far does not take it too seriously. In addition to the nodding reference to Kafka, there are clear parallels with Sartre's *La Nausée*, although Handke has said that he only read this after completing his own novel. There are, in addition, some similarities with Hitchcock's *Vertigo*, the 'dicke Schriftsteller' has affinities with both Hitchcock and Dürrenmatt, there is an element of near-quotation from Goethe's theory of the 'Novelle' and the final scene not only presents Keuschnig as a sort of Werther (through the way he is dressed), but could also be seen as mocking the ending of the Socialist Realist 'Entwicklungsroman'. Such instrumentalisation of motifs, scenes and figures from literature and the cinema, however, has long been an integral part of Handke's prose style. More importantly in this connection, the theme of liberation from pre-scribed social roles and the attainment of some authentic individual identity has formed the corner-stone of this writer's work from the beginning and on into the Eighties (and his treatment of this theme has shown elsewhere, e.g. in *Kindergeschichte*, 1981, the same ten-dency to lapse into the mystical). In addition, our understanding of *Die Stunde der wahren Empfindung* would seem to be reinforced by the fact that Handke expressed his preference for the 'Geborgenheit unter der Schädeldecke' as against the external world very clearly in his Büchner-Preis speech, and the sense of his attraction to the 'Weg nach Innen' to be found in this novel is reinforced by his *Langsame Heimkehr* (1979).

In a severe attack on *Die Stunde der wahren Empfindung* and other works of so-called 'Neue Subjektivität', Roman Ritter took the view that the subjectivity represented in this novel gave no sort of 'Einsicht in die gesellschaftlichen Verhältnisse', but reflected, rather, a 'Konzeption der Innerlichkeit als . . . der narzißtischen Isoliertheit des innerlichen Ichs' that revealed nothing of the social causes of Keuschnig's irritation and suffering.[13] Heinrich Vormweg

13. Ritter, 'Die Neue Innerlichkeit . . . ', p. 246.

makes a similar distinction to Ritter between 'Innerlichkeit' and a subjective literature which aims to deepen the reader's awareness of the interaction between the individual psyche and society: he approved of 'eine überraschende, keineswegs einfach den alten Individualismus wiederherstellende Hervorhebung des einzelnen, des Ich, der Person', in which the individual is shown 'in seiner Abhängigkeit, seiner Verstrickung in soziale Realität, seine Klassenzugehörigkeit . . . '. Vormweg's examples of such subjective literature include Karin Struck's *Klassenliebe* and Hans J. Fröhlich's *Im Garten der Gefühle*, but he expresses strong disapprobation of Handke's fiction and Karin Struck's second novel, *Die Mutter*, which for him stands 'im Zeichen der Subjektivität des einzelnen, einer überstürzt wieder als Wert installierten, teils kruden Spontaneität und dem Drang nach einer gefühlshaften Übereinkunft mit den Lesern'. Even Frisch's *Montauk*, so favourably reviewed by many critics when it appeared in 1975, is seen as merely using 'die Form des *journal intime* zur weltläufig-dekorativen Aufbereitung einer Vorstellung seines Ichs, die nicht enthüllt, sondern eine Pose festigt'.[14] Both Ritter and Vormweg offer a more precise understanding of the term 'Neue Subjektivität' (also known, confusingly, as 'Neue Sensibilität' and 'Neue Innerlichkeit') based on their reading of works widely included in that category, which helps to identify within it more than one type of literature. An amalgamation of their ideas would suggest that we should distinguish here between 'Neue Innerlichkeit' and 'Neue Subjektivität', with the former indicating a turning away from affairs of the day and a withdrawal into what is portrayed as a more or less autonomous inner self, or into hypochondriac self-observation; this sort of writing could in turn be regarded as beginning with Bernhard, as an essentially Austrian literature — where, of course, it has to be seen in a different literary context — and adopted by West German writers following the example of their Austrian colleagues. 'Neue Subjektivität', as we understand it, would then signify the presentation, in the literature of the Seventies, of experiences produced by the collision of the self, with all its hopes, dreams, doubts and emotional needs, with the outside world. A comparison between Handke's *Die Stunde der wahren Empfindung* and Uwe Timm's *Kerbels Flucht* offers, we would argue, the possibility of evaluating how far the suggested distinction is plausible.

Uwe Timm's first novel. *Heißer Sommer*, ended with the hope of a better future, with the belief, indeed, that there was 'ein realisierbares Glück für alle'; *Kerbels Flucht*[15] concerns the consequences for a

14. 'Noch kein neuer Morgen', *Jahresring* (1975–6) p. 239.
15. Königstein, 1980. All quotations from this edition.

contemporary of Ullrich Krause of the loss of such optimism. Kerbel is unable to come to terms with the sense of emptiness that many people felt on the demise of the Student Movement. Moreover, looking back at the time of his 'wirkungslosen Betriebsamkeit', as he now calls it, Kerbel comes to the conclusion that he has merely wasted time. Like many of his generation, he belatedly becomes aware of having neglected personal needs in his enthusiastic work for social change and so, when he meets Karin, he invests his whole emotional energy in their relationship, much as Schneider's Lenz did with L. When she leaves him it is 'die Katastrophe' for him. The agreed basic principle of this modern affair had been that each wished to avoid the 'Gefahr der Erstarrung, [der] Abtötung neuer Erfahrungen', had expressed themselves anxious not 'am gegenseiti-gen Überdruß ersticken, sondern sich auch für den Widerspruch offenhalten, für das Neue . . .' (34). Karin has apparently retained this attitude, and she regards the break with Kerbel as offering her 'einen neuen Lebensentwurf': this she exploits to the full, while his response is withdrawal into moody introspection. The novel consists in the main of diary entries and other reminiscences left after Kerbel's death, which show how he turned in upon himself and record his preoccupation with self, his grief and his wild hopes of starting again. In addition, as he himself notes down, the act of writing makes 'alles erträglicher, auch das Selbstmitleid' (14). He begins to analyse the roots of the personal stagnation leading up to Karin's going and begins to see that his problems can, to some extent, be traced back into childhood; he is also forced to admit that the sense of the purposelessness of his life had emerged long before the 'catastrophe'. In Karin's new friend, 'ein von seinem Beruf fanatisierter Mann', Kerbel sees qualities that he has now lost, the man is, he feels, an after-image of his former self, 'und zwar in dieser energischen Zukunftsplanung, etwas zu bewirken, etwas zu ändern' (73). While most of his contemporaries have by now either remained politically active or conformed to society by finishing their studies and entering a profession, Kerbel — feeling torn between his emo-tional needs and 'was man abstrakt als richtig einsieht' — rejects any purposive action, such as taking his examinations, 'als Abtötung meiner Begierde und damit meiner Selbst' (103). He admittedly writes of work as a crucial component of self-realisation, but is unable, particularly in his highly unstable state after Karin's depar-ture, to tolerate the demands and petty constraints of a career. He has visions of discovering his 'radikal Anderes', his 'Mehr an Lust, an Phantasie, an Freundlichkeit' by either joining in the civil war in Nicaragua ('Wäre ich dort, mir wäre — vielleicht — geholfen'), purchasing a cork plantation in Portugal, becoming involved in a rural commune or, just before his death, apprenticing himself to a cabinet-maker. These are the left-over romantic dreams of the Student Movement and Kerbel is, in any case, incapable of the commitment necessary to realise them. In the relationship with Karin he can delude her — and himself — that he is open to new ideas and shares her 'Gier nach einem anderen Leben', but he is, in reality, far more like the girl from East Berlin. Her depression frightens even Kerbel and she embodies, he says — without seeing the similarity to himself — a 'melancholische Endzeitstimmung . . . , die das Glück im kleinsten Kreis sucht, im ganz Privaten' (86). Without being able to admit it, he has projected all his hope on to the relationship with Karin and, when he loses her, his 'Krankheit', observes the friend and narrator who tells us of Kerbel's last months, is 'lediglich verstärkt und damit fühlbarer: eine allgemeine Lustlosigkeit, die langsame Auszehrung der Zuversicht, eine Bleichsucht der Wünsche und eine Atrophie des Willens' (102). Kerbel loses his casual work as a taxi-driver when he has an accident whilst drunk ('Sie fahren wie ein Lebensmüder', his passenger tells him); he is then a disastrous failure in editing a publisher's news-sheet, a job secured for him by a university friend. He turns to the rural commune, on which he has now set his hopes, but finds it taken over by drug-taking drop-outs; when he leaves for home the communards warn him of an intensive security check in the area, he accelerates away from a police barrier, instead of stopping, and is shot.

In Handke's *Die Stunde der wahren Empfindung*, we were confronted with an inexplicable break with the familiar which unleashed a movement into the self, but only in the sense of an acutely sensitised inward preoccupation with, as far as the reader is concerned, apparently arbitrary aspects of external reality. It told us nothing of Keuschnig's thought-processes or of the nature of the change in him. *Kerbels Flucht*, instead of depicting a seemingly random caesura in the life of the central character, revolves round a turning-point for him that unleashes a fateful decline which can, in the main, be explained from his earlier life. The withdrawal into the self, the intensified inner life, can be explained as the result of a deep-rooted, but latent, ontological crisis triggered off by a decisive personal tragedy (Karin's leaving). This difference in the type of inwardness portrayed is also reflected in the form of the two novels. While Handke depicts Keuschnig's transformation through the interpretative voice of a third-person narrator, *Kerbels Flucht* presents the range of causes of Kerbel's inherent alienation and the final phase of heightened despair from his own point of view, through the immediacy of diary entries, letters, jottings and even parts of an uncompleted authobiographical novel, all bearing direct witness to his neurotic and total introspection, particularly after the 'catastrophe'. *Die Stunde der wahren Empfindung* essentially makes reality mysterious, with Keuschnig's relationship to it being conveyed by a 'Sprachteppich, der als solcher rein *ornamentale* Funktion hat', as Jean Améry has so aptly observed,[16] so that we cannot reach to the interpersonal and social causes of his breakdown or the nature of his regenerated existence. In *Kerbels Flucht*, on the other hand, we are confronted with a sensibility caused by a specific outer world and heightened ever further through suffering in that world until it reaches breaking point. The emotional sensitivity of Kerbel, the intelligent, upwardly mobile student, is increased by university and his study of literature; he is captivated by the dreams of the Student Movement and clings to them, failing to recognise that the gulf between its heady formulations and social reality is even wider than before. The unrealised human needs identified by the Student Movement may well be, in themselves, fully justified, but Kerbel's inability to distinguish between them as a distant goal and existing reality makes him a neurotic. When his only prop, Karin, leaves him he is thrown back on his own anxious, unworldly self; to make matters worse, his studies have alerted him to recognising the symptoms of his own illness, so that his knowledge, far from helping him, only hastens his demise: 'Das Quälende aber ist, daß ich durchaus die Mechanismen kenne, die zu dem führen, was man ausflippen nennt, aber deshalb den Vorgang nicht abstellen kann' (144). Kerbel, by now a failed academic, is sunk by that imbalance that threatens the equilibrium of all intellectuals, from which Peter Schneider's Lenz was able, in the event, to save himself. The inwardness of the novel is thus in no way purely private, nor does it signify a narcissistic concern with one's own sensibility; the component parts of Kerbel's crisis and of the strands of the narrative 'fügen sich . . . zum Bild einer privaten wie allgemeinen Orientierungslosigkeit und Krise zusammen'.[17] In this sense *Kerbels Flucht*, which we would consider a highly illuminating example of 'Neue Subjektivität', represents a splendid demonstration of the way in which it is still possible in the contemporary novel to portray the experiences and suffering, the needs and fears of the individual subject realistically, i.e. in their interaction with existing society.

The literature of 'Neue Innerlichkeit', in our sense of the term,

---

16. 'Grundloser Ekel', *Merkur*, 29, 1975, p. 470.
17. Stephan Reinhardt, 'Mutlosigkeit', *Frankfurter Hefte*, 36, 1981, Heft 1, p. 72.

includes both the hypochondriac or narcissistic concern with the self, as found in the works of Bernhard or Handke, and the new 'Biedermeier' of Nicolas Born or Richard Schroubek, the first-person narrator of Botho Strauß's *Die Widmung* (1977). The striking and refreshing feature of *Die Widmung*, also widely understood as an example of 'Neue Subjektivität', in its undifferentiated sense, is the mocking, critical tone of Strauß towards his central character. All these novels (which we would designate as 'Neue Innerlichkeit'), have in common an understanding, on the part of the author, of the self as essentially autonomous and able to realise itself only in the authentic inner world of the self, rather than in the sham external world. The bulk of the novels in this area of subjective writing in the Seventies and Eighties consists, however, of those included in 'Neue Subjektivität', in our more precise understanding of the term, i.e. as subject-centric literature that attempts to portray the individual's search for self-realisation within the framework of the social forces that determine that quest. A widespread and long-lasting after-effect of the Student Movement and the impulses emanating from it (which include a deeper interest in social-scientific subjects like sociology and psychology) was the break with the traditional concept of the autonomous self, as put forward by traditional philosophical and aesthetic theories and continued by the writers of 'Neue Innerlichkeit'. The whole range of personal life-histories at the end of the Sixties point to the new interest in the force of social indoctrination in shaping the development of the individual, and this was in turn reflected in the various forms of realist writing after 1973. *Kerbels Flucht*, as a late representative of this type, adds a keen awareness of the problems of modern narration, using the montage technique to present the various kinds of information about Kerbel: it also has close affinities with the psychological realism which emerged strongly in the second half of the Seventies. The foremost exponent of this type of realist writing is undoubtedly Dieter Wellershoff: his first two novels of the Sixties demonstrate a fascination with psychological problems that is continued in his 'Hörspiele' and deepened in his theoretical writings, which are increasingly preoccupied with the ideas of Freud and R.D. Laing. His prose of the Seventies and Eighties directly reflects this concern (cf. Chapters 3, 5 and 9). Perhaps the most striking work of this type is, though, Heinar Kipphardt's *März*, which, again drawing on Laingian ideas, reconstructs the life and suffering of März and presents his 'illness' as the product of the normative constraints of a 'geistesgestörten Gesellschaft'. But the concern with pathological states of mind, found in *März*, Wellershoff's *Einladung an alle* and *Die Schönheit des Schimpansen* and the work of Günter Steffen, has ultimately more in common with our category of 'Neue Innerlichkeit' — as revealed by a comparison of Steffens *Die Annäherung an das Glück* with Born's *Die erdabgewandte Seite der Geschichte* — than with 'Neue Subjektivität', which uses psychological insights to inform and illuminate the attempt, through reconstructing individual — even highly personal — experience, to understand the interaction between social reality and the self. Not untypical of such an interest is the desire expressed by Franz Xaver Kroetz, 'meine eigenen biographie-immanenten, existenziellen Ruinen . . . als gesellschaftliche Phänomene zu begreifen und darzustellen'.[18]

Autobiographical writing as part of 'Neue Subjektivität' consists essentially in the working out of this interaction, rather than in the conventional presentation of the individual personality as being of exceptional interest, or in monomaniac rumination. It has much in common with that other frequently-met German form of autobiographical writing, the 'Lebenslauf', but the choice of the potentially more open and flexible form of the novel allows the experiences of the individual personality to be seen all the more easily as part of a more general social pattern. Perhaps the clearest and most important example of such writing in the period since the early Seventies is given by women's literature, which, through the concern in the autobiographical novel with questions of personal identity and the depiction of subjective experience, places such texts in the wider context of a broadly based concern for the development of collective consciousness and comradeship amongst women. Verena Stefan's *Häutungen*, Margot Schroeder's *Ich stehe meine Frau* and Ingeborg Drewitz's *Gestern war heute* all have their place in such writing, as does the first, to feminists somewhat controversial, example of this type of novel, Karin Struck's *Klassenliebe* (1973).[19]

Klassenliebe represents the efforts by a narratorial voice, clearly Karin Struck herself, to tell her life-story in a way which makes it 'klar und durchsichtig' to herself, so that it helps to sort out her own identity problems. Her lack of self-assurance is rapidly seen to be connected with her social background and gender-specific difficulties. Karin comes from the working class, but now feels 'abgeschnitten von der Arbeiterklasse. Geschnitten von beiden Seiten. Kaum bin ich eine "Intellektuelle", stoßen mich die Arbeiter weg, intellektuellenfeindlich aus Angst und Minderwertigkeitsgefühl, stoßen

18. 'Ich schreibe nicht über Dinge, die ich verachte', *Theater heute*, 21, 1980, Heft 7, p. 18. Cf. further in this connection: Moray McGowan, 'Das Objekt entdeckt seine Subjektivität: "Innerlichkeit" in den neueren Kroetz-Stücken?' in K. Bullivant and H.J. Althof (eds.), *Subjecktivität — Innerlichkeit — Abkehr von Politischen?*, Bonn, 1986.
19. Frankfurt, 1973. All quotations from this edition.

mich die andern weg, weil ich gar keine "richtige" Intellektuelle bin und nie sein werde' (49). Speaking 'eine Niemandssprache in einem Niemandsland', she is at times so desperately uncertain of herself as to contemplate suicide, at others she clings to the relative security of a negative role — her refusal to conform 'ans fette Bürgertum'. The narrator firmly rejects the 'Typ der degeneriert-sensiblen, modischen, "emanzipierten" Frau' represented by Fassbinder's Petra von Kant, 'die nicht begreift, daß sich das, was sie unter Emanzipation versteht, lediglich aus den sozialen Privilegien bürgerlicher Bildung und Herkunft ... zusammensetzt' (164), but recognises that she cannot return to her working-class roots. She also longs for meaningful intellectual work, but is at the same time aware of the pressure of hitherto suppressed sensual needs; she wants to be both 'Hirn-Mensch und Sinn-Mensch'. During the time of the Student Movement, when Karin was politically active, this aspect of her personality was particularly neglected, as she now recognises through the contrast between her life with her new lover and that with his predecessor: 'Hätte mich H. nicht mit Sensibilität unterernährt. Die heruntergekommene marxistische Theorie hat H. sterilisiert. Ich wäre nicht auf Z.'s Sinnlichkeit und Anschaulichkeit hereingefallen. Meine jahrzehntelange sinnliche Unterdrückung' (226). It is, however, the act of writing itself that confronts the narrator with the full extent of her personal problems and thus offers, in the reconstruction of experiences and emotional reactions during a critical phase of her life, the chance 'zu sich selbst zu kommen und sich über diesen Vorgang zu verständigen'.[20]

A similar concern with the problems of self-realisation has long been the major theme of Gabriele Wohmann's novels. Her work in the early Seventies, up to *Schönes Gehege* (1975) presented these problems, however, as emanating from a conflict between the self and an everyday world experienced as inherently disgusting and inducing a withdrawal into the self (the 'schöne Gehege' of the title); this places her work within our category of 'Neue Innerlichkeit'. In her more recent novels, on the other hand, she has located the search for identity firmly in a precise social world. *Ach wie gut, daß niemand weiß* (1980), the work with the closest affinities to women's literature, focuses on the reactions of Marlene Ziegler, a young psychotherapist, to the personal consequences of accepting a temporary position in Switzerland, followed by a lecture tour of the United States, and necessitating separation from her partner and her normal

---

20. Heinrich Vormweg, ' ... kein verkrüppelter Mensch', *Süddeutsche Zeitung*, 30–31.5.1973.

life. In this new situation she has time to reflect on her identity problems, which stem essentially from the conflict between her professional ambition and her femininity, but which are intensified by the introspection stemming from the nature of her work. By 'dropping out' of her familiar social world and extricating herself from personal ties for a few months she is able to scrutinise herself at a certain distance; she also attempts to examine her own needs in the relationship with Herbert, her vacillation between libidal urges and sexual hatred and her feelings on the roles of men and women in general. She is torn between dreams of self-autonomy and social conformism, between a feminist notion of self and the traditional role of woman, with the result that, even by the end of her 'leave', she cannot come to a clear decision, even though Herbert has now suggested marriage. The novel is weakened, however, by a tendency for it to follow the path of Marlene's new existence and merely drift from one situation to another, with the quest for self-enlightenment unconvincingly interwoven with her travel experiences. It lacks the sharp and precise concern with the problem of identity — this time as exemplified in the personal crisis of a man — of her earlier *Frühherbst in Badenweiler* (1978).[21]

The protagonist of that novel, Hubert Frey, is a successful composer who, sensing that a nervous breakdown is imminent, withdraws to Badenweiler, the spa town where Chekhov and Conrad Aiken died. The project 'HUBERTS KRISE' seems, on first sight, to be highly self-indulgent, but the retreat does have the effect of inducing examination of self and its relationship to his social world. Behind the grand artistic gesture — Hubert is, for example, fully aware of the symbolism of the time of year he has chosen for his impending breakdown — there is a genuine mid-life crisis, which appears as a neurotic concern about his state of health and fear of death, as well as in a radical scrutiny of the value of his life up till then. He begins to see that his personal problems are partly rooted in his childhood (we again note the influence of psychological realism), but stem essentially from his relationship to his wife Selma. Unlike him, she has grown in self-assurance over the years, particularly since establishing herself as a successful journalist: 'Strotzend vor Selbstverwirklichung blieb sie in einer Art Overal, der ihr wie aufgenäht und aufgebügelt anlag, frisch, kühl, lebensfähig' (24). But Hubert also realises that he is disturbed by the state of the cultural milieu in which he works and that his general sense of unease is linked to the mood of the country: 'Ich fühle mich nicht mehr

---

21. All quotations from the edition in the Fischer Bücherei, Frankfurt, 1980.

behaglich in diesem Staat. Ich habe einen harten Geschmack auf der Zunge bei Begriffen wie HÄRTE, OPFER, DURCHGREIFEN, AUSDAUER, eine Wörterliste, die sich verlängern ließe, und deren Einzelposten sehr verräterisch und verhängnisvoll die schlimmste Epoche in der deutschen Geschichtsschreibung beschwören' (48). Ultimately, though, his mind keeps dwelling on his fear of death, which emerges ever more clearly as the root cause of his mid-life crisis. One day, however, he comes across a terrified mouse and suddenly comes to the recognition that his stay in Badenweiler is indefensible: 'Mit was für Luxusfragen er sich doch in den vergangenen Wochen herumgequält hatte. . . . Hier galt kein Zaudern. Hier konnte nichts auf die lange Bank geschoben werden. Hier mußte gehandelt werden' (170). As a result, Hubert is filled with determination to start afresh with his 'entsetzlich kurzen Leben'.

Like most of the novels of Gabriele Wohmann, *Frühherbst in Badenweiler* is narrated in the third person by a figure clearly well disposed towards, but not uncritical of, the protagonist, much in the manner of Martin Walser's novels from *Jenseits der Liebe* (1976) onwards. A blend of direct, indirect and free indirect speech concentrates the reader's attention on Hubert, while the narrator's ironic intrusions invite quizzical examination of his behaviour. The critical stance of the narrator comes out particularly strongly in the ending of the novel — the confrontation with the mouse — which can only be understood as irony. In one sense, indeed, the novel can be read as a sustained criticism of the narcissistic concern with inner life in the novels of 'Neue Innerlichkeit', with the intrinsic plea, brought out in the contrast between Hubert and Selma, for the self to be defined through interaction with the active world.

Self-assessment, the examination of the quality of individual personal and social life and critical scrutiny of established patterns of relationship between men and women, all providing the main focal points of a number of the novels discussed above, were central to the thinking of the generation which, caught up in that complex entity called the Student Movement or influenced in some way by what it stood for, found itself involved in the late Sixties in radical re-evaluation of its personal values. It is, therefore, not at all surprising that these themes are taken up time and again in the novel of the Seventies and Eighties, which is dominated, in the main, by writers strongly influenced by those earlier experiences. The Seventies were, moreover, a time when such people were finishing their studies and beginning to establish themselves in careers, with the result that they were now in a position to begin putting the high ideals of the Student Movement into practice.

This latter theme, which is central to a number of works from the Seventies examined in this and other chapters, is also taken up by Hans J. Fröhlich in his *Im Garten der Gefühle* (1975),[22] in which his particular concern is the human consequences of such an attempt to realise the ideals of 1968. The first-person narrator of the novel is in his mid-thirties and has been enabled, through the generosity of his rich parents-in law, to give up his work in the archives of a Hamburg advertising agency and to pursue the life of a freelance essayist and translator, while living in idyllic surroundings at M. on the shores of Lake Garda in northern Italy. His earlier life in Hamburg has been dissatisfying — he calls it 'eine gescheiterte Existenz' — so that he feels that 'im Leben so ziemlich alles daneben gegangen [ist]', but in Italy he has found a 'tiefe innere Ruhe' (cf. in this connection also Fröhlich's *Anhand meines Bruders*, 1974). His financial independence has enabled him to achieve a private 'Befreiung von der Überflußgesellschaft', in Marcuse's term, to free himself from the material constraints of capitalist economy on the individual; he and his wife Dorothee are envied by many of their friends for having put into practice one of the dominant utopian dreams of the Student Movement. But the life they lead is not quite as idyllic as it seems, the narrator not knowing 'wie lange ich mir ausreiche, wie lange diese Ruhe dauert. . . . Es gut zu haben, kann doch nicht genug sein' (32). This danger of the potential emptiness of their existence is compounded by his fear that he may sink back 'einmal wieder in meine frühere Erbärmlichkeit' and his sense of the danger of the house being destroyed 'von innen her', by which he is referring to personal difficulties with Dorothee that are only now emerging. For her part, Dorothee, when she married and moved to Italy with him, seems to have fallen prey to her dream of being half of an 'idealen Liebespaar'. Now, however, she is becoming conscious of her need for a sense of individual freedom and for confirmation — through the attention of other men — of her continued sexual attractiveness. For several years she has projected all her emotions on to the family (they have a small daughter), but notions about alternative forms of cohabitation, much in discussion during her student days in Hamburg, come flooding back to her, until the point is reached where she dismisses the nuclear family as 'inzestuöse Scheiße'. It is at this point in their relationship that the summer flood of guests starts and the contact with their visitors brings the incipient conflict into the open. Protracted conversations with their friends, all apparently preoccupied with similar problems, lead to a

---

22. Munich, 1975. All quotations from this edition.

deepening of the couple's rift and a heightened activity in the narrator's inner life. Both consider flight into another relationship: the narrator is captivated by a significantly younger woman, but, at the end of the summer, he and his wife decide to remain together, partly because of the child. He cannot promise himself that this will mean the start of a new and better existence together: they have chosen, rather, to make the best of their existing style of life.

This novel was strongly attacked by Reinhard Baumgart, in terms that would suggest that it has greater affinities with 'Neue Innerlichkeit' than with 'Neue Subjektivität', as we understand it: 'Sosehr hier auf Privatheit und Subjektivität gesetzt wird, das Buch bleibt so anonym, als würde es in gar keinem bestimmten Jahrhundert oder Land spielen, sondern wirklich nur in irgendeinem "Garten der Gefühle". Subjektivität, derart ins leere Nirgendwo-Nirgendwann wuchernd, ohne zeitgenössische Schärfe, wird dann unverhofft etwas vollkommen Unpersönliches'.[23] We would argue, on the other hand, that the novel is located in a quite specific social and temporal context. The couple around whom the novel revolves and their various friends can only be from a West German middle-class, university-trained background and their ideas are unambiguously based on late-Sixties utopian thinking in the Federal Republic. The narrator and Dorothee have been able to put into practice one of the central utopian visions — opting out of the rat race and establishing a rural existence based on a sense of their own needs. While their friends envy a life style to which theirs can only approximate during holidays, the reality of everyday life throws the married couple back on themselves as individuals and in their relationship together. The liberation from external constraints and ties is seen to promote neuroses and unpredictable behaviour, and in the company of their friends, who all to some extent seem to share their problems, difficulties are observed more clearly and, as a result of intense conversations, pushed almost to crisis-point. This holiday grouping is, moreover, no mere summer ephemeron; it reflects bourgeois society in miniature but, more importantly, it represents society as it increasingly is in this post-technological age. Man's long-established self-image as worker of some sort is ever more at variance with the reality of him as man of leisure, with increasing amounts of time available for individual interests. Fröhlich's novel portrays the visitors to M. as no longer in need of holidays for relaxation in the traditional sense; their stay there is an extension of, or, we might say, a concentrate of their daily life, rather than the break it would

23. 'Freizeitmenschen unter sich', *Die Zeit*, 10.10.1975.

once have been. It is striking how each member of the group is preoccupied with problems of self-realisation; the constant self-examination and obsessive analysis of individual needs are manifested, above all, in lengthy, intense conversations ostensibly about the problems of others, but really outpourings of their own anxieties. The educated middle class is portrayed as characterised by increasing abstraction and, significantly, extrovert guests from a different background are made to feel uneasy and leave. Everything that confronts them is discussed and, in effect, reduced to words; the latest news on the situation in Chile is, for example, chewed over in a way that ultimately removes it from real events. Frenetic discussion seems to fill in the sense of something lacking in their lives and, at the same time, is evidence of their search for 'bei aller Disparatheit des Erlebens Zusammenhang, Ordnung, Einsicht'.[24] Instead of the leisure offered by modern society being utilised in the cause of true self-fulfilment — and they delude themselves that this is what they *are* doing — it is filled with neurotic inwardness expressed as empty chatter (which in Heidegger's understanding of the word is an indication of unauthentic existence). It is 'wie wenn wir Heutigen am Wort krankten . . . , wodurch Gefühle und Gefühltes unentwegt und zunehmend ermittelt, dingfest gemacht, auseinandergenommen, bis in die Wurzeln hinab zerlegt und ins Leere getrieben werden'.[25]

The externalisation of inner life in conversation, which is seen particularly clearly in the case of the narrator, but of which *Im Garten der Gefühle* essentially consists, is undoubtedly a concomitant feature of the change to post-technological society in all developed countries. However, it appears here in specifically West German guise, in that the neuroses induced by the collision between life style and utopian thinking, even in the language used by the group in M. (and this linguistic precision is Fröhlich's particular achievement in this novel), can be traced back without difficulty to the spectrum of debates in the Federal Republic of the late Sixties. The stimulus provided by various aspects of the Student Movement to realist writing in the Seventies has already been observed in a number of the areas examined; another manifestation of 'Neue Subjektivität', the probing of problems of identity through confrontation with one's own childhood in the Third Reich, also clearly goes back to the uncompromising and wide-ranging examination of National Socialism that the Student Movement demanded and helped to bring

24. Werner Ross, 'Geometrie der Unordnung', *Merkur*, 31, 1977, p. 1122.
25. Werner Helwig, 'In die Einsamkeit zurück', *Frankfurter Hefte*, 31, 1976, Heft 10, p. 72.

about. In the so-called 'Väterromane' of the Seventies and Eighties (cf. Chapter 7) and the 'Deutsche Chronik' of Walter Kempowski (cf. Chapter 9), writers attempt to re-create their childhood and family background and thus to close the gap in their identity left by suppression or ignorance of the Nazi past. The intensive concern with this period in the Seventies, while undoubtedly stimulated to some small degree by the then current trials of minor war criminals, owes much to the body of scholarly analyses of fascism produced after the Student Movement, the extensive number of non-fictional publications on aspects of everyday life in the Third Reich and the range of documentary and historical novels on this subject; at the end of the decade, the film *Holocaust* was instrumental in bringing to the generation born between 1935 and 1945 an increased sensitivity to the importance of understanding the significance of National Socialism. At the same time, as in other forms of autobiographical writing in the Seventies, the use of personal experience as the direct source of material for the novel helped to re-establish confidence in the narrative form: indeed, the reception of many autobiographical novels at the time served to indicate that the categorical statements made a little earlier, declaring that the individual story could no longer give insights into more general social patterns, was not necessarily true in practice: 'in der prismatischen Brechung durch ganz Individuelles' in such writing '[wurde] Repräsentatives für eine ganze Generation eingeholt'.[26] The way in which autobiographical (and, to a lesser extent, biographical) writing led to a renewed confidence in depicting, even in fiction, individual life histories can be seen in the work of a number of writers examined here; a particularly apposite example, in the context of this analysis of problems of identity and the Nazi past, is provided by Peter Härtling's *Hubert oder Die Rückkehr nach Casablanca*, a fictional analysis of an individual case of uncertain identity, clearly drawing on autobiographical material that Härtling had been working on for some time (cf. Chapter 9).[27]

Throughout his life Hubert Windisch has suffered from the consequences of a particular manifestation of patriarchal society, the authoritarian male in the role of soldier. His father is a 'Deutsch-Nationaler' who, determined to help rid Germany of the 'Schmach von Versailles', takes part in the attempted *Putsches* after the First World War; soon afterwards he joins the NSDAP and starts to make ready for the next war. As a result, family life is subordinated to

26. Bernd Neumann, 'Die Wiedergeburt des Erzählens aus dem Geist der Autobiographie?, *Basis 9*, 1979, p. 96.
27. Darmstadt & Neuwied, 1978. All quotations from this edition.

military exercises and, later on, to actual preparation for war; the house is dominated by the image of man as sturdy warrior. Hubert's elder brother Wilhelm is, physically and in his basic attitude, a copy of his father, while the sickly, dreamy Hubert disappoints paternal expectations and is rejected as inferior: 'Aus dir wird nie ein richtiger Mann. Das war der Kehrreim seiner Kindertage. . . . In ihm steckte der Mann nicht, den Vater erwartete' (12). From early on Hubert — who is not excused from joining the Hitler Youth — learns to escape from the 'väterlichen Zuchtstelle' by taking refuge in role-playing, in which he 'die Wirklichkeit verließ und sich durch Phantasie stärkte' (36). The cinema is a favourite retreat and, at the same time, a stimulus to his imagination.

Hubert's instinctive reaction is to rebel against his father's world: nevertheless, one side of him is fascinated by the machismo apparently embodied in the military; he voluntarily enlists but, disappointingly, everyone treats him 'als wäre er, der Sohn, nur ein Schatten, ein kläglicher Ableger' (82). Far from being sent to the front, he is given an office job, but here he learns once more to cut himself off; he puts on a mask that enables him to stand apart from the war. When Anna, his first real love, whom he regards as an island of peace and security amidst the chaos, tells him of the horrors Auschwitz and Theresienstadt, he refuses to acknowledge what is happening in a world that has cast him out and which he, in his turn, rejects: 'Was sie sagt, will er nicht sehen. Es ist Vaters entsetzliche, von Planern und Tätern aufgewühlte kriegerische Welt' (111). This is truer than he realised at the time: it emerges that his father, Hauptsturmführer Windisch, who commits suicide in Holland in 1944, was a mass murderer.

When the end of the war finally comes, Hubert deludes himself into thinking that, although he 'zwanzig Jahre nicht er selbst gewesen [ist]', he will now be able to lead his own life, but in the rapidly ensuing process of de-Nazification he has to flee from his father's ghost and give the latter's occupation as 'Landwirt'. He cannot hide for long, though: an acquaintance soon discovers that he is the son of the man responsible for the death of so many Jews in Holland and Hubert is forced to defend himself, 'sich rechtfertigen für etwas, das er nicht gewesen war' (223). He fears that he will 'Vater nie verlieren' and once again takes refuge in disguise, hiding behind a series of roles from American films. Over the years, the camouflaged Hubert is able to build up a successful career in a newspaper concern. While, however, all around him adjust quickly to 'normalisation' and respond with alacrity to increasing affluence, Hubert, the apparent success, is ill at ease. He misses 'ein Stück meines Lebens, die Zeit hat mir meine Vergangenheit verdorben und ich leide darunter. Meine Phantasie reicht nicht aus, mich neu und anders zu erinnern' (250–1). The sense of lacking a past and the consequent identity problems result in his leading an inadequate, although far from tragic, false life; but with the death of his mother, the only person who knew his true life-story, he finds himself confronted once more, and far more intensely, with his father. He can now recognise that, since the end of the war, he has 'auf einer Insel gelebt und angenommen, daß seine Zeit auch die Zeit der anderen sei' (271). He is brought up against a past that he has essentially suppressed, the re-emergence of a 'Trauer, die er allein nicht aushalten konnte'. Soon afterwards, Hubert's essential difference from those around him is confirmed by the fact that he is the only one at an editorial meeting to oppose the rearmament of the Federal Republic. For his colleagues the — then very recent — past is no longer of importance; unlike him they have lost the capacity for grief over the horrors of the Third Reich.

In order to make himself 'unanfechtbar' in his now confirmed isolation Hubert retreats ever more into role-playing, identifying in particular with Rick Blane in Michael Curtiz's film *Casablanca* (hence the subtitle of the novel. The choice of Blane/Bogart indicates, of course, the strong subliminal influence of the paternal image and, indeed, a female colleague soon notices the way in which he begins to behave 'übertrieben männlich'). His increased involvement in a fantasy world causes his work and marriage to suffer. His increasing inability to live in a society devoid of history and to distinguish between dream and reality comes out most vividly in his attempt to explain his problems to his wife by appropriating a past from *Casablanca*. She, totally immersed in the world of the 'Wirtschaftswunder', has little sympathy for the decline of this 'Schlappschwanz'. Hubert allots himself, significantly enough, the role of someone who shoots 'einen namenlosen Mörder' (freely based on Rick's shooting of Strasser, the Gestapo major), but his desperate effort to shape his existence, 'der er einen Grund geben wollte', by, in effect, killing his father and acquiring a sense of personal past, is a disaster: his private and professional lives fall apart completely. Unlike Rick, who had the chance to escape from an unauthentic existence by action — surrendering his seat on the plane and entering the resistance movement — Hubert can only drift along; he is demoted by his employers and given the job of travelling salesman, where he can bury himself in the pose of 'männlicher Einsamkeit' that he has taken over from Rick. But this — as Laszlo (the Nesvadba of the film) says — is essentially the role adopted by someone trying to escape from himself.

Hubert lives in a world of imagination run riot, until he picks up a young girl hitch-hiker and spends the night with her. It is not long before he feels the need to tell her his story and pour out his sense of guilt for his father's crimes, but she is not interested: it was all 'ewig lange her' and should not concern him in any way at all: 'Sie hatte ihm erklärt, es sei egal. Mit einem Satz hatte sie die Narbe aufgerissen und den Schmerz gestillt' (385). He experiences a sense of immediate relief and feels that, for the first time, he can discuss his past honestly and openly with someone: 'Er könnte ihr, sagt er sich, von dem Jungen erzählen, dem alle Spiele verdorben wurden, von dem Garten in Kassel und den Männern, die auszogen, die Welt in Trümmer zu legen, und von Edith und Anna und' (386-7).

Hubert oder Die Rückkehr nach Casablanca portrays the cumulative psychological burden placed on someone who, from childhood onwards, can only exist in an intensive inner life. The character's early problems with the male role expected of him are compounded both by the suppression of part of his own self, necessitated by his father's appalling war crimes, and by his sense of alienation from a society that has shed its sense of past and lives only for and in a consumer present, (*Hubert . . .* has here clear affinities with the new historical novel). The third-person narrator is far from omniscient, nor is he concerned to present a balanced account: his interest is in Hubert and his suffering, which he portrays in the manner of a sympathetic friend. His gaze remains fixed in a continual close-up portrait and the perspectivisation of narration, so reminiscent of Walser — other people's statements or opinions are given in either direct or indirect speech, while those of Hubert are given in the preterite, for the most part, otherwise in the present tense — is clear evidence of his closeness to his protagonist. The narrow focus corresponds, of course, to the latter's preoccupation with his personal problems and to his tendency to withdraw in on himself, but the narratorial voice makes it clear that this is far from self-indulgent introspection or clownish role-playing: it is rather the result of suffering induced by external causes. The structure of the novel allows the narrator to sift and organise the complex body of material in a way impossible for Hubert; by and large he restricts himself to information that has come from Hubert, but the ending of the novel indicates that the narrator and the character himself have different interpretations of the latter's future development: Hubert feels a sense of liberation in the presence of Effi and is sure that, in time, he will be able to tell her everything, but the exceptionally direct intervention at this point ('sagt er sich') clearly expresses the narrator's doubt as to whether he can, in fact, emerge successfully from his life of fantasy — a doubt seemingly confirmed by the fact that Hubert still clings to his Bogart-style fedora.

In a certain sense the Seventies represent the third phase of the response in West German literature to the legacy of Nazism. The so-called 'Bewältigung der Vergangenheit' of the Forties and Fifties initially addressed the immediate past in essentially metaphorical terms: only later was it concerned with personal moral aspects for the generation immediately involved, when the documentary drama of the Sixties turned its attention to much thornier questions about the nature of National Socialism; in the Seventies comes examination of the psychological consequences of the Third Reich for the generation born just before, and during, the war. Although the next generation, represented by Effi, may take the view that people of Hubert's age are free from the burden of guilt, *Hubert . . .* and the 'Väterromane' show the extent of the psychological damage caused by the past. A further example of suffering in the present caused by being brought up in the Third Reich is provided by Hermann Peter Piwitt's second novel, *Die Gärten im März* (1979).[28]

On one level the work is marked by a double subjectivity, in that the narrator, a typesetter and would-be writer, hopes to discover the real meaning of his own life and thus to be able, 'noch mal von vorn anzufangen', by attempting to discover something of the past of his missing friend Ponto. Left-wing associates regard this activity as 'unsolidarisch': he is wasting time on someone who is 'ein hoffnungsloser Fall' at a time 'wo doch die großen Themen auf der Straße lägen. Löhne, Preise, Mieten. Wohnraumvernichtung' (7). For the narrator's wife Lea, who — like Hubert Windisch's second wife — finds the meaning of her life in money and possessions, her husband's concern with Ponto is 'ein privatistischer Luxus'; it would make far more sense if he would write 'mal'n Bestseller'. Stylistically and in terms of literary motifs the novel recalls Raabe's late work *Die Akten des Vogelangs*, in that, although his family cannot comprehend the importance of the undertaking, the narrator tries to take stock of his own life through preoccupation with that of an outsider. Like Krumhardt, Raabe's narrator, he seems to have accepted the values of his own social world only with difficulty and has long been fascinated by the eccentric and anti-social Ponto. The latter's disappearance, like the death of Velten Andres for Krumhardt, provokes in the speaker an intense concern with his friend's life. In reconstructing that life with the aid of

28. Reinbek, 1979. All quotations from this edition.

Ponto's papers and possessions, he finds confirmed his dissatisfaction with the prevailing work ethos and various other aspects of
existing society. On the other hand his study teaches him how to go
about the process of self-definition without, as Ponto did, becoming
a recluse.

At first sight Ponto does, indeed, seem to be a hopeless case: a
drinker who seems to destroy even the pleasant things in his life, a
man who has long since ceased trying to make anything of himself.
But the narrator, who has spent many an evening chatting at the bar
with him, identifies him as a different sort of drinker and, indeed,
Ponto is repelled by the 'männerbündlerische Kameraderie des
Alkohols'. He sees himself as anything but a 'Säufer', but, as 'die
gequälte Natur selbst', who cannot forget 'daß, wenn es den Rausch
nicht gäbe, man die Nüchternheit erträglich machen müßte' (92–3).
He also drinks in order 'sich von innen [zu] begucken'. Ponto's real
process of self-examination takes place, however, in the attic of his
parents' house, into which he withdraws to sort through old photographs and postcards and to pour out his thoughts on paper, in
order 'sich selbst auf die Spur [zu] kommen, indem er dem Kind auf
die Spur kommt, das er gewesen war' (10). Ponto's father had been a
high-ranking SA officer who ordered his wife and children around
the house, forced his eldest son to volunteer for army service (during
which he lost a leg on the Eastern Front) and even put forward the
names of neighbours as candidates for sterilisation. Even after the
war, the father had taken a stern stand against allowing the poison
of 'Abtrittsliteratur wie "Im Westen nichts Neues"' in the house,
and so driving Ponto's crippled brother away from home. The
domestic reign of terror is complemented by the experience of
school: 'Wenn er allerdings an seine Schulzeit denke, sagt er, könne
er sich nur daran erinnern, Angst gehabt zu haben. Angst, dranzu-
kommen. . . . Angst vor dem Zynismus und der bloßstellenden
Grausamkeit der Lehrer' (145). Bizarrely enough, though, Ponto's
memories of childhood were happy ones, 'bis er nachzudenken
begann', and it is only in retrospect that he becomes aware of the
coercion on him, which is to exert such destructive psychological
pressure on him later:

> Sei anständig, wahrhaftig, gerecht, hilfsbereit, mitleidvoll, opferbereit' —
> als ich endlich begriffen hatte, sagt Ponto, wie das von meinen Eltern
> gemeint gewesen war, nämlich als Weisung, wie man denen da oben
> angenehm auffiel und denen da unten gegenüber bei gutem Gewissen
> blieb, kurz, wie man sich am glattesten in seinen Stand, in seinen
> Mittelstand schickt — als ich das endlich durchgeschaut hatte, war es
> schon zu spät. Ich hatte schon alles in den falschen Hals gekriegt. Und

heute — wollte ich sie noch beim Wort nehmen, die Eltern, Lehrer, Pfarrer — müßte ich ein paar Konzernherrn mindestens erschießen (147–8).

Ponto comes to recognise that he has, from the very beginning, been programmed to act in the interests of others and that, as a result, he had been robbed of an authentic childhood and later life. He now has no individual identity to which he can cling, and so is condemned to an anxiety-ridden and utterly inadequate existence. His drinking represents the attempt not only to make this reduced life more bearable, but also to muffle the full expression of the anger that has built up within him: 'Ein Satz: "Die Katatonie ist der letzte Versuch, Gewalt zu vermeiden"'. Ein Spruch, einer unter vielen, auf einen Zeitungsrand gekritzelt. Er hebt die Hände, ganz Abwehr und Übergabe in einem und senkt den Kopf, in komischer Verzweiflung ihn schüttelnd. Ausweichen, sich totstellen, sich einnebeln, ein bißchen von sich zu verstehen geben, ohne Gewalt zu riskieren' (123–4). His last effort at self-definition is withdrawal into the parental home; when this fails, Ponto disappears. One friend thinks that he has joined the terrorists and the reader cannot exclude the possibility of suicide, but the narrator, who knows him so well, is convinced that he has now moved on to continue his search for identity, while living somewhere close to his childhood home.

Die Garten in März presents us with two processes of personal stock-taking, since the narrator learns so much about himself in his concern with Ponto. In addition, his investigation — akin to Krumhardt's sorting through Velten's papers, and with a similar result — enables him to recognise that Ponto's problems are very different from his own. He also, to some extent, comes to terms with his own life and the very act of writing seems to have had a therapeutic effect, in apparently reconciling him to his job as a typesetter. On another level, however, *Die Gärten im März* represents a criticism of 'Neue Innerlichkeit'. A sort of counter-figure to Ponto is the writer Pocher, who has made a name for himself through his preoccupation with death and his exploration in the narrator's words, of the 'zarten Irrgärten der Seele, die falschen Zirkel des Gefühls, die alten Ausgänge ins Nichts' (29–30). Pocher dismisses the literary efforts of the narrator and stresses quite different concerns of literature: 'in dich hineinlauschen! Die inneren Kontinente! und vor allem: keine politischen Pflichtübungen' (83; this is, of course, an unambiguous reference to Nicholas Born). Before his disappearance Ponto had strongly criticised Pocher for seeing the world as moribund and for wanting 'keine Demütigungen, keine Schmerzen, keine Herausforderungen mehr, die einem zu verstehen geben, daß man noch lebt'. Ponto did, admittedly, seem to have very fixed views on the state of things in the world, but this apparent assurance was easily explainable: he lacked 'die Kraft dazu, daß es in dir noch arbeitet' (96). Ponto's notes, the conversations with him, the reconstruction of his life and the narrator's attempt to learn thereby something of himself all add up to a plea for such people not to cut themselves off from the world. Also stressed is the necessity of seeing the self not as an autonomous entity, but as a being defined by social and historical conditions. The narrator's evocation of his environment, recreated in lively conversations and a whole range of still lifes — in which Piwitt's brilliant command of language is seen to maximum effect — is, indeed, a sort of reconciliation on his part of himself with the world in which he lives. He also comes to realise that an active inner life is necessary as a defence against stagnation and, more importantly, as the means of constantly redefining the self in its interaction with society. The author, like every realist writer, also clearly intended to show how, by representing the experiences of other persons, the individual subjects as readers and social beings can be helped to relate to themselves the interaction in the novel between the protagonists and society.

The novels examined in this chapter and categorised as 'Neue Subjektivität' — as opposed to 'Neue Innerlichkeit', in our definition — may be considered in conjunction with Walser's recent books, novels of political realism, such as Schneider's *Lenz*, Margot Schroeder's *Ich stehe meine Frau* and Baroth's *Aber es waren schöne Zeiten*, and recent historical fiction such as Döbler's *Kein Alibi* and Ingeborg Drewitz's *Gestern war heute* — which, given their extreme subject-centricity, could all be regarded as being closely related to those of 'Neue Subjektivität'. Whatever the theories of the late Sixties and the early Seventies may have said, all these works demonstrate, probably better than any other West German novels of recent years, that the portrayal of individual lives can indeed still put over to the reader experiences by no means unique to the fictional characters, but of much wider relevance. The diverse 'Lebensläufe' that appeared at the end of the Sixties, as well as other documentary works, may well have prepared the way, to some extent, for this resurgence of subjective realism. However, many exposés of, for example, the lot of the socially underprivileged tend, as Christa Wolf argues in *Lesen und Schreiben*, to present society as essentially static. They lack the progressive element, the utopian dimension of realist fiction that encourages readers to address themselves to the question, in modern times increasingly difficult, of their own self-realisation. The novel of

'Neue Innerlichkeit' renews that German tendency, examined in Chapter 1, to flee from the vicissitudes of the outer world into the seductive and apparently richer world of an autonomous self. In contrast, the novels of 'Neue Subjektivität' examined in this chapter again bring to the fore the vision which lies at the heart of the great nineteenth-century realist novels: that of individual self-fulfilment within the framework of a wider search for a more humanitarian and dignified society, contained within the negative utopia evidenced by the experiences of the protagonist in a society that still falls short of that standard.

9

The Resurgence of Traditional Realism?

'Es läßt sich nicht mehr erzählen'
(Theodor W. Adorno, 1954)
'Es darf wieder erzählt werden'
(Siegfried Unseld, 1972)

Apart from the occasional isolated — and essentially early — attempt to rehabilitate the traditional epic form of narration, the nature of the West German novel up to the Seventies was strongly influenced by an antipathy towards realism (cf. Chapters 2 and 3). Both in literary criticism (Jens, Adorno and others) and in the novel itself (in the work of Grass, Walser and Johnson, for example) an avant-garde view of literature (Jens's 'abstrakte Literatur') seemed to have established itself as the determinant of quality. During the Sixties this anti-realism was complemented by criticism of the epic form itself, made by the proponents of concrete literature, notably Helmut Heißenbüttel and Jürgen Becker, and becoming very prominent towards the end of the decade. After 1970 a relatively traditional realist novel emerged to play a major part in the literature of the decade: this development has been seen as marking a radical break with preceding literary tendencies. Our opening remarks above make it clear that this is, in a way, true, but it should not be forgotten that one consequence of the peculiarly German tradition of the idealist novel (cf. Chapters 1 and 2) has been the identification of the social novel with 'Trivialliteratur'. We are not here concerned with the catalogue of neglected nineteenth-century authors or the odd status, in German literary history, of writers from the earlier twentieth century like Heinrich Mann, Döblin, Arnold Zweig, Fallada, Remarque and Kästner (the first three being seen as important but difficult to accommodate within the main stream of literary development, while the others are thrust into the 'popular' category). However, the general tendency to label non-idealist works as 'trivial' has had its effect on received wisdom with regard to West German literature and makes it highly relevant here. The slide into critical obscurity of Richter and Kolbenhoff, the low regard initially paid to Böll's early novels — not all of which can, in any case, be taken as examples of traditional realism — and the more recent assignment of Walser and Lenz to 'bessere Unterhaltungsliteratur' are evidence enough of this tendency.[1] (It may be noted that in 1961 *Der Spiegel* labelled Böll a 'katholischer Fallada'.) The established picture of the literary history of the Federal Republic also ignores the highly competent skills of writers like Kirst, Simmel, Habe, Willi Heinrich and Konsalik; some of their works would undoubtedly have been accorded a different reception in countries with a more catholic concept of literature. Publications by such writers as Max von der Grün, Matthias Mander, Wolfgang Körner, Angelika Mechtel and others from the Dortmunder Gruppe 61, and by isolated individuals like Günter Herburger and Günter Seuren, are further indications of a growing interest in realist prose during the Sixties.

Previous chapters have given clear evidence that we see the Student Movement as the major stimulus to the body of realist writing in the Seventies, but other influences should be noted that helped to kindle interest and new-found acceptance regarding realist narration. Undoubtedly, one major factor was the translation into German of foreign writers such as Solzhenitsyn, Doris Lessing, V.S. Naipaul, John Updike, Bernard Malamud and, above all, the South American authors Borges and Marquez: all showed, in differing ways, that a relatively conventional narrative literature is still possible today. More detailed examination of how this influence worked would require a separate study, but it is noticeable that a considerable number of critics and writers who took a firmly anti-realist line in the late Sixties and early Seventies were soon writing favourable reviews of these foreign works. Another apparent stimulus was the discovery of the popular by literary critics — originally by the student generation. This is reflected in anthologies such as *Super Garde* (1969) and *Trivialmythen* (1970) and is also to be found in the literary theory of, amongst others, Heißenbüttel and Wellershoff; the 'popular' is taken throughout to include both the novel and film, in the sense of the Hollywood cinema. Reflecting this influence of an American cinematic style that has essentially remained true to its realist roots, the stylisation of the early 'Neue Deutsche Film' has, from the mid-Seventies onwards, increasingly shown traditional realist characteristics — examples include Fassbinder's *Effi Briest*,

---

1. Cf. in this connection Christa Bürger, *Textanalyse als Ideologiekritik. Zur Rezeption zeitgenössischer Unterhaltungsliteratur*, Frankfurt, 1973, and Manfred Jurgensen, 'Der deutsche Unterhaltungsroman der Gegenwart' in Manfred Durzak (ed.), *Deutsche Gegenwartsliteratur*, Stuttgart, 1981, pp. 252–69.

Die Ehe der Maria Braun and *Lola,* Schlöndorff's *Die verlorene Ehre der Katharina Blum* and *Die Fälschung,* Margarete von Trotta's *Die bleierne Zeit* and *Rosa Luxemburg* and Wolfgang Petersen's *Das Boot.* Perhaps the most decisive example of the tendency towards realist narration in the cinema was Edgar Reitz's essentially conventional *Heimat* (1984): its reception revealed a widespread positive response, even in previously anti-realist circles, to its epic spread and its faithful re-creation of a segment of social reality. Perhaps the most striking instances of the influence of such filmic narration on the novel are provided by works of novelists who were earlier proponents of an experimental prose style, such as Peter Handke (*Der kurze Brief zum langen Abschied* and *Die linkshändige Frau*), Peter Härtling (*Hubert oder Die Rückkehr nach Casablanca*) and Gerhard Roth (*Ein neuer Morgen* and *Der große Horizont*).

A further stimulus to realist writing after 1970 was also set in motion by the Student Movement: this was the revival of interest in the 'Expressionismusdebatte' of the Thirties, which helped to focus attention, within and outside the Werkkreis Literatur der Arbeitswelt, on the question of realism; it brought about, too, the republication of virtually forgotten novels from the Weimar Republic, as well as the translation into German of a number of important foreign texts (the role played here in the Seventies by the Autoren-Edition, in particular, has tended to go unnoticed). The superficial politicisation of intellectual life, including literature, may have faded quickly after 1969, but it had engendered an increased awareness towards the impact of social and political conditions on the life of the individual and this is continued and reflected in the novels of the Seventies, as well as affecting critical attitudes towards experimental prose. Mon, Heißenbüttel and others had in the Sixties made vague assertions as to the capacity of experimental literature to illuminate the relationship between the individual and his social world. Younger critics dismissed such statements, with the result that experimental writing soon disappeared from the centre of the literary stage. This rapid change, obvious by 1973, is most graphically reflected in the programme of the Luchterhand-Verlag, in the latter Sixties one of the major supporters of such writing: the contracts of Heißenbüttel and Mon were cancelled and great play was now made of the social novels of Michael Scharang (who had made his own literary début with experimental texts) and Max von der Grün. It is most noticeable that, while the latter's work was received in the Sixties with good-natured condescension or as being of little more than curiosity value, his — admittedly vastly superior — *Stellenweise Glatteis* (1972) was highly praised by Heinrich Vormweg, hitherto a vigorous opponent of the realist novel, for having 'keinen beliebigen Ausgangspunkt', but being, rather, 'konsequent an einem immer nur vage bekannten Realen orientiert . . . , das authentische Befragung dringlich fordert: an den gesellschaftlichen Verhältnissen'.[2]

For these and other reasons, which might well include a general reaction against the dominance of documentary literature, the beginning of the Seventies is marked by an upswing in narrative fiction. The re-emergent novel, however, clearly reveals that the doubts of the Sixties cast on the viability of traditional realism by the theories of (amongst others) Barthes, Adorno and the rediscovered Brecht had left their mark. Novelists seem to have taken particularly to heart the questioning of what had appeared self-evident, the representative nature of individual experience in the modern world and the consequences for narrative techniques of this change of view. Although Siegfried Lenz, somewhat self-effacingly, tends to describe himself as a traditional realist novelist and is certainly dismissed as such by his critics, his work in the last decade or so fully reflects his awareness of the problems relating to modern narration: *Deutschstunde* (1968), *Das Vorbild* (1973), *Heimatmuseum* (1978) and *Der Exizierplatz* (1985) are all narrated in the first person and avoid the preterite. Heinrich Böll would seem to have followed the arguments amongst literary theorists with a little mocking amusement, to judge by his highly ironical use of the far from omniscient 'Verf.' in *Gruppenbild mit Dame*, but the form of his later novels, *Die verlorene Ehre der Katharina Blum*, *Fürsorgliche Belagerung* and *Frauen vor Flußlandschaft* (a 'Roman in Dialogen und Selbstgesprächen'), indicates that, in his latter years, he intensified a formal experimentation, clearly springing from an awareness of the limitations on the conventional novel form (a knowledge that had been present in his work from an early stage, but for which he is rarely given due credit).

The example of *Gruppenbild mit Dame* illuminates particularly clearly the narratorial stance adopted by many writers in the more traditionally constructed novels of the Seventies and Eighties. Although, as we have indicated, Böll's narrative technique in novels such as *Haus ohne Hüter* and *Billard um halbzehn* is anything but rigidly conventional, his earlier work nevertheless betokens a firm authorial stance towards the social theme contained in his chosen material. The protagonists are at times little more than ciphers or embody some part of a system of metaphors that dominates the novels, so that, despite apparent modernism, they evince the moral attitude of an essentially omniscient narrator in the manner of the nineteenth-

2. 'Einladung an alle', *Jahresring*, 1972–3, p. 249.

century novel. *Ansichten eines Clowns* in many ways marks a turning-point in Böll's writing, in that the critical voice of the author is heard only in undertone, but the novel is narrated by Hans Schnier and reflects his egocentricity. *Gruppenbild mit Dame*, despite its thematic links with Böll's earlier work, differs radically from its forerunners, since the experiences of Leni and her acquaintances are re-created by bringing together their individual points of view, with the narratorial voice, the 'Verf.', anxious at every turn to stress that his function is merely that of someone organising and presenting the material. Such a sharp focus on subjective experience and the concomitant fading of an omniscient narrator is nothing new in the so-called traditional novel: Barthes claims to detect something similar in the later novels of Flaubert, while, within the German novel, Fontane (for example, in *Irrungen, Wirrungen* and *Effi Briest*) and Raabe (cf. Chapter 1) exemplify this tendency and, we have argued, point the way for the appropriate representation in literature of individual experience in modern society. This subject-centric realism is characteristic of a whole series of relatively conventional novels in the Seventies and Eighties, including — apart from those examined in this chapter — the novels of Siegfried Lenz, Wellershoff's *Die Schönheit der Schimpanse* and *Die Sirene*, Michael Scharang's *Der Lebemann*, Gerhard Roth's *Der stille Ozean* and F.C. Delius's *Adenauerplatz*. Perhaps the most obvious and important example, however, is provided by the recent novels of Martin Walser.

All Walser's novels, from *Ehen in Philippsburg* onwards, have centred on the existential problems of a single individual, the author's major theme being the damaging effects on the subject of modern achievement-orientated society. While his first book is, indeed, a highly conventional social novel, he soon adopted a quite different narrative style, with the first two volumes of the Anselm Kristlein trilogy (*Halbzeit* and *Das Einhorn*) being marked by a linguistically inventive playing with Anselm's identity problems and social existence. We have already examined the growth of Walser's dissatisfaction with such 'puren Sprachspiel' and his championing of the documentary prose writing of Erika Runge, Ursula Trauberg and Wolfgang Werner, as well as his subsequent participation in the discussions on realism within the Werkkreis; the important thing in the context of this chapter is the way in which, after the first efforts at literary reorientation in *Fiction* and *Die Gallistl'sche Krankheit* and the completion of the trilogy with *Der Sturz* (1974), he channels his ideas on realist writing into a new and distinctive, but nevertheless basically traditional narrative form, starting with *Jenseits der Liebe* (1976). Although the style of his recent novels would seem far removed from that put forward under the label of 'Realismus X' — essentially a redefinition of abstract literature — a degree of continuity in Walser's theoretical position is provided by the continued stress of the crucial importance in realism of the category of experience, indeed, after 1976 this becomes the key feature of his writing. Realism, he says in 1976, is essentially concerned with demonstrating 'das Verhältnis von einem Bewußtsein zu der Umgebung, die dieses Bewußtsein andauernd konditioniert'.[3] In the traditional bourgeois novel — at least in the ideal-type understanding of it — this relationship of the protagonist to his social world is basically positive, movement of the novel consisting in the process of his gradual development towards self-recognition and, thus, the possibility of eventual self-fulfilment; from the middle of the nineteenth century onwards, however, the social world produced by industrial and urban change is increasingly depicted as making the protagonist's relationship to society problematic and his chance of self-realisation much more difficult. Walser's portrayal of the state of things in the contemporary world shows the individual, in the process of interaction with social forces, as engaged in nothing short of a struggle for survival. The recent novels are typified by a concentration on the inner life of the protagonist, provoked by a process — brought about by experiences in the outside world — of gradual awareness as to the nature of his own position. The existential necessity of such an inner life — which can manifest itself in flight into failure and extroversion, as well as in reflection ('Seelenarbeit') — is here confirmed by further confrontation with the demands of hostile modern living.

The prototype of Walser's anti-hero is Franz Horn, a sales executive with a firm of denture manufacturers in *Jenseits der Liebe* (and *Brief an Lord Liszt*, 1982). In the early years of the company he would seem to have worked energetically and with considerable success, but now, in his middle years, he finds himself incapable of coping with the intense competition provided by other, usually younger, colleagues. Without being fully aware of the causes of his behaviour, he has made a sort of unconscious protest against the change in his position within the firm by excessive drinking, heavy weight gains, involvement in union activities inimical to the management and support for a Communist shop-steward, but it is not until a business trip to England that he really becomes aware of his deep-seated lack of satisfaction in his work. He does make, it is true,

---

3. *Marburger Blätter*, 4/5, 1976, p. 27. Cf. further in this general connection Ulrike Hick, *Martin Walsers Prosa*, Stuttgart, 1983.

a further, more open protest at the end of the novel by taking a — less than fatal — overdose of sleeping-pills, but he learns to find a sort of contentment in his now conscious role as failure: 'Er wollte doch nichts als in seiner von ihm selbst überhaupt nicht mehr bestrittenen Nichtswürdigkeit in Ruhe gelassen werden. *Und* er wollte diese seine eigene Nichtswürdigkeit noch ein bißchen übertreiben, um dann das Gefühl zu haben, auch ihm sei ein wenig Ungerechtigkeit zugefügt worden'.[4]

Das Schwanenhaus provides a sort of variation on the character of Horn.[5] Gottlieb Zürn, an estate agent, believes that he can find the peace he seeks by making his fortune: 'Geld, das hieße, Leben ohne Stoppuhr und Peitsche. Geld, das wäre das Gefühl der Unsterblichkeit' (87). For this reason he determines — even though, like Franz Horn, he feels inferior to his dynamic competitors and is incapable of 'mutig sein' — to secure the sole rights to the sale of the 'Schwanenhaus', a magnificent villa in the locality. Zürn is all the more handicapped *vis-à-vis* his colleagues Schatz and Kaltammer by the fact that the placing of the commission is to be determined by two women, for he feels all women, including his wife and his mother, to be inherently superior to him. Nevertheless, Gottlieb Zürn begins to dream of the sample particulars that he will draw up, his triumph over the competition and the money that he will make. But he fails to keep his first appointment with Frau Dr Leistle, although he regards his 'Desertion vom Schlachtfeld' as a veritable triumph, and, in the crucial interview that he does secure and keep with her, he is unable to bring himself to show her his draft layout. His various defeats (as estate agent, husband and father) do not depress him overmuch, however — indeed, he 'wunderte sich öfter darüber, daß dann alles doch irgendwie ging' (193) and he can still recognise 'in den schlimmsten Momenten . . . wie schön es war zu leben'. The symbolic moment of his ultimate defeat, the demolition of the 'Schwanenhaus', induces a rapprochement between himself and his wife that imbues him with the strength 'die man zum Einschlafen braucht' — a recurrent motif of survival in this phase of Walser's writing.

These motifs are extended and deepened in *Seelenarbeit* (1979), the novel preceding the rather slight *Das Schwanenhaus*; here[6] the social causes of the protagonist's personal problems emerge far more clearly,and the psychological contours of the figure are more defined. Xaver Zürn's wife, Agnes, has no direct superior at work and

4. *Jenseits der Liebe*, Frankfurt, 1976, pp. 112–13.
5. Frankfurt, 1980. All quotations from this edition.
6. Frankfurt, 1979. All quotations from this edition.

therefore has a 'gutes Arbeitsverhältnis', but he himself suffers, like Franz Horn, from the power relationship at his place of work and his own sense of inferiority — heightened by his having risen from being a normal worker to the position of chauffeur to the managing director. His work isolates him from his fellow-workers and he has difficulty in communicating with his employer, Dr Gleitze, (from whom, to make matters worse, he is separated by a glass partition for much of the time), while at home communication with his wife and daughter is increasingly problematical. He manages to pretend to others that he has great self-control and is admired for his 'Ruhe' and 'Ausgeglichenheit', but the man behind this mask is constantly reflecting on the spiritual damage inflicted on him by these problems; this manifests itself in psychosomatically-induced intestinal pains and an increasing tendency towards paranoid behaviour. Zürn obtains some relief from the difficulties caused by his hours on the road when he is demoted and sent back to his old job as a fork-lift truck driver, but this inevitably affects his inferiority complex, exacerbated by the failure of his daughter Julia in school examinations: 'Plötzlich war Gleitzes Maßnahme unkritisierbar geworden. Die Schule, die ganz hohe Instanz, hatte Dr. Gleitze rechtgegeben. Die Zürns sind Versager' (264). Only sexual intercourse with Agnes can bring any sort of tranquillity and only in the relationship with her, still far from close, 'war er möglicher als ohne sie. Ohne sie käme er sich schädlicher vor. Sie machte etwas wieder gut' (282). This motif of the short moments in which the individual can forget himself temporarily, even in an intrinsically problematic relationship, recurs in Walser's work and undoubtedly reflects a widespread experience in an increasingly atomised society.

Walser's concern with man's contemporary existential problems and their interaction with the marital relationship is expressed most forcefully in his greatest commercial success in recent years, *Ein fliehendes Pferd* (1978).[7] Like the other anti-heroes, the protagonist Helmut Halm, a school-teacher in Stuttgart, suffers from the pressure imposed upon him by the competitive ethos of society, which forces him into a sort of controlled schizophrenia (he lives 'doppelt'), whereby superficial conformism at school enables him to safeguard his 'wirkliche Person'. The many ramifications of social 'Dressur' — which are brought out with greater economy and clarity in this work than any other of the period — include not only the

7. Frankfurt, 1977. All quotations from this edition. Walser designates this as a 'Novelle' and it does, in part, conform to certain features of the genre, but there is, in other ways, little to distinguish it from a number of his novels and so we feel justified in including it within this analysis.

pressure at the workplace, 'etwas zu werden', but extend into the intimacy of personal relationships, making relaxation at home impossible — hence, in these recent works, Walser's particular focus on interpersonal problems. Sexual relations between Helmut and his wife Sabine are frustrated by the way in which the 'Sexualgebote dieser Zeit und Gesellschaft', in the form of statistics as to average activity, provoke in him feelings of 'Widerwillen und Ekel'. He is highly conscious of the pressure to prove himself 'wettbewerbsfähig', feels that he is 'ununterbrochen am Pranger' and renders his sexual self immune from these external forces by trying to avoid all close contact with Sabine. Halm retreats into an internalised existence, which is one form of response to social constraints on the self, whereas Klaus Buch, his former school friend and *alter ego*, whom the couple meet during their annual holiday on Lake Constance, responds to conformist pressures with total *extro*version. Buch seems superficially to be the ultimate embodiment of a competitive society, and it is only later that we discover his true state of constant stress from his wife Hel:

> Er hat nicht viel gehabt von seinem Leben, sagte sie. Es war nichts als eine Schinderei. Jeden Tag zehn, zwölf Stunden an der Maschine. Auch wenn er nicht schreiben konnte, hockte er an der Maschine. Ich muß auf dem Posten sein, hat er gesagt. Ihm ist alles, was er getan hat. furchtbar schwer gefallen. . . . Er hat oft aufgeschrien, nachts. Und immer öfter hat er Schweißausbrüche gehabt, mitten in der Nacht (136–7).

Klaus regards every sphere of his life — work, sex, leisure (particularly sport) — in an intensely competitive light. He embodies, with an intensity unmatched by any other figure in Walser's novels of the Seventies and Eighties, the full extent of the engulfment of the individual by society in all its manifestations and through him the writer, with remarkable economy, presents the reader with the full complexity of the modern interaction between society and personal consciousness.

The force and narrative tightness of *Seelenarbeit* and *Ein fliehendes Pferd* stem from the way in which the experiences of the protagonists in the external world are thematically relevant, i.e. play their part in the inner process of growing self-knowledge. *Jenseits der Liebe* and *Das Schwanenhaus*, on the other hand, suffer at times from digression into detailed and lively scenes not always germane to the main theme. This is particularly true of the former book, as far as the trip to England is concerned: an episode in the Cheylesmore Working Men's Club shows off Walser's brilliant command of language and would have made a very satisfactory separate sketch, but, as with so many scenic descriptions in his later books, it is extraneous to the main thrust of the novel.

The danger of drifting off into elegant 'Kabinettstücke' or superior travelogue is particularly evident in this author's *Brandung* (1985), although this weakness was ignored in the flood of positive reviews. Walser, drawing not for the first time on experiences gained at an English-speaking university, here continues the life of Helmut Halm, now in his mid-fifties, who has been invited to spend a semester as guest lecturer at a Californian university. While it must be admitted that Walser's descriptive powers are seen in this novel at their most brilliant and that his sketches of California and college life in the United States provide the reader with a series of vivid cameos, these have the effect of piling one scene or description of a locality on top of another, without in any way advancing the movement of the novel. In addition, the focus is further blurred by the re-emergence of Walser's literary playing with problems — so central to *Halbzeit* and *Das Einhorn* — which were presented in *Ein fliehendes Pferd* as having clear social origins. The result is that Helmut's drinking or his fear of sexual contact with his wife Sabine come over as leitmotifs that can, ultimately, only be understood by reference to the earlier work. The mid-life crisis, shown there as induced by the competitive ethos and youth cult of modern society, has given way to a very general concern with ageing that is pushed even into the realms of the absurd. The death of parents and friends is certainly a personal problem that comes with age, but in *Brandung* Halm has to endure in a matter of weeks the death of his father-in-law, the suicide of a friend of student days, Rainer Mersjohann (the person who invited him to California), and the drowning in the Pacific surf of Fran, a young student with whom he has been infatuated; to cap everything, the family dog is run over and killed shortly after his return to Stuttgart. Another problem, induced initially by a competitive society and then intensified by age, is the fear of failure: this comes out in this novel in Halm's concern about the public lecture he has to give, but is rendered absurd by his becoming unconscious almost as soon as he has begun it. *Ein fliehendes Pferd* presented fear of sexual inadequacy as a specifically modern anxiety, brought about by the emphasis placed on sporting activity and youthfulness, and this theme is continued here, in that Helmut avoids this problem by shunning sexual contact with Sabine. Suddenly, however, he finds that control over his neuroses, already shaken by the move to California, vanishes in the face of his infatuation with Fran. He can feel his ordered life start to come 'ins Rutschen' and, do what he may, cannot stop the slide. The potential for a perceptive analysis of Halm's reaction to this new situation is obvious, but Walser in no way attempts to explore its psychological dimensions. He depicts Halm's new-found passion and its consequences purely externally (whereas he had, in *Ein fliehendes Pferd*, shown the outer shell of Klaus Buch, only then to reveal the anguish beneath it), resorting here to the motif of role-playing that characterised his portrayal of Anselm Kristlein. Halm is shown as Malvolio, buying himself a cognac-coloured suit (rather than yellow stockings) to impress his new love, and consciously making himself the laughing-stock of the faculty. At the farewell party given for him he trips and gashes his face badly, but in the incident Fran's ankle is broken — he is thus, in all probability, responsible for her drowning, since it appears that she was unable to escape from a car stranded in the surf. In the manner of Franz Horn, Halm's response to the pressures put on him in California (where he emerges briefly from the protective cocoon of his routine existence in Stuttgart) is to flee from them by precipitating and embracing total failure.

This recurrent motif is complemented by another from Walser's recent novels: the comfort Halm finds, after returning home, in his relationship to Sabine. But whereas, particularly in *Ein fliehendes Pferd* and *Seelenarbeit*, these themes were previously presented in an extremely real social context, they are here, very much in the manner of the slight campus novels of Malcolm Bradbury and David Lodge, merely used as pegs on which to hang the humour. It would be wrong to infer from *Brandung* that Walser has moved away from the sensitive and sympathetic realism of recent years, although we cannot help noticing weaknesses here that are present in *Jenseits der Liebe* and, to a lesser extent, *Das Schwanenhaus*. The shortcomings of the novel undoubtedly stem from the fact that California is, as Halm himself says, not his reality, and the problems that face him in this essentially holiday environment are either exotically different or of little relevance to his normal social existence in Stuttgart.

Despite the fact that *Brandung* differs in not reflecting the neuroses induced by life in modern society 'in dem seismographisch funktionierenden Bewußtsein des Betroffenen',[8] the novel has much in common with its predecessors. Apart from the thematic links and the continued use of familiar motifs already indicated, the essential style continues that of all the novels from *Jenseits der Liebe* onwards. Apart from the epistolary *Brief an Lord Liszt*, all these works are narrated in a relatively conventional manner in the third person, but the narrator is by no means omniscient: he restricts himself to

8. Anthony Waine, *Martin Walser*, Münich, 1980 (Autorenbücher), p. 175.

219

reproducing — through a blend of direct and free indirect speech, together with occasional use of the preterite — the protagonist's experiences in external reality, as processed in his inner life. While, however, the first-person narration of the Anselm Kristlein trilogy gave no indication of the narrator's views, the subject-centricity of the later novel is fused with narratorial undertones that evince a warm sympathy, but a far from uncritical attitude, towards the protagonist. Through the use of the third person the reader's gaze follows the characters' tendency towards introspection, with experiences in the outer world being internalised and assessed as to their significance for the self in an inner world which, at the same time, is felt to be the seat of their 'wirkliche Person'. Like Raabe, to whose figures these have a certain affinity, Walser understands why they retreat into the self in order '[ihre] Menschenwürde zu retten' and realises too that the 'Herabwürdigung der Erscheinung zugunsten der Seele' has, within the context of the German novel, made a virtue out of necessity.[9] He nevertheless makes it clear that for him this 'Kleinbürgertendenz', as he calls it, of the Zürns and the Halms is a fatal mistake. His choice of a subjective variation on the traditional novel is, it would seem, not only intended as criticism of the new inwardness of the Seventies, but it is also designed to highlight the general tendency in the main stream of the German novel to focus on, and justify, the inward path. At the same time Walser is anxious to alert the 'Kleinbürger' (whom he knows well and by whom he wishes to stand in his suffering) that by finding no place 'die ihm den Eintritt in die wirkliche Geschichte erlaubte', he has failed, and continues to fail, to defend his own interests. In this concern to emphasise the negative utopia in existing society blighting the life of his anti-heroes, and the intent to demonstrate thereby the necessity for social change, are visible the lasting after-effects of Walser's intense politicisation in the late Sixties and early Seventies.

Like every important German novelist of the last two decades, Walser has found himself having to address himself very much to problems of narration in the modern novel: but the latter part of our analysis of his recent work is indicative of the way in which he has, over and above this, concerned himself with the German novel tradition. As with many other writers at the time, the radical questioning of the established form of the novel — in which he himself played a leading part — produced a hiatus in his writing career and, again like those other writers, his return to narrative

9. Martin Walser, 'Goethe hat ein Programm, Jean Paul eine Existenz', *Literaturmagazin 2*, Reinbek, 1974, pp. 108–9.

fiction was assisted by the model offered by autobiographical and biographical writing. Large sections of *Jenseits der Liebe* and *Brandung* are closely based on his experiences at the universities of Warwick and California, and the influence of the 'Lebensläufe' of the late Sixties is clearly evident in the form and intent of the recent novels. Further indications of the keen interest of leading novelists in biography is reflected in the literary publications of the Seventies, which include Peter Härtling's *Hölderlin* (1976), Adolf Muschg's *Keller* (1977), Wolfgang Hildesheimer's *Mozart* (1977), Dieter Kühn's *Ich, Wolkenstein* (1977), Hans. J. Fröhlich's *Schubert* (1978) and Gerhard Zwerenz's *Tucholsky* (1979). Prominent amongst the flood of avowedly autobiographical novels are Hildesheimer's *Zeiten in Cornwall* (1971); Grass's *Aus dem Tagebuch einer Schnecke* (1972); Karin Struck's *Klassenliebe* (1973); Handke's *Der kurze Brief zum langen Abschied* (1972), *Wunschloses Unglück* (1972), *Das Gewicht der Welt* (1977) and *Kindergeschichte* (1981); Max Frisch's *Montauk* (1975); Thomas Bernhard's *Die Ursache* (1975), *Der Keller* (1976), *Der Atem* (1978) and *Die Kälte* (1981); Koeppen's *Jugend* (1975); Bernward Vesper's *Die Reise* (1971/7); and Zwerenz's *Das Großelternkind* (1978). After a time of intense attention to objective external conditions, there is a widespread return to the 'Ich als d[er] einzige[n] Quelle der Wahrheit' (Dieter Wellershoff):[10] at this point the 'Dichterbiographien' help further to re-establish a damaged sense of personal identity, while the questioning of fictional writing is in many cases followed by a conscious reaffirmation of what has long been a common basis for narrative prose — personal experience. Much has been made of the role of artistic creativity, but, as long ago as 1906 Thomas Mann made the claim, which the recent German novel seems to confirm, that such experience is the true source of literary material: 'sehr große Dichter [haben] ihrer Lebtage nichts erfunden', he stated, 'sondern nur überliefertes mit ihrer Seele erfüllt und neu gestaltet'.[11]

In their concern with their own past, as the first stage of returning to the narrative, many authors seem to have established the truth of some theories prevalent at the end of the Sixties, in so far as it was by no means accepted as self-evident that individual experience reflected objective truths about life in society in general; Thomas Bernhard observed at the time: 'Wir wollen die Wahrheit sagen, aber sagen nicht die Wahrheit. Wir schreiben etwas wahrheitsgetreu, aber das Beschriebene ist etwas anderes als die Wahrheit'.[12]

10. Dieter Wellershoff in *Frankfurter Allgemeine Zeitung*, 12.11.1974.
11. In a letter to Kurt Martens. Cf. *Briefe 1889–1936*, Frankfurt, 1962, p. 62.
12. Thomas Bernhard, *Der Keller*, Frankfurt, 1976, p. 44.

Once again, there is a danger here of theory going too far, this time in the assertion that no experience has any relevance beyond its meaning for the individual, since it soon become clear from the response to many autobiographical novels of the Seventies that they were widely received as reflecting personal problems typical of, at the very least, the generation of '68 (cf. Chapter 8). This was, in any case, no handicap for the individual writer, whose primary concern was for self-discovery. For many of the young writers who made their débuts in the Seventies, in particular those who had gone more or less directly from their parents' home into the collective of the Student Movement, the authentic self was unknown. It is therefore not surprising that so many of them are concerned with basic problems of establishing a sense of identity by re-creating their past, as a means of defining, orientating and complementing an as yet reduced or disconcerted self. Within the autobiographical novel examples of such themes are given by a number of feminist works, by Karin Struck's *Klassenliebe*, Elisabeth Plessen's *Mitteilung an den Adel* (1976), Hermann Kinder's *Der Schleiftrog* (1977), Roland Lang's *Die Mansarde* (1979) and Bernward Vesper's *Die Reise*. The latter novel most clearly brings out an additional existential problem: the burden of the parental Nazi past.[13] Aided by 'die versuchsweise genaue Aufzeichnung eines 24-stündigen LSD-Trips', Vesper recorded his childhood, the anxious process of his freeing himself from the conservative (by then 'deutsch-national') ideas of his father, the Nazi writer Will Vesper, and his 'Rebellion gegen die zwanzig Jahre im Elternhaus, gegen den Vater, die Manipulation, die Verführung, die Vergeudung der Jugend' (44). His account does, in part, enumerate 'die Gründe, warum wir [he and Gudrun Ensslin, KB] aus Deutschland weggehen' (544), but the basic concern is 'für mich und meine Geschichte und meine Möglichkeit, sie wahrzunehmen' (26). In Vesper's case he decides against the novel in favour of the diary form (although there is nothing to distinguish the form of *Die Reise* from that of many other so-called novels of the Seventies), the latter representing for him 'ein ungeheurer Fortschritt, weil der Mensch sich weigert, seine Bedürfnisse zugunsten einer "Form" hinanzustellen' (36). The problems created by his family's Nazi past were, in his case, insurmountable (he committed suicide in 1971), but by the time *Die Reise* was published posthumously in 1977 it had become clear that his theme, taken up in the series of 'Väterromane' of the latter Seventies, had formed the substance of a new sub-genre within the orbit of the social novel.

---

13. *Die Reise*, Jossa, 1977. All quotations from this edition.

The wider currency that this sort of work acquired is reflected in the fact that it was adopted by the somewhat older and established Peter Härtling, in his *Nachgetragene Liebe* (1980). In this autobiographical novel Härtling is, however, in one sense offering only one more variation on the theme dominating his writing since the Sixties — his concern, 'Geschichten gegen die Geschichte zu erzählen': nevertheless his work in the Seventies is vivid testimony to the shift in patterns of narration at that time. Härtling's early books (*Niembsch oder der Stillstand*, 1964, *Janek*, 1966, and *Das Familienfest*, 1969) are essentially experimental novels that reveal the influence of the body of ideas represented by the Wiener Gruppe, Max Bense and Heißenbüttel: those of the Seventies, on the other hand, move ever closer to the tradition of the social novel. The unifying factor is Härtling's rejection, based on his own experience, of what he regards as a falsely harmonising and homogenising tendency in the writing of history in general, and in modern historical accounts of Germany's recent past in particular. His counter-interpretation, attempting to take fully into account individual experience of so-called historical events, is based essentially on the story of his own family; his father, Härtling writes in *Nachgetragene Liebe*, 'hinterließ mich mit einer Geschichte, die ich seit dreißig Jahren nicht zu Ende schreiben kann'.[14] The novels of the Sixties do not narrate in the strict sense of the word, but consist of rapid shifts in the temporal and narrative perspectives, the interweaving of at times contradictory half-sentences and fragmentary phrases, collages, flashbacks and jumps forward in the narrative flow, and the mingling of various voices within apparent dialogue. Instead of the location and the characters being fixed in time and place, the novels create a 'flimmerndes Mosaik' (Karl Krolow) corresponding to the process of memory itself, whereby the narrator as individual subject attempts to re-create the past by sifting through personal experience and the testimony of others. The move to a more conventional form of narration in the Seventies is, however, by no means as abrupt in Härtling's case as it is with Walser. His next novel, *Zwettl. Nachprüfung einer Erinnerung* (1973), follows its predecessors to a considerable degree in operating with a blend of monologue, dialogue and quotations and is, in addition, narrated from three perspectives (first and third person, as well as neutral documentary commentary): the mosaic pattern, however, gives way to a more formalised block structure along the lines of, say, Arno Schmidt's *Das steinerne Herz*. In its turn, this leads to a more comprehensible —

14. Darmstadt & Neuwied, 1980, p. 7.

admittedly limited, yet all the more realistic — reconstruction of the past, as experienced in childhood and youth. In contrast to the earlier novels, the locations and the characters are very precisely fixed, but, at the same time, the attempted re-creation of the past in literature is qualified and, ultimately, left open by the 'Korrekturen', an account of the narrator's visit to the town of Zwettl in 1971, supplemented by various documentary reports.

Within a year of the appearance of this novel, Härtling had moved on to attempt a basically chronologically structured 'Roman einer Generation'. *Eine Frau* (1974) still retains much of the style of his previous works, in that it is made up of diary entries written by the main character, Katharina Wüllner, later accounts of her past, memories, letters, quotations, free indirect speech and reconstructed conversations, but these are here located within the relatively conventional framework of a family chronicle. Information gleaned from *Nachgetragene Liebe* would suggest that here is a fictionalised account of the life of the author's mother: it appears to confirm that this book and its predecessor together comprise attempts on Härtling's part to come to terms with recent family history. His mother's life and his own memories of her enable Härtling to construct a graphic picture of a middle-class German family's life between 1902 and 1970, though the events of the day are consistently depicted from the point of view of an individual woman. Her memory enables her to grasp from the perspective of the then near-present the significance of things which, at the time, she 'nur zum Teil verstand'.[15] Even now, much remains unexplained, especially the time before her diary entries begin in 1917, life in the confusion of the end of the Second World War and its aftermath and — in a way that convincingly reproduces the failing memory and rather confused mind of a very elderly person — the latter stages of her life, when she seems ever more preoccupied with significantly earlier events. This incomplete and highly subjective record of the past rings true, however, precisely because it approximates to the fallible nature of human memory; it should also be said that, despite the obvious gaps in her recall, certain aspects of Katharina's story — for example, the portrayal of prosperous middle-class life in the first half of the century in areas now lost to Germany, her experience of the war as an increasingly frightened half-Jewess and the picture of life in Dresden in the letters from her Jewish Uncle David — add vigorous flesh and blood to somewhat pale and insubstantial chapters in the accounts of recent German social history, so that *Eine*

15. *Eine Frau*, Darmstadt & Neuwied, 1974, p. 79.

Frau, in the very best tradition of the family chronicle, enriches the dehumanised historical record of the period.

Eine Frau marks a crucial turning-point in Härtling's development, in that the reworking of family history into a convincing but clearly subjective account, commensurate with the limited and highly personal experiences of the individual, gives him faith in the communicative powers of narrative fiction and thus determines the shape of his future writing. *Hubert oder Die Rückkehr nach Casablanca* (cf. Chapter 8) continues the reworking of personal experience, in an even more fictionalised form: but the structure of the narrative, clearly influenced by the cinema, is now more conventionally linear. As in Walser's later novels, the protagonist here is an anti-hero, who follows with dismay the development of West Germany — the shedding of the Nazi past, the period of restoration, the rearmament. Nor can he settle into the system of values defined by the newly affluent consumer society that his country has become. Similar personal difficulties beset the two central characters in *Das Windrad* (1983), seemingly based in part on aspects of Härtling's later autobiography (his campaign against the building of the Startbahn West at Frankfurt Airport). The structure and narrative technique of this novel are still more conventional than *Hubert . . .* , and can be understood, to some extent, as a sort of modern 'Entwicklungsroman': Georg Landerer, a hitherto successful printer, finds himself brought up short by a physical collapse, diagnosed as stemming from hypertension; thus suddenly alerted to the short span of time left to him, he turns his back on his career and family, having up till now tolerated the frustrations involved, and takes up residence in a Swabian village. There he makes friends with the local drop-outs, above all with Baldur Kannabich, an eccentrically talented sculptor and inventor, who has developed an ecologically sound windmill for generating electricity. Despite the lack of planning permission, this is built, but the authorities soon tear it down after a violent large-scale police action. The distraught Kannabich commits suicide, leaving a letter in which he tries to explain to Landerer that the destruction of the windmill was only the last straw and that the real cause of his despair was the 'Unverstand' and 'Arroganz' of his own generation. He had seen how former Nazis were transformed overnight into sincere democrats, how even 'heimkehrende Neinsager' had become contented citizens, whose 'leere Sätze' simply accelerated the development of the country into a spiritual and physical wasteland. Looking back on the course of his life, he could now see that members of his generation

die Köpfe und die Seelen und die Leiber vergifteten, daß wir die Erde mißbrauchten, daß wir die Zukunft verplanten, daß wir Elende sind. . . . Aber die Jungen, und nicht nur sie, sind hellhörig geworden, empfindlich, aufsässig. Sie brechen das ohnedies fatal gewordene Gespräch mit den Pfründenhaltern, Schönrednern, den Bonzen und Machtverteilern ab und fangen ein anderes an: Mit den Verletzten, mit den Suchenden, mit den Vergessenen, mit den Empfindlichen. Auf die setze ich.[16]

Landerer embarks on a lecture tour, his theme being Kannabich's legacy: he can now work out what he had meant for himself and, as a result of the insights he gains, joins a local cooperative of young printers as a typesetter. The integration into his new life is complete.

Das Windrad continues some of the major thematic aspects of its predecessor, while opening up a way out of the malaise that had incapacited Hubert. Its shape, as already mentioned, recalls the 'Entwicklungsroman', but also has affinities with a particularly German variant on the traditional novel, the 'Heimatroman'. It should be said straight away that, as Härtling himself has stressed, 'Heimat' (in Bloch's sense) has always been a key concept to him. It is noticeable how this term, hitherto almost unusable because of the negative associations of its misuse by the Nazis, has reacquired a positive meaning in recent years: it has become an important cultural concept (with Edgar Reitz's film putting the final seal on its rehabilitation). It has, indeed, been argued that the novels of Böll and Grass have always had something of the quality of the 'Heimatroman' (certainly this has some validity in the latter case), but there can be little doubt that the East Prussian novels of Siegfried Lenz, the Gleiwitz trilogy of Horst Bienek, Kempowski's 'Deutsche Chronik' (set in Rostock), August Kühn's Munich novels and those of a number of Austrian novelists all evoke a firm sense of a partly lost 'Heimat', with all that that implies. Härtling is also not alone in portraying the small community as offering refuge to a self threatened by, or not able to realise itself in, a hostile society: this idea is central to Walter's *Die Verwilderung* and Karlheinz Frank's *Willi kalt und heiß* and, it could be argued, occurs with varying degrees of intensity in the recent work of Martin Walser (who has also written on the subject of 'Heimat' outside the realms of fiction). The loosely-knit Horn–Zürn clan that provides the central characters of his later novels clearly has very strong roots in Swabia, and in *Seelenarbeit* the longing of Xaver Zürn for his Wigratsweiler Hof and the solace it brings him is matched by the sense of void in the life of his employer, Dr Gleitze, who still yearns for, and speaks constantly

16. *Das Windrad*, Darmstadt & Neuwied, 1983, p. 146.

of, his lost Königsberg home. Perhaps the closest similarity to *Das Windrad* is provided by the first in a planned trilogy of village novels by Gerhard Roth, another former 'experimental' novelist whose work has become increasingly conventional since the mid-Seventies. In *Der stille Ozean* (1980) the central character, Asche, flees from the collapse of his professional life in the city into a village in the Steiermark, where he comes to recognise his authentic needs and the personal possibilities offered by the community, where he finally decides to stay.

The re-emergence of interest in 'Heimat' undoubtedly played its part in the tremendous commercial success of *Tadellöser und Wolff* (1971), the first novel in Walter Kempowski's 'Deutsche Chronik'. He designates it, interestingly enough, 'ein bürgerlicher Roman' and indeed his work, set against that of other West German writers, can be seen as the most conscious harking back to the traditions of that form. At the same time, his novels are clear evidence of the way in which the traditional form was regenerated in the Seventies by the blending of new and old elements — in his case, family saga and 'Heimatroman' were combined with the elements of the documentary and the autobiographical novel, together with a critical perception of the new historical novel. As with other writers, Kempowski's later novels of the chronicle have moved away somewhat from this mix of new and old and have also tended to leave behind the modern narrative techniques deployed early on, becoming ever more traditional in terms of form and authorial intent.

From a number of autobiographical sketches, we know that from early in the Sixties it was Kempowski's intention to write a family saga. *Tadellöser und Wolff* and *Herzlich willkommen* both stress his love of Thomas Mann's *Buddenbrooks*, but the second book describes, significantly, his purchase of Galsworthy novels, 'diese riesige Familiensaga, von der man nicht genug kriegen kann'.[17] The historical model chosen for his own work would seem, therefore, to be fairly clear. We also know that he started very early on to question members of his family and others about their past in Rostock and Hamburg and to record these conversations; he collected family letters, conducted research in various city archives and disciplined himself to note down in detail his own memories. Within the planned series of novels, he intended to cover the family history from 1900 until 1963, but after several other literary efforts — still unpublished — he began in earnest by working in the relatively secure area of his own recent life-story. In *Herzlich willkommen*

---

17. *Herzlich Willkommen*, Munich & Hamburg, 1984, pp. 277–8.

Kempowski describes how he set to work on this: 'Die Vergangenheit rekonstruieren: alles aufschreiben, solange das Gedächtnis noch Kleinigkeiten hergibt, die bösen, einsamen Stunden der Untersuchungshaft, in denen es jedoch Lichtblicke gegeben hatte'.[18]

In *Im Block. Ein Haftbericht* (1969) the narrator, unambiguously Kempowski himself, presents the reader with 'erlebte und bezeugte Tatsachen'. The story of his arrest and imprisonment in Bautzen is narrated more or less chronologically, the time-sequence being of no particular significance in itself. The narrative moves from one bundle of ideas — made up of either fragments of thoughts, conversations, descriptions of occurrences in the prison or near-quotation from letters received — to another, with these arranged in blocks, in the manner of the early Arno Schmidt. At times, but by no means always, there are associative links between the blocks. The narrative perspective is confined to the point of view of the narrator at the time of his imprisonment, with the restricted world around him perceived only through the filter of the narrator's consciousness. It is a sort of 'Kunstkopfroman', in which the reader is plunged by the narrative technique employed into the totality of the prison experience — the isolation, the immersion in a dull routine and the emotional paralysis gradually induced by those two forces.

Im Block is, thus, a far from conventional novel, but an innovative one that recreates with utter conviction the subjective response to six years' imprisonment. Kempowski's second novel, however, represents a decisive shift towards the conventional form of narrative fiction. While the initial critical response to *Tadellöser und Wolff*[19] was to question whether such a work, written in blocks and seeming to lack any overall structure, could be understood as a novel at all, Kempowski's own designation of it made clear his intent. Indeed, close analysis reveals that, despite the superficial impression created by the layout, the book marks a revival of the family novel. Through the life history of the narrator, who is actually called Walter Kempowski, a whole segment of family history is paraded before the reader: in a manner that immediately recalls the opening of *Buddenbrooks*, we begin with the move into the new family apartment, this scene being followed by detailed descriptions of the various family members, the house, family rituals, school, friends, leisure time and holidays. Only the programmatic chapter titles, so usual in the traditional novel of this type, are missing. Together with the continuation volume, *Uns geht's ja noch Gold* (1972), which follows the

---

18. Ibid., p. 57.
19. *Tadellöser und Wolff*, Munich, 1971. All quotations from this edition.

family's story from the end of the war up to the time of Kempowski's arrest in 1948, *Tadellöser und Wolff* conjures up a lost world, the disappearance of which is seen as synchronous with the decline of a middle-class mercantile family: again, the similarity to *Buddenbrooks* is obvious. The prosperity of the Kempowskis, ship-owners and shipping-agents in Rostock, is slowly undermined by the changes taking place in the twentieth century, with the Second World War sealing their demise: their last freighter is sunk, a Hamburg branch of the family has its ancestral home destroyed in the bombing, Kempowski's father is killed in the closing months of the war and all their remaining property in Rostock is commandeered by the occupying Russian forces. The final destruction of the family comes in 1948, with the arrest of its last Rostock members — Kempowski, his mother and brother.

This adoption of key features of the traditional genre is reinforced by the narrative technique employed in *Tadellöser und Wolff*. While *Im Block* was narrated rigorously from the perspective of the central character, in this novel Kempowski clearly views himself as the chronicler of his family and, to a lesser extent, of the social world in which they lived and worked in Rostock. The epic flow of some types of traditional novel is missing — although this can be seen as existing in the 'Deutsche Chronik' as a whole — but the loose structure of the blocks enables the author to range widely and present the reader with precise details of the family and its members; the numbered sections merely lack, but nevertheless imply through their particular focus, the conventional title — 'Das Haus', 'Im Kontor', 'Ein neuer Freund', 'Sommerferienzeit', etc. The novel does break with the traditional form of the novel, though, in the narratorial stance adopted: it is not the older and far wiser Kempowski telling the story as an omniscient interpreter of his own past, but the boy of the time commenting on events as he experienced them. As the chronicler he is but one voice amongst many and he lets the other players speak for themselves — in direct or indirect speech. He builds up a detailed linguistic model of the age with whole scenes or conversations being reproduced mimetically (as was confirmed by the film of the novel), complete with the accent of the speakers or the favouring of particular turns of phrase, much in the manner of 'phonographic' Naturalism. In keeping with this, the narrative language of Kempowski himself is that of a boy — he uses simple syntax, short sentences and his speech is littered with childish expressions and slang of the time: his brother is a 'Schatzfink'; his grandfather 'grabbelte' for coins in his pocket; his sister puts her 'Ratzefummel' in her handbag; 'Scheiße mit Reiße', he curses. The child's perspective is maintained throughout, there is no attempt made to colour what he remembers or has been told by others with the knowledge or possible moral assurance of an adult looking back on this time; the epoch is re-created without prior interpretation by a present-day commentator, but as it was experienced at the time, with all its attendant contradictory attitudes and imponderabilia. In this respect, Kempowski's narrative technique is close to Arno Schmidt's views on realism (a debt he acknowledges), not only in the obvious use of index cards, but, more importantly, in the 'Foto-Text-Einheiten' created, the amalgam of objective (E I) and subjective (E II) reality to be found in a novel like *Das steinerne Herz*, E I being represented here by documentary material and other people's statements, and E II by the 'Sich-Erinnern' of Kempowski himself.

The advantages of this approach emerge most clearly in the treatment of the relationship of the various Kempowskis to National Socialism, which serves to illuminate the inevitable differences of opinion and inconsistencies within such a family. Uncle Richard, for example, is a convinced Nazi:

> Onkel Richard erzählte von Hitler. Stahlharter Händedruck, Augen wie Friedrich der Große. Wir ahnten ja gar nicht, was der Mann für Vorräte angelegt habe. Den Krieg, den hielten wir noch Jahre um Jahre durch. Gewaltig. Alle Turnhallen in Polen beschlagnahmt. Büchse auf Büchse, ganze Türme.
>
> Dann paßte er einen Moment ab, wo der Bräutigam nicht in der Nähe stand und flüsterte: demnächst gehe es wieder aufwärts. Er wisse das aus absolut sicherer Quelle. Die ganze Kraft des Reichs werde konzentriert, um noch in diesem Jahr die Entscheidung zu erzwingen. Ein einziger, gewaltiger Schlag (289–90).

Walter's father, on the other hand, is uncertain in his attitude, tending to respond opportunistically to the pattern of events. We note that, by the time of his daughter's wedding to the Dane Sörensen in 1944, he is at pains to explain to him 'den Unterschied zwischen "Deutscher" und "Nazi"' and to reject National Socialism: 'Wer hätte das gedacht, daß es noch mal so kommen würde. Dieses Pack. Nicht einmal richtig deutsch sprechen. Der Gauleiter Hildebrandt, der sei ja direkt Viehhirte gewesen. Säh auch danach aus' (230). Back in 1941, however, the fall of Verdun had produced a different sort of reaction from him: '"Donnerwetter!" rief mein Vater, "großartig!" eines Tages würde man doch wohl ein Führerbild kaufen' (132). His enthusiasm had been even greater at the invasion of Poland and we know, moreover, that before the war he had pictures of Bismarck, Hindenburg and Hitler hanging on his office wall (23), while the young Walter remembers (or the narrator has in front of him) a photograph of his father 'sogar als SA-Mann unter einer Birke' (15). The information to be gathered from the text would suggest that the involvement of Walter's father was greater than it seemed; his mother, on the other hand, is resolutely unpolitical — even before 1933 she had found things 'ja nicht zum Aushalten', because of constant political meetings. Her concern is for human decency, with the result that the outbreak of war, far from striking a nationalist chord, makes her think only of the consequences for ordinary people: ' "Daß die Menschen nicht in Frieden leben können", sagte meine Mutter. "Die Großen sollten in den Boxring gehn und die Sache selbst austragen, dann würden *sie* aber zukucken" ' (92). When Sörensen is arrested by the Gestapo she does not hesitate to go and plead (successfully) for his release (197).

Given the attitude of some members of the family and the inescapable external presence of the Third Reich, the children grow up with it as an integral part of life. On his way to school one day Walter is told by his friend Manfred all about the Jews: 'Im Patriotischen Weg habe man abgeschnittene Finger gefunden, das Werk Israels. Die mordeten Christen, zerstückelten sie und schmissen sie weg. Das war für die eine gute Tat. In jeder Synagoge ein verkrusteter Blutkeller. Dafür kämen sie in'n Himmel' (37). The present-day commentator, fully aware of the significance of such a statement, would undoubtedly pounce on it, but for the young Walter, as he then was, such things were merely one small part of his life — he immediately moves on to say how his brother Robert caught the two of them up. The casual, unstressed mention of aspects of Nazism as part of everyday life at the time builds up into a convincing picture of the age as experienced by a child, contrasting strongly with more heavy-handed treatments of the period. We can deduce from the novel that Walter does not care much for the Hitler Youth, but he nevertheless plays war games with his Halma men, is very interested in colonial novels and 'Lanzerhefte' and has pictures of 'Ritterkreuz' holders pinned up over his bed; but this is far from being a sign of nationalism on his part — the pictures, for example, could just as well be those of footballers or pop stars. His older sister Ulla is capable of having her own views on the Nazis — she is delighted to lose her German citizenship on marriage, when her first instinct is to throw away the copy of *Mein Kampf* she receives — but the younger Walter is wrapped up in his own world; he does, admittedly, eventually rebel against the Hitler Youth, but this is a completely unpolitical act, stemming as it does from his desire to keep his hair long.

231

The treatment of the family under National Socialism shows the full potential of the narrative technique and stance adopted by Kempowski. The various facets of the material in this segment are presented in scattered fashion and without commentary, in a way that demands the critical involvement of the reader, if he is to unravel it, but this quality is, sadly, absent from whole sections of the rest of the novel. Large parts consist of scenes, admittedly vivid, but — and here, behind the use of blocks may be sensed the enthusiasm of the collector who cannot bear to leave anything out — they repeat themselves or pile up one on another, without adding anything new. *Tadellöser und Wolff* does compensate for this to a large extent, it should be said, in that the material presented by the child narrator is in itself fascinating. However, in the sequel, *Uns geht's ja noch Gold*, the piling up of pictures is merely continued and the lack of economy and sharpness inherent in the method becomes particularly apparent. The full disadvantages of the (increasingly uncritical) style are seen in the latest novel in the sequence, *Herzlich willkommen* (1984), which concentrates on the time (1956–7) immediately following Kempowski's release under an amnesty. It is very similar to the first two: we are presented with one scene or image after another, but — undoubtedly because the author is an outsider to the Federal Republic — they give nothing of the spirit of the age. The rigorous subject-centricity of the narrative in *Im Block* would have brought out this isolation very adequately, while the psychological realism of Härtling or Walser would have produced a critical picture of the values or the political climate of the Adenauer era, deriving its sharpness from the alienated position of the narrator. In the event, Kempowski's amalgam here of personal experience and documentary material, devoid of any emotional or other subjective — e.g. socio-political — position on the part of the narrator, is merely tedious.

The remaining novels of the chronicle exemplify different problems produced by the author's gradual move away from his initial subjective realism. *Ein Kapitel für sich* (1975), a reworking of his experiences in prison, breaks with the narrow focus of *Im Block* by including the voices of his mother and brother and letters from his sister and uncle. The structure of the novel is now given by cinematic cuts from one perspective to another, with a consequent weakening of the intense feeling of isolation. The originally bleak narrative has been enlivened by the strewing of adjectives and adverbs and at times the events are commented on, if only unintentionally, from a point of view which can demand hindsight. The 'enriching' of the text, as Kempowski undoubtedly saw it, makes it inferior to the original as a work of literature.

The move away from a consciously subjective narrative position towards the more traditional form of the novel, already detected in *Tadellöser und Wolff* and which we note again here, comes out most forcefully in those volumes which portray the childhood experiences of the adult generation of Kempowskis and de Bonsacs who appeared in *Tadellöser und Wolff: Aus großer Zeit* (1978) and *Schöne Aussicht* (1981). These novels are different from all their predecessors in that, although they depict social history through the story of the family, this does not enmesh with the autobiography of the author and narrator. Kempowski's approach to these earlier periods remains the same — he has burrowed his way through city archives and family letters, interviewed surviving relatives and family friends and collected a host of contemporary photographs — but he is clearly conscious of a lack of personal knowledge of the world he describes. In *Schöne Aussicht* he goes so far as to underline the authenticity of the material by prefacing each section of the novel with various quotations, designed to show the typicality of the events depicted in that part of the novel, underlining thereby his intent to produce a representative picture of the time. The narrative of the two novels is made up of statements by members of the family, friends and acquaintances, presented in the mix — by now familiar — of direct and indirect speech, but the structuring into blocks has been severely eroded: many blocks containing lengthy stories have the effect of conventional chapters, and the element of contrast, which gives whole sections of *Tadellöser und Wolff* their real quality, is completely absent. The narrator, clearly identified in *Schöne Aussicht* as still being Kempowski himself, seems to operate as compiler of, and occasional commentator on, the family history that he evokes, very much in the manner of someone turning the pages of an old photograph album. Yet he alone is in the position to distinguish between authentic material (as produced by the memory of others) and fictional reconstruction: he operates, in other words, as an omniscient narrator presenting the reader with (he maintains) a representative re-creation in literature of a past social world, presented to us as a totality. As in much modern architecture or stage design, we are shown, in modernist fashion, the basic structure on which it rests, but the actual edifice is fundamentally conventional. The various voices we hear do not add up to a polyperspectivity that keeps the narrative fluid, but merely offer variety from the pattern of indirect speech, while the narrator, in the manner of a Galsworthy, lovingly reconstructs a bygone age in what he believes to be its entirety. The novel lacks the distortion produced by the foreshortened perspective of the youthful narrator in *Tadellöser und Wolff* and which, in turn, stimulates the reader's critical faculties. Perhaps unintentionally, the young Walter is devoid of the nostalgia that characterises the narrators in later volumes; his concern is essentially the discovery of his own self through the recreation of his past. It is the discovery of his youthful straightforwardness, in its interaction with the values and attitudes of the adult world in the Third Reich, that brings about the illuminating critical perspective of the best parts of the novel.

The qualified success of *Tadellöser und Wolff* and the persuasive power of other more or less conventional novels discussed in this chapter, particularly Walser's *Ein fliehendes Pferd* and *Seelenarbeit* and Härtling's *Eine Frau*, derive from the way in which they portray what is essentially a highly individual experience of reality. The body of Kempowski's work demonstrates, on the other hand, the problems brought about by the attempt — conscious or unconscious — to lay claim to the omniscience enjoyed by the traditional narrator of the bourgeois novel and to the totality that it was seen to embody. The dangers of uncritically adopting such a conventional narratorial stance, with all that it implies regarding the tacit claims made for the status of the subject-matter, emerge with particular force in Dieter Wellershoff's *Der Sieger nimmt alles* (1983).[20]

The critical reception of this novel provides a fascinating case-study of professional literary criticism at work in West Germany. In the so-called quality press it was uniformly savaged, while reviews in regional newspapers were on the whole very favourable. Thus Rolf Becker (in *Der Spiegel*) saw it as proof that Wellershoff was 'kein Balzac der deutschen Mark', while Christel Heybrock (in *Mannheimer Morgen*) claimed that, 'um etwas Vergleichbares zu finden, muß man zurückgehen zu Tolstoi, Fontane, Flaubert, Zola'.[21] It is not our concern, though, at this juncture, as to whether or not this pattern points, as has been suggested, to an anti-realist cartel amongst the upper echelons of West German literary criticism. The important thing here is that both camps were agreed in seeking to compare it with the great nineteenth-century European novels, which gives an immediate indication as to the style of *Der Sieger nimmt alles* and the implicit claim it makes about the significance of its theme.

The central character of the novel, whose life — according to the

---

20. Cologne, 1983. All quotations from this edition.
21. Cf. here Rolf Becker, 'Ein Balzac von der deutschen Mark', *Der Spiegel*, 5.9.1983 and, in the wider connection of the reception of this novel, Lothar Baier, 'Ceterum censeo: Wellershoff ist zu verreißen', *Merkur*, 38, 1984, pp. 360–4.

dust-jacket — is meant to be 'von exemplarischer Gültigkeit', is Ulrich Vogtmann, a man who makes his way up from modest beginnings to an important position in commerce during the extreme social mobility in the era of the 'Wirtschaftswunder': in this sense, then, we are indeed dealing with a figure that is important within the social history of the Federal Republic. Having managed to enter university, Vogtmann is far from enthusiastic about his studies and has no idea where they might lead, until Reichenbach, a friend from his early days at university, who has now achieved success, opens his eyes to the possibilities that lie before him: 'In diesen Jahren passieren die entscheidenden Dinge. Die Wirtschaft expandiert, überall wird aufgebaut. Wer jetzt einsteigt, der wird vom allgemeinen Aufschwung hochgerissen. . . . Du darfst nur nicht den Start verschlafen. Mach endlich diese blöde Examen, und stürz dich auf die realen Dinge' (29–30). When Vogtmann stands in for Reichenbach during his absence on secondment, he attracts the attention of the owner of the milk condensery where he is working; he is invited to a party and there finds himself pursued by the owner's daughter. He sees his chance, 'das große Geld' zu machen and, after persuading his current girlfriend Jovanka to have an abortion, abandons her to marry Elisabeth Pattberg, his key to fortune. Over the years he advances through the firm to become managing director and, after the death of old Pattberg and the suicide of Elisabeth's alcoholic and, in any case, unbusinesslike brother, he finds himself in total control. By now this is not enough for him; he takes out huge loans and buys up a chain of Bavarian grocery stores. He also puts huge sums of money into a speculative venture involving the sale of drugs to Zaïre. His questionable business methods and the gambles he takes with funds raised on the strength of the parent firm bring the company to the brink of bankruptcy; Elisabeth, as the major share-holder, dismisses him and he then finds out how completely he has been duped in his other ventures. Now totally ruined, Vogtmann despairingly tries to persuade a wealthy and successful contemporary from school to find a position for him, but, before he can be told that there is no such opening, he dies of a heart attack in a lonely hotel room.

Wellershoff is clearly intent in this novel — some of the very obvious inadequacies of which come through in the clichéd story line — in producing more than a well researched and factually convincing picture of commercial life, which parts of it undoubtedly do provide. The aim is to chart the 'Psychographie' of Vogtmann as a 'von Bereicherungsphantasien getriebenen, von "Niemandsgefühlen" verunsicherten Karrieristen'. Brought up in a boarding school, where he was rather a loner, his only hope of escape from the misery that was his early life is the wild hope 'daß etwas geschah, ein Ereignis, das Bedeutung für ihn gewann und sein Leben veränderte, irgend etwas, das ein neuer Anfang war' (13). He can see that he is leading a merely 'vorläufiges Leben' and desperately wants to change, but an inherited passivity causes him to feel 'unzusammenhängend und aufgelöst, weil niemand da war, an den er sich halten konnte' (38). His rise, which, in the later stages, he ruthlessly forces through against family opposition, is initially dependent on the intervention of others — Reichenbach and Elisabeth. His studies, which he finishes only after the former's prompting, provide him with information about the workings of money, 'mit dem man die unzulängliche, verschlossene Welt öffnen und beherrschen konnte' (15); when Elisabeth offers herself to him, he realises that she embodies the realisation of his dreams: 'Gleich würde er sie haben, sie und alles, was sie war. Die Millionen, die man nicht von der Bettkante stieß. Sie, das Falsche und das Richtige, und alles, was an ihr anhing, was dazugehörte' (86). Despite his rapid financial advancement, the marriage is in a sense indeed 'das Falsche', in that, even when he has total control of the firm, he is forced to ask himself: 'Was sollte diese Anstrengung? Er wollte es nicht. Er steckte immer in einem falschen Leben. Das falsche war das einzige Leben und man mußte sich darin bewähren' (124). The purchase of the chain of stores is an attempt to solve this dilemma by freeing himself from his continued financial dependence on Elisabeth: 'Er würde Geld haben und sich frei fühlen. Geld war ein anderes Wort für Leben, für den Rausch des Lebens, denn fast alles, was begehrens- oder wünschenswert war, war auch käuflich' (185). He buys himself a flat in Munich, acquires a mistress there and through her gains entry to the city's smart social scene; he seems for a time to have attained a sort of happiness — if only superficial — but the rapidly ensuing financial difficulties turn the last phase of his life into nothing more than a desperate struggle for survival. The reader has, in any case, long since concluded that he is in some way incapable of finding real happiness.

Vogtmann is not the exclusive focus of the novel: substantial sections of two chapters ('Auf der Schaukel' and 'Schwarze Löcher') are narrated by Elisabeth. Unlike her husband, she is very much an idealist, whose basic philosophy is that one has to 'sich selbst und seine wirklichen Werte kennen'. Her love for Ulrich and the progress of his career are of great importance to her: 'sie hatte seine brachliegenden Energien gespürt. . . . Er war den Weg gegangen, den sie ihm eröffnet hatte, und er sollte sich immer auf sie verlassen können' (103). The two of them live on totally different planes; after twenty years of marriage she is still deeply in love with him, whereas he views their relationship as one of suppressed conflict and believes that she is only waiting for his downfall. To convince her of the measure of his commitment in marrying her, he at last tells her about his abandonment of Jovanka (which was, in reality, far from hard for him); this fills her with horror and significantly alters her view of their life together. Their alienation from each other is accelerated by his frenzied work-rate and, later, his ruthless use of the family fortune, which forces her to admit at last that 'sie seien auf dem falschen Weg, und alles würde allmählich zerstört werden, außen und innen. Innen konnte es in den Menschen nur so aussehen wie in ihnen selbst' (235). When she is alerted to his ruinous conduct of the family concern she has him dismissed and obtains a formal separation.

The parts of the novel concerned with the problems between Ulrich and Elisabeth take up the theme of inter-personal relationships, central to Wellershoff's 'Hörspiele', his 'Novelle', *Die Sirene* (1980), and a range of short stories up to, and including, his volume, *Die Körper und die Träume* (1986). The Vogtmann's marriage breaks down as a result of irreconcilable differences in outlook and ideals: this could have formed the nucleus of a different and tighter novel, but, although the passages narrated from Elisabeth's perspective are some of the best in the novel, they remain superficial. Deep psychological analysis of the mental and emotional life of the couple is made impossible by the novel's vast sweep, and their personal story becomes but one of several subplots.

The most important back-cloth to the drama is the world of finance. The bulk of the novel consists of the ultimately chequered path that Vogtmann takes through the — as far as this reader is concerned — unknown realm of the world of financial dealing and commercial speculation, including a very detailed and highly convincing demonstration of one way to make money by speculating in the Third World (the Zaïre transaction). It is not clear, however, what these closely observed and lengthy episodes are meant to achieve. It is suggested briefly, at one point only, that his experiences open Ulrich's eyes to the fact that even the world of big money is false and unsatisfying: 'Alle kennen sie die Regeln des Spiels, aber keiner den Inhalt, keiner den Sinn. Alle spielen sie ihre Rolle. Es ist noch das Beste, was man tun kann' (282). This point is never touched upon again and, indeed, we gain the impression that the big fish, those who make really large sums of money, enjoy their work and its financial rewards, while only the social upstart Vogtmann, condemned as such to remain an outsider, finds no satisfaction in his uncertain life on the fringes of this world. This too could have been a splendid topic for a novel. A further suggestion is that Ulrich is tricked because he has somehow failed to learn the rules of a game that he does not fully understand. He himself, when his ruin becomes clear, speaks of traps having been set for him and — if we think, for example, of the way in which he is defrauded over the sale of the chain of stores and duped in the Zaïre speculation — there does seem to be some sort of system, controlled by faceless individuals, which exploits the gullible until they are no longer useful. This theme, too, is not developed further. The reader has the impression that while the author completely understands the roles played by various characters in the financial dramas, in the novel they remain ciphers. It lacks scenes that would take us into this unknown world and real insights into the mind of the key figures. Instead, we have to be content with the labels attached to them by the author. It is sadly true that, as Peter Gillies has put it, the novels of Harold Robbins, Simmel and Konsalik ultimately reveal far more about the world of finance.[22]

This labelling of characters, which denies the reader understanding of the workings of their mind and their motives, is also evident in the treatment of Vogtmann's family life. His son Christoph, to whom an entire section is devoted, is a problem child: he becomes a kleptomaniac and, having been punished by being sent to boarding school, sprays the slogan 'No future' across the front of the school. His problems are clearly to be understood as stemming from the tension within the family and the attitude of his father towards him. Nevertheless, as with the figure of Klaus Jung in Wellershoff's earlier novel *Die Schönheit des Schimpansen* (1977), we do not catch sight of the family life which has induced the neurosis; the cause is merely asserted and we are only presented with its consequences. The figure of Vogtmann himself, despite the length devoted to him, is similarly foreshortened. From the opening scene of the novel, which describes the manner of his death, concluding with a sort of close-up of his deformed feet, we are given to understand that he is both a physical and a psychological cripple: he is an orphan and has great difficulties in his boarding school, particularly because of his lack of family and the disability that prevents him from taking part in games. This existential anxiety is compounded by the inheritance from his mother of a very passive nature, for which he later tries to compensate through frenetic activity. The first twenty-seven years of

---

22. In a review in *Die Welt*. Quoted in Baier, p. 360.

his life are merely sketched in, but — as the opening scene emphasises — predestine his later life, despite all apparent advancement, to
failure. The omniscient narrator reveals himself to be fully convers-
ant with the combination of psychological problems that dictates
Ulrich's behavior in adult life — he knows, for example that Ulrich
is deluding himself into thinking that self-fulfilment will come with
money, since 'wenn sich der Anfang einer möglichen Veränderung
zeigte, würde er ihn kaum erkennen können' (13). The reader,
however, is denied such knowledge of the character, with the result
that his rise and fall tends to read like a pale copy of the trite
patterns in popular novels.

The combination of fateful flaws that mar *Der Sieger nimmt alles*
stems essentially from Wellershoff's clear determination to write an
exemplary novel of his time, complete with the epic breadth and
narratorial omniscience of the traditional novel. Instead of deciding
on one of the various aspects of the web of plots that could have been
the stuff of a good novel — a full examination of the experience of
childhood and school, leading on to the portrayal from Ulrich's
perspective of his subsequent difficulties in a hostile and alien world,
for example, or the analysis from the point of view of both participants in his marriage — , Wellershoff is unambiguously resolved to
present the reader with the spectrum of West German society; this
alone explains, for example, the detailed and lengthy description of
chic Munich life, which is of little relevance to the fate of Vogtmann,
the born loser. There are other indications as to the author's
intentions in this novel than its length (506 pp.) and the spread we
have indicated: the motif of 'Auf der Schaukel' may well be a purely
coincidental reminder of Fontane's *Effi Briest*, but the way in which
the progress of the stories is marked by appropriate weather and the
indication of character traits through physical attributes (in the
cases of Ulrich and Christoph) have distinct affinities with well-
known models. Thematically and, at times, stylistically *Der Sieger
nimmt alles* has parallels with Balzac's 'Comédie Humaine' cycle, as
so many critics recognised. The destruction of the Pattenberg company cannot but evoke key aspects of *Buddenbrooks*, marked as it is by
the demolition of the ancestral villa at the hands of a new financial
world with new and different values; the destruction signifies both
the decline of the family and of an older social world with, it is
implied, better values (as indicated by the past evident in the picture
of Soloturn station square compared to modern reality, pp. 233–4).
Der Sieger nimmt alles is proof, however, of the problems that beset
any writer attempting to emulate such models today; the more
successful novels examined in this and other chapters underline the

vital necessity for the contemporary realist novel, be it modernist or relatively traditional in form and concept, to take full cognisance of the nature of modern existence, to abandon any claim that the novel can represent the totality of social life and instead to address, and to reflect, the subjective experience of reality by the individual subject.

Conclusion:

Realism Today

If we look back from the present at the history of the German novel since 1968, the year of the so-called 'death' of literature, it is clear that it has recovered and, indeed, flourished during the past two decades. The works examined in this study, which represent but a part of the total picture, are testimony to the emergence in the period since 1968 of a substantial body of realist novels of consistently high quality, which, in quantitative terms, can only be compared to the Twenties' boom in the realist novel. The literary achievement represented by these novels goes against the major emphasis of literary theory and critical debates of the late Sixties, which, as we have shown, tended to continue the German anti-realist tradition: today, however, there are signs that the realist novel has played a part in changing, to some extent, the climate of critical opinion in West Germany. It is true that, in literary scholarship (in the sense of 'Germanistik'), realism still tends to be understood as coterminous with a specific period of German literary history, but in the area of literary criticism the old antipathy to realism as such would seem to be on the wane. Undoubtedly, there is still a strong lobby for what is left of experimental literature (Jörg Drews, the most prominent member of this group, still dismisses realist novels — he specifically mentions Walser in this connection — because they 'nur grau und kleinlich an eben den Verhältnissen kleben, die sie beschreiben').[1] So strong is this lobby, indeed, that Lothar Baier, Jürgen Lodemann and Klaus Ramm talk of a 'Stimmungskartell gegen Realismus' and Dieter Lattmann was still writing in 1985 of there being a general opposition to realist writing, but these are not views we would now share.[2] Although it provoked talk of an anti-realist monopoly, the criticism of Wellershoff's *Der Sieger nimmt alles* was fair, in that it drew attention to the serious flaws in the novel (cf. Chapter 9), while

1. Jörg Drews, 'Über einen neuerdings in der deutschen Literatur erhobenen Ton', *Merkur*, 39, 1985, p. 949.
2. Cf. Baier's article, 'Ceterum censeo: Wellershoff ist zu verreißen'. Ramm and Lodemann agreed with Baier's position in discussion at the II. Internationales Germanistentreffen of the DAAD, Wissenschaftskolleg zu Berlin, 28.9.1985. Cf. also: Dieter Lattmann, 'Literatur auf der Flucht?', *UZ-Magazin*, October 1985, p. 2.

Lattmann's attitude is influenced by the equally critical response to his *Die Brüder* (1985). Rather like Wellershoff, Lattman utilises the completely unmodified traditional form — in his case the family novel — to attempt a broadly based analysis of post-war German society in East and West, with the inevitable result: incredible coincidences, heavy narratorial interventions and, above all, the 'coverage' of all crucial phases of the period since 1945 by the members of just one family render the novel clichéd and, ultimately, laughable. Criticism of the two novels identified the inappropriate choice of literary model by both authors, but did not evince a position dismissive of realism as such. Indeed, in contrast with the early Seventies, when such an antipathy could still be observed, contemporary literary criticism in West Germany would seem to be essentially pluralist; Siegfried Lenz was awarded the Thomas Mann-Preis for 1985, and the positive reception accorded to realist novels such as Eva Demski's *Scheintod* (1984), F.C. Delius's *Adenauerplatz* (1984) and Martin Walser's *Brandung* (1985) was, if anything, over-generous. Cynical observers of the West German literary scene may be tempted to attribute such apparent tolerance to the general stagnation of experimental literature since the mid-Seventies, but the increasing openness of Helmut Heißenbüttel and Heinrich Vormweg, leaders of the attack on realism in 1969, with regard to recent realist writing, seems to be clear evidence of a real shift having taken place.[3]

Despite the change in the reception of realist works and the quantitative and qualitative achievement of the realist novel since 1968, a reduced impetus can be detected in the last few years. There are, of course, works that retain the innovative verve of the Seventies, but the flood of realist novels starts to dry up after 1982. Explanations for this change, which has not gone unobserved, have tended to relate it to disillusionment and resignation caused by the so-called 'Bonner Wende', the sensed conservative shift in governmental social policy during the chancellorship of Helmut Kohl, just as the 'Neue Subjektivität' of the Seventies was attributed to the 'Tendenzwende' of 1972–3. Yet again, there is a sense in which this interpretation of the situation is not entirely wide of the mark: the bulk of the literature produced in the Seventies, especially by new writers, stemmed from a generation strongly influenced by experiences and debates of the late Sixties, even if individual authors were

---

3. Cf. in this connection Heißenbüttel's reviews of Böll's *Gruppenbild mit Dame* and *Fürsorgliche Belagerung*, Vormweg's contributions to *Jahresring* 1970–6 and his 'Laudatio für Brigitte Kronauer' on her award of the Kunstpreis Berlin for 1985 (published by the Akademie der Künste).

not part of the Student Movement itself. The literature of the Seventies is shaped by the enthusiasm and the energies of that time, but, even for the most optimistic writers, the election result of 1982 is the final, decisive blow. Neo-conservatism, already a force in the West as a result of the coming to power of Ronald Reagan and Margaret Thatcher, now comes to dominate public life in the Federal Republic. This is undoubtedly the major — but by no means the exclusive — reason for the prominence in recent literature of the themes of resignation, tiredness or spiritual stock-taking, some prominent examples being Jürgen Theobaldy's *Spanische Wände* (1984), Heinrich Böll's *Frauen vor Flußlandschaft* (1985) and Ingeborg Drewitz's *Eingeschlossen* (1986). Clear indication of the change in the general mood of the time is given by the fact that, while many novels of the Seventies were politically engaged, in one sense or another, those novels of the mid-Eighties which tackle directly political themes — such as F.C. Delius's *Adenauerplatz* and Max von der Grün's *Die Lawine* (1986) — are the exceptions. It is also striking how a competent descriptive literature, skilfully using realist techniques from the novel of the Seventies, has established itself and been well received: yet it lacks the utopian element that is a hallmark of true realism. The loss of this dimension in such literature emerges vividly from the contrast between Eva Demski's *Scheintod* and Lothar Baier's *Jahresfrist* (1985), perhaps the most striking instance in the recent West German novel of the process of self-examination and loss of utopian vision induced in a man of '68 by the changing social and political climate of the Federal Republic. Eva Demski's novel consists in the reconstruction of life in the Seventies by 'der Frau', following the premature death of her estranged husband, an 'alternative' solicitor: while it evokes an accurate and familiar picture of the time, it fails to add anything new to our image of that era or to help the woman in reorientating her life; its undoubted appeal would seem to be essentially nostalgic. Baier's 'Erzählung' (as he chooses to call it, though it is indistinguishable from a novel), on the other hand, continues the spirit of the Seventies, in that the self-orientation of the main character involves a critical re-evaluation of his own recent past and leads on to a new sense of personal direction, defined by a revival of engagement in worthwhile causes. A further indication of the shift from the more or less direct political or socio-critical appeal of the novels of the last decade is a turning away from contemporary social themes, or historical ones with present-day relevance. The trend now is towards an artistically accomplished and entertaining novel, of which Patrick Süskind's *Das Parfum* (1985) and Uwe Timm's *Der Mann auf dem Hochrad*

(1984) are but two examples, or towards mythical material and the mythological as such — a tendency begun by Handke in the Seventies. Examples here are the keen interest in Tolkien and in the work of Michael Ende (*Die unendliche Geschichte* and *Momo*), Handke's *Über die Dörfer* (1981) and *Der Chinese des Schmerzes* (1983), and Botho Strauß's *Der junge Mann* (1984); the clearest indication is provided outside the novel by the latter's 'long poem' *Diese Erinnerung an einen, der nur einen Tag zu Gast war* (1985).

Given the fickle and volatile nature of the present-day West German book trade, it would be wrong to rule out here the factor of the constant search by publishers for the new and different. Nevertheless, our understanding of the nature of realism — as determined essentially by a fusion of epistemological notions and utopian thinking, rather than by a particular style of writing — would suggest that, just as the upsurge of realism in the Seventies was induced by the continued utopianism derived from the Student Movement and a (false) hope for significant social change, the apparent switch away from it undoubtedly reflects a response by writers today to a change in the understanding of extra-literary reality. At this point certain ideas from outside the literary world, which also proceed from the observable lessening of utopian energies in recent years, help to awaken understanding of this development and to enhance awareness of its consequences for literature.

In an essay published in 1985, entitled 'Die Neue Unübersichtlichkeit', Jürgen Habermas addresses himself to the increasing despair of intellectuals, which — under the impact of poverty and human degradation in the Third World, the striking social inequality in the so-called developed countries, the arms race and other threats to world peace — 'an die Stelle von zukunftsgerichteten Orientierungsversuchen tritt'.[4] Habermas rejects the post-modernist hypothesis that earlier utopian visions, which were secularised during the eighteenth century, are today increasingly taking on religious garb; the sense of the 'Neue Unübersichtlichkeit' of the world is attibuted, instead, to a situation, in which 'eine immer noch von der arbeitsgesellschaftlichen Utopie zehrende Sozialstaatsprogrammatik die Kraft verliert, künftige Möglichkeiten eines kollektiv besseren und weniger gefährdeten Lebens zu entwerfen' (4). It is, he argues, particularly difficult for the legal and administrative machinery of the modern industrial state to accept 'postmaterielle Werte', especially 'die expressiven Bedürfnisse nach Selbstverwirklichung und die kritischen Urteile einer universalistischen Aufklä-

---

4. Jürgen Habermas, 'Die Neue Unübersichtlichkeit', *Merkur*, 39, 1985, pp. 1–14.

rungsmoral', since these collide with the power system of the functional social state (10). He identifies three forms of response to this impasse: in the cases of the 'Legitimisten' of the social state (such as Social Democrats) and the 'Neokonservativen' (the Republicans in the USA, the Conservatives in the United Kingdom and the CDU/CSU in the Federal Republic) he observes the emergence of a defensive consciousness, 'das seiner utopischen Dimension beraubt ist' (12). Even the non-functionalist response, dissidence, can only be utopian if it can mobilise the resource of 'Solidarität' against the forces of 'Geld' and 'Macht' in a way that leads to the formation of a political will intended to influence 'den Austausch zwischen diesen kommunikativ strukturierten Lebensbereichen auf der einen, Staat und Ökonomie auf der anderen' (13). He sees this as being made possible by dissident movements coming together to form 'öffentliche Diskursen und höherstufige Intersubjektivitäten', i.e. 'autonome Öffentlichkeiten', which only then might have the effect of making the 'Selbststeuerungsmechanismen von Staat und Wirtschaft', as they have undoubtedly become, 'gegenüber den zweckorientierten Ergebnissen radikal-demokratischer Willensbildung hinreichend empfindlich' (13). Modern society, firmly based on the principle of the social state, has, in Habermas's view of things, lost contact with the masses, whose interests it notionally represents: in particular, the economic and administrative spheres have become incapable of responding to ideas arising, and deriving their support, from the mass of the populace. To escape from this situation, Habermas claims, it is necessary to establish 'ein Verfahren der diskursiven Willensbildung . . . , welche die Beteiligten *selbst* in die Lage versetzen [könnte], konkrete Möglichkeiten eines besseren und weniger gefährdeten Lebens nach *eigenen* Bedürfnissen und Einsichten aus *eigener* Initiative zu verwirklichen' (14).

The social manifestation of Habermas's category of utopian dissidence would be, in the first instance, the formation of groupings essentially outside the legislative structure, designed to counter dangers to human life or deteriorations in its quality, brought about by the interaction of the now autonomous resources of money and power: the Peace Movement and the Greens clearly fit this category. In the Seventies, a whole series of authors, still fired by their belief in the utopian and didactic potential of literature, viewed the novel as a similar means of establishing a public discourse. In recent years, however, we detect a shift towards a divorce between activist intentions and the writing of literature — something which Günter Grass has, in fact, always insisted upon. The quiet message inherent in the later novels of Otto F. Walter, Lothar Baier's *Jahresfrist* and Ingeborg Drewitz's *Eingeschlossen* seems to be a sense of the need for extra-literary social engagement. For Martin Walser, glad 'daß die Grünen entstanden sind, daß also unser Herumempfinden einen politischen Ausdruck oder eine politische Form gefunden hat', the formation of an opposition that stands above established parties means relief for him as an author, enabling him to retreat once again into 'das Hinterfeld', the true domain of literature.[5]

This wider sense of the need for literature to move back from the attempt at direct political engagement that characterised much writing in the Seventies is yet further confirmation that in a number of ways — sometimes contradictory — that period was very special. Perhaps the most important factor that marks it off from this present decade is the strong adherence to the utopian hopes of the Student Movement, borne along in many quarters by the illusory sense — induced by the application of a simplistic notion of fascism to the present, on the one hand, and disturbing threats to civil liberties on the other — of being able to identify the political and social forces opposed to the creation of a better life in West Germany. The enemies of true democracy — identified as the police, the press, the ex- and neo-Nazis in control of finance and industry and, ultimately, state institutions themselves — seemed for many to have been smoked out. Looking back on the period, the so-called 'Tendenzwende' of 1972–3 appears to have had far less influence on the weakening of utopian thinking than the pragmatic government of Helmut Schmidt and the resurgence of the conservative opposition, capped by election victory in 1982. These developments and the lack of social change brought with them a new and at times intense feeling of disillusionment, and this has produced various literary reactions, including a return to literature as diversion from the existential strains of life and the new mystical tendency already mentioned. While this can, in certain cases, be understood as a response to what Habermas calls 'Neue Unübersichtlichkeit', 'als Erklärung des Unbegreiflichen, als Zuflucht vor dem Unübersehbar-Unvorstellbaren',[6] elsewhere it is clearly of different provenance. It can involve a conscious renunciation of rationalism — and thereby, in literature, of the realist novel — and a concomitant turning to a view of the writer as seer and of literature as a world of magic. Thus the narrator of Botho Strauß's novel *Der junge Mann*

---

5. In conversation with Ulf Erdmann Ziegler, *die tageszeitung*, 30.9.1985.

6. Moray McGowan, 'Unendliche Geschichte für die Momo-Moderne?', *Theaterzeitschrift*, 15, 1986, p. 100. This article is highly informative on Strauß's mythical tendencies, particularly as exemplified by his dramas. Cf. further in this connection K.H. Bohrer (ed.), *Mythos und Moderne*, Frankfurt, 1983.

claims that only 'ein mehrfaches Bewußtsein [u
migen und zwanghaften Regimen des Fortschrit
jeder sogenannten "Zukunft" schützen kann, wir
lich die lebende Eintracht von Tag und Traum, vo
Sachverstand und geringfügigem Schlafwandel'.
schiedener Ton' which this narrator requires of his
(and which is certainly attained in Strauß's *Diese Erinn*
der nur einen Tag zu Gast war) corresponds very much to ⸗röße
durch Ansonderung' which Peter Handke demands of tne poet as
priest, who in that role has far more to teach the world than any
'professioneller, vor Durchschau-Zwang blickloser Denkpolizist mit
Aufklärungsfimmel'.[8] Rationalism is, he claims, 'ein Denkfaulheit',
and so, to act against it, the function of the poet is 'den Mythos
ein[zu]*bürgen*' (88). Before every act of writing, seen by Handke as a
'mythisches Abenteuer', the poet should receive the 'glühende Kohle,
die der Seraph dem Jesaja an die "unreinen" Lippen legt' (99).

The major response in recent German literature to what Peter
Schloterdijk has called 'das Zwielicht einer eigentümlichen existenziellen Desorientierung' has been the presentation of doubt and
despair themselves. The first indications of this were in poetry, in
so-called 'Katastrophenliteratur', as represented by Enzensberger's
Der Untergang der Titanic and the work of Günter Kunert. This theme
has since been taken up and deepened in the novel, in Christa Wolf's
Kassandra (1983; here, not for the first time, one of her works is
central to the West Germany literary scene) and Günter Grass's *Die
Rättin* (1986), which, amongst other things, addresses itself to the
'Abschied von den beschädigten Dingen' demanded by Grass in
1982.[9] Heinrich Böll's last novel, *Frauen vor Flußlandschaft* (1985)
should also be understood as an expression of this new mood of
despair. The novel was widely misunderstood by literary critics as
failed realism, but, like those of Christa Wolf and Grass, is essentially not a realist work. The decision taken by Böll and Wolf, two of
the major exponents of the German realist novel since 1945, to turn
away from the style that has dominated their writing is indicative of
a major problem that affects realism today: the major themes of the
present-day, which Habermas and others have identified, are enor-
mously and increasingly complex and horrifying in their possible
consequences for the human race. Given that, over and above this,

7. Botho Strauß, *Der junge Mann*, Munich, 1984, p. 11.
8. Peter Handke, *Phantasien der Wiederholung*, Frankfurt, 1983, p. 68.
9. Günter Grass, 'Die Vernichtung der Menschheit' . . . , *Die Zeit*, 3.12.1982. Cf.
further in this connection Peter Härtling, *Finden und Erfinden*, Darmstadt & Neuwied,
1984 and Michael Schneider, *Nur tote Fische schwimmen mit dem Strom*, Cologne, 1984.

ospects for a diminution of the various threats to mankind are from bright, it is difficult, if not impossible, for them to be treated adequately in the realist novel. Realism, after all, proceeds both from the premise that the author as subject is able to comprehend the nature of reality, to some extent, and from the utopian belief in progress, with the fictional world contributing to the constant amelioration of the human condition. While, interestingly enough, the great themes of the day can be taken up in the popular novel, which is unburdened by such expectations (as shown by Frederick Forsyth's *The Devil's Alternative*, 1979), it would seem that utopian demands in this domain are now better expressed through the form of the bold allegory (*Kassandra*) or the conscious simplification of the morality tale (*Frauen vor Flußlandschaft*).

The drift of this reading of the present situation inevitably raises substantial doubts as to the future of realism. One limited possibility is suggested by Habermas's essay through two examples he gives of dissident public discourses: the feminist and ecological movements, within which, it would seem, literature could play its part. While there has been little literary response to ecological debates, apart from certain aspects of Peter Härtling's *Das Windrad* and Grass's *Die Rättin*, it is noticeable that, at a generally barren time for realist writing, feminist literature represents a vigorous exception. The role of literature within the women's movement has in a way resembled that of 'Arbeiterliteratur' within the working class, in that it has contributed to the development of a sense of solidarity amongst women and can help to point forward to ways in which they can develop further. The first phase (solidarity), represented by works like Verena Stefan's *Häutungen* (1975), is now undoubtedly over, but a highly realist novel like Brigitte Kronauer's *Rita Münster* (1983) indicates the role literature can play in establishing a broadly based intersubjective discourse within the context of a long-term movement defined only by the goals of self-exploration and self-fulfilment. Another social area, within which something similar might develop, is defined by the 'Gastarbeiter' and, indeed, there are now definite signs of the emergence of a literature written in German by this under-privileged group.

A further, very different light on the possibilities open to the contemporary realist novel is shed by Theodor Adorno's ideas put forward in his essay 'Der Standort des Erzählers im zeitgenössischen Roman' (1954). While this formed the corner-stone of attacks on realism mounted by Walter Jens (1961) and Jörg Drews (1974), we would argue that the concern in the late Sixties with the criticism of traditional realist fiction, particularly as exemplified by the theories of Brecht, Adorno and Heißenbüttel, played a major part in the upsurge of a modern realist novel in the Seventies. It could now be argued that other ideas put forward by Adorno in that essay but regarded, understandably enough at the end of the Sixties, as exaggerations and irrelevancies, now start to acquire plausibility. In 1954 he claimed: 'Wie die Malerei von ihren traditionellen Aufgaben vieles entzogen wurde durch die Photographie, so dem Roman durch die Reportage und die Medien der Kulturindustrie, zumal den Film. Der Roman müßte sich auf das konzentrieren, was nicht durch den Bericht abzugelten ist'.[10] In the Seventies the precise opposite was the case, with the narrative range of the realist novel being extended by techniques taken over from the 'Neues Hörspiel' and the cinema, while the reportage played its part in setting the example for a range of documentary, autobiographical and biographical novels, as well as in the widespread adoption of the montage technique. Things look rather different today. The use of filmic techniques in the novel itself has become somewhat tired and hackneyed, with Wellershoff's *Der Sieger nimmt alles* and Max von der Grün's *Die Lawine* demonstrating the particular danger inherent in writing a novel with an eye to its adaptation into a screenplay (both have been filmed); it can mean attention to surface and visual detail at the possible expense of character or linguistic analysis. Perhaps even more important in this context is the way in which Edgar Reitz's *Heimat* has once more brought to the fore just how well the film can narrate, and if it is compared with another German chronicle, Siegfried Lenz's *Exerzierplatz*, there is little doubt as to which tells its story more convincingly. As far as documentary prose is concerned, it is noticeable how Wallraff's publications, from *Der Aufmacher* (1974) up to *Ganz unten* (1985), have moved ever further away from the more 'literary' montage style of the early Seventies, but have, in the process, made far more public impact than any work of realist fiction could ever achieve. If this analysis of present trends is accepted, then it suggests that the novel is indeed likely to be thrown back on what is unique to it, which for us is the explorative concern with the experience of reality, as reflected in language, in a way that widens the perception of that reality by the individual subject as reader. Even in the rather exceptional circumstances of the Seventies it was noticeable how works approaching the category of 'Sprachrealismus' seemed to offer the most satisfactory treatment of current themes, and this ought to be much more true now, if our reading of the contemporary situation of the novel is correct. Clearly,

10. Adorno, *Noten zur Literatur 1*, Frankfurt, 1968, p. 62.

it is too early to tell, but there are already one or two indications that the realist novel is indeed pointing in this direction. In Brigitte Kronauer's *Rita Münster* (1983) and Gernot Wolfgruber's *Die Nähe der Sonne* (1985), two examples that come to mind here, we find the retention of the intense subject-centricity that characterised the novel of the Seventies, allied to a significantly more thoroughgoing concern with language than was the case earlier.

Wolfgruber's earlier novels — *Auf freiem Fuß* (1975), *Herrenjahre* (1976), *Niemandsland* (1978) and *Verlauf eines Sommers* (1981) — all depict the anguish of the real victims of Western society, characters born in the working class who have moved up and away from their social roots, only ultimately to fail. These novels have generally been attributed to that Austrian wing of the 'Literatur der Arbeitswelt' which includes Franz Innerhofer and Michael Scharang, and there are, indeed, fundamental similarities between these writers. The inner life of Wolfgruber's protagonists, like those of Innerhofer and Scharang, is dominated by the desire for happiness and its correlative, the nightmare of life as unfulfilled existence, as expressed in interaction with a closely observed environment and in neuroses induced by the frustrations of life in the outer world. In *Die Nähe der Sonne*, too, there are reasons enough for Stefan Zell's misery — his father's Nazi past, his own inability to complete his studies, a lack of professional satisfaction and problems in his personal life; in this sense, the 'Achterbahn der Gefühle' (Ulrich Greiner) which Wolfgruber describes in no way lacks psychological motivation, but Stefan's real anguish, with which the author is ultimately concerned, stems from very different roots. The range of aids available in an 'Überlebensladen' confronts him with the extent of general anxiety in the society, an anxiety apparently caused by the existence 'eines undurchdringlichen Gespinstes aus Staatsmacht und Geld und Militärs . . . , einer Macht, die alles endrückend umschlingt, allgegenwärtig und unsichtbar'.[11] The novel is, as such, clearly a response to what Habermas calls 'Neue Unübersichtlichkeit', but the question is as to whether it is simply an expression of the despair this induces, or whether it can be seen as part of the formation of a public discourse. Our view is that, even though individual social experience may no longer be representative, the life of a single person can still tell something of the wider nature of social existence and the existential problems caused by aspects of the given society. While the social sciences and the statistical evaluation of aspects of modern life have a certain value, they are complemented and enriched by the

11. Gernot Wolfgruber, *Die Nähe der Sonne*, Salzburg, 1985, pp. 333, 196–7.

reader's confrontation with the highly personal nature of individual interaction with society in the literary treatment of the individual's experiences and socially-induced anxieties. Moreover, the inter-subjectivity produced by the response of the reader to the subject of the novel enables individual experience to assume a limited paradig-matic character and, thereby, to help build up a public discourse that can take a stand against the negative features of society and thus contribute, in the longer term, to renewed social progress. Realist writing such as this can avoid the drift into superficial verism and continue that link — the attainment of which is the achievement of the West German realist novel of the Seventies — with the major thrust of realism in the second half of the nineteenth century, namely, to represent the deformation of the individual by modern society, thereby participating in an (admittedly slow) process of growing public awareness and keeping alive the hope of continuing progress towards the goal of a life of true human dignity.

Select Bibliography

It is not possible to attempt to give here a comprehensive bibliography of the vast body of scholarly literature on realism, nor, indeed, necessary, as the publications by Pohl, Aust and Martini, listed below, all contain extensive bibliographical information. The works listed here are those which have been of particular help in the writing of this book. For secondary literature on the various authors examined in the context of this study readers are referred to the comprehensive bibliographies contained in the *Kritisches Lexikon der deutschsprachigen Gegenwartsliteratur (KLG)*, edited by Heinz Ludwig Arnold.

General works on realism

Auerbach, Erich, *Mimesis*, Princeton, 1971 (3rd edn.)

Aust, Hugo, *Literatur des Realismus*, Stuttgart, 1977

Borgerhoff, E.B.O. '*Réalisme* and kindred words: Their use as terms of literary criticism in the first half of the nineteenth century', *PMLA*, 53, 1938, pp. 837–43

Brecht, Bertolt, 'Über den Realismus', *Schriften zu Literatur und Kunst 2*, Frankfurt, 1967

Brinkmann Richard (ed.), *Begriffsbestimmung des literarischen Realismus*, Darmstadt, 1969

Demetz, Peter, 'Zur Definition des Realismus', *Literatur und Kritik*, Heft 16/17, 1967

——, 'Über die Fiktionen des Realismus', *Neue Rundschau*, 88, 1977

Halperin, John (ed.), *The Theory of the Novel*, New York and London, 1974

Kahler, Erich, 'Übergang und Untergang der epischen Kunstform', *Die neue Rundschau*, 64, 1953, pp. 1–44

Knüfermann, Volker, 'Realismus und Sprache', *Zeitschrift für deutsche Philologie*, 89, 1970, pp. 235–9

Kohl, Stephen, *Realismus. Theori und Geschichte*, Munich, 1977

Lukács, Georg, *Essays über Realismus*, Berlin, 1948

——, *The Historical Novel*, London, 1962

Steinmetz, Horst, 'Der vergessene Leser' in Ferdinand von Ingen et al. (eds.), *Dichter und Leser*, Groningen, 1972, pp. 113–33

Stern, J. Peter, *On Realism*, London, 1973
Wellek, R. and A. Warren, *Theory of Literature*, London, 1949

German realism: general

Brinkmann, Richard, *Wirklichkeit und Illusion*, Tübingen, 1957
Hatfield, Henry, 'Realism in the German Novel', *Comparative Literature*, 3, 1951, pp. 234–52
Kinder, Hermann, *Poesie als Synthese*, Frankfurt, 1973
Lämmert, Eberhard (ed.), *Romantheorie in Deutschland seit 1880*, Cologne, 1975
Lukács, Georg, *Deutsche Realisten des neunzehnten Jahrhunderts*, Berlin, 1951
Martini, Fritz, 'Zur Theorie des Romans in deutschen "Realismus" 'in, *Festgabe für Eduard Behrend*, Weimar, 1959, pp. 272–96
——, 'Deutsche Literatur in der Zeit des "bürgerlichen Realismus"', *Deutsche Vierteljahresschrift*, 34, 1960, pp. 581–666
——, *Deutsche Literatur im bürgerlichen Realismus*, Stuttgart, 1964 (2nd edn.)
Pascal, Roy, 'Fortklang und Nachklang des Realismus im Roman' in W. Kohlschmidt (ed.), *Spätzeiten und Spätlichkeit*, Berne and Munich, 1962
Preisendanz, Wolfgang, *Wege des Realismus*, Munich, 1977
Ruckhäberle, H.J. and H. Widhammer (eds.), *Roman und Romantheorie des deutschen Realismus*, Kronberg, 1977
Swales, Martin 'Zum Problem des deutschen Realismus' in F.N. Mennemeier & C. Wiedemann (eds.), *Kontroversen, alte und neue. Akten des VII. Internationalen Germanisten-Kongresses 1985*, Band 9, Stuttgart, 1986, pp. 116–21
Traeger, Claus, *Studien zur Realismustheorie*, Frankfurt, 1972

German realism: the post-war novel

Arnold, H.L. (ed.), *Positionen im deutschen Roman*, Munich, 1974
Baumgart, Reinhard, *Aussichten des Romans oder Hat Literatur Zukunft?*, Munich, 1970
Bense, Max, *Die Realität der Literatur*, Cologne, 1971
Heißenbüttel, Helmut, and Heinrich Vormweg, *Briefwechsel über Literatur*, Neuwied–Berlin, 1969
Laemmle, Peter, (ed.), *Realismus — welcher?*, Munich, 1976
Lerch, Fredi, (ed.), *Vorschlag zur Unversöhnlichkeit: Realismusdebatte Winter 1983/84*, Zurich, 1984
Powroslo, Wolfgang, *Erkenntnis durch Literatur. Realismus in der westdeutschen Literaturtheorie der Gegenwart*, Cologne, 1976
Reinhold, Ursula, 'Realismus in der Diskussion', *Weimarer Beiträge*, XXV, 2, 1979 pp. 32–55

Thieß, Frank, *Dichtung und Wirklichkeit*, Wiesbaden, 1952

Timm, Uwe, and Gerd Fuchs (eds.), *Kontext 1. Literatur und Wirklichkeit*, Munich, 1976

Trommler, Frank, 'Der zögernde Nachwuchs' in Thomas Koebner (ed.), *Tendenzen der deutschen Literatur seit 1945*, Stuttgart, 1971, pp. 1–116

——, 'Realismus in der Prosa' in ibid., pp. 179–275

Vormweg, Heinrich, *Eine andere Leseart*, Neuwied and Berlin, 1972

Index